THE CANDIDATE'S 7 DEADLY SINS

THE CANDIDATE'S

DEADLY SINS

USING EMOTIONAL OPTICS TO TURN
POLITICAL VICES INTO VIRTUES

DR. PETER A. WISH

LIONCREST
PUBLISHING

THE CANDIDATE'S 7 DEADLY SINS

Using Emotional Optics to Turn Political Vices into Virtues

ISBN   978-1-5445-0729-3 *Hardcover*

       978-1-5445-0727-9 *Paperback*

       978-1-5445-0728-6 *Ebook*

FOR TWO VERY SPECIAL PEOPLE IN MY LIFE,
DR. LESLIEBETH WISH AND JUDGE CARLY S. WISH.

CONTENTS

FOREWORD

There are three distinct times during a presidential campaign when candidates have an opportunity to make a significant impression on voters and move the dial of public opinion in a significant way: their announcement, the debates, and, if they are the nominee of their party, their speech at the convention. Before their convention speeches, it is tradition that they are introduced with a short bio film. It was my job to produce that film for George W. Bush when he ran for president in 2000. Voters in the Republican primary who had voted for him had a pretty good idea about who he was and what he stood for, but all the rest of the country knew about him was that he was the son of a former president.

The film was a pretty big deal for the campaign and a huge responsibility for me. So, imagine the reaction of the future president and campaign staff when I intentionally left a scene in the film where Bush completely mangled what he was trying to say. Even though I had another perfect version.

Here's what happened.

I was filming George W. and his wife, Laura, at his ranch. Because he was not very good at reading a script, I was conducting interviews to try and just get spontaneous natural moments from him. I asked a question about the birth of their twin daughters, and he just completely mangled what he was trying to say. He and Laura cracked up laughing, as did the film crew. We went back and rerecorded the line, and this time he got it just right.

A few weeks later we were editing the film together, and we got to that section with the bad take, and I said, "Take it out and put in the good take." The editor did, and we started to move on. Then I reflected for a moment and said, "I've changed my mind; put back in the scene he screws up." The editor was a bit baffled, but not nearly as confused as the senior staff of the campaign. They thought I'd lost my mind. "McKinnon, are you kidding?! You're intentionally having our guy screw up in a film we control and are paying for? What are you thinking?"

I was thinking that the moment was real. That it was human. That it was vulnerable. That it showed he could laugh at himself and not take himself too seriously. Most importantly, it was authentic. People could relate to a guy with imperfections. Finally, I said to my colleagues, "Let's admit the obvious. Our guy isn't the best orator in the race, so let's just lower the bar of expectations."

And it worked.

That's the kind of observation that Dr. Peter Wish had when he saw the poster for the movie *Mitt*, a documentary about the now-senator from Utah looking back on his run for president in 2012. In the poster, Romney's hair is out of place, not perfectly coiffed like it always seemed to be during the campaign. Dr. Wish had the same reaction I did after viewing the documentary, which revealed a bunch of behind-the-scenes moments of Romney being very human: "Where was *that* guy during the campaign? I like *that* guy!" He was thoughtful, candid, generous, humble, funny, and self-deprecating. In other words, he was real. Not the stiff that we all saw on the campaign.

The campaign was so worried about things like Romney's Mormonism that they kept him on a tight leash and totally on script. But the story of his faith is a huge part of what makes Romney who he is. It's a compelling and important part of the narrative of his life. And they ran from it.

Dr. Wish understands all of this better than anyone I've encountered in politics. He knows that in order to win in modern politics, it's not enough to be the smartest person in the race or the most qualified (hello, Hillary Clinton). Voters aren't looking for talking points or plans. They're looking for an emotional connection. For a narrative, a story.

It's remarkable to me that until now, no one has really written a knowledgeable, insightful, and comprehensive treatise on what voters really look for in a candidate, and how candidates can capture the hearts and, therefore, the support of voters. Dr. Wish is a psychologist, a therapist, and a political coach who understands that in order to be successful candidates need to create a relationship with voters.

This book is the ultimate catalog of political persuasion. It should be a must-read for anyone thinking about running for office, or anyone who wants to help someone become a better candidate. It's the best how-to book about getting elected.

—MARK MCKINNON, CHIEF MEDIA ADVISOR TO GEORGE W. BUSH AND JOHN MCCAIN AND CREATOR AND CO-HOST OF *THE CIRCUS* ON SHOWTIME

INTRODUCTION

"The political brain is an emotional brain...In politics, when reason and emotions collide, emotion invariably wins."

—DR. DREW WESTEN, *THE POLITICAL BRAIN*[1]

Despite the freezing temperature outside, guests inside the Westin Marriott Hotel Ballroom in Boston were sweating. Campaign staff and volunteers poured in off the buses, fresh from the last campaign stop in Pittsburgh. They were on a high. Their internal polling had convinced them the election was in the bag.

Was I the only one who knew Mitt Romney was in trouble?

When Governor Romney arrived, his surrounding entourage was beaming, certain of victory. Mitt himself was calm and unruffled. As exhausted as he was, he still looked, as he always did, terminally handsome—like an eight-by-ten-inch glossy photograph, not a hair out of place.

---

1   Westen, Drew. *The Political Brain: The Role of Emotion in Deciding the Fate of the Nation.* New York: PublicAffairs, 2016.

There's the problem, I thought to myself. A concern had been gnawing at me throughout the campaign: he was *too* perfect, and therefore unreachable. Romney never revealed to Americans the real Mitt behind the eight-by-ten-inch photo. He had failed to establish an emotional connection with voters.

Americans want to see their candidates laugh, tell personal stories, and appear relaxed in natural everyday settings. The word "relaxed" never came to mind with Mitt—but the words "controlled" and "remote" did. I knew too much about human behavior from my decades as a psychologist to ignore this fatal flaw.

Romney, his wife Ann, and their family quickly exited to his suite. Donald Trump sequestered himself somewhere in the hotel. The rest anxiously watched as the votes tallied on the big screens. I joined Ken Langone, the billionaire co-founder of Home Depot, outside one of the VIP rooms. We felt growing uneasiness about what we were seeing on TV.

Slowly, the maps started to turn red and blue as votes were counted. By 9:00pm, there was a tug of war in Ohio. Karl Rove, the iconic conservative political pundit, former senior advisor and deputy chief of staff for President George W. Bush, and architect for Bush's 2000 and 2004 campaigns, held on the longest: "Ohio hasn't been called yet!" But the minute it was, we knew the election was over. From Abraham Lincoln to Donald J. Trump, no Republican has ever won the presidency without carrying Ohio.

We'd lost.

What went wrong? Those of us gathered at the Marriott knew without question that Mitt Romney would have excelled in leading America. His character was impeccable—his competency, outstanding. Why hadn't voters seen that too?

Even before Mitt came down to address the crowd, many of the dejected Romney team members, including me, made their way back into the freezing November night. Trump headed for his plane to fly back to New York. The electoral maps confirmed the truth: Romney had built an invisible wall between himself and the voters. He failed to sell them on his personal qualities. Not enough voters got to *know* or *trust* him.

Michael Kranish, author of *The Real Romney*, wrote in the Boston Globe, "Exit polls told a stunning story. The majority of voters preferred Romney's visions, values, and leadership. But he had clearly failed to address the problem that Romney's own family worried about from the start. Obama beat Romney by an astonishing 81 to 18 percent margin on the question of which candidate 'cares about people like me.'"[2]

No doubt Mitt Romney had cared about everyday Americans—but he'd failed to clearly articulate that message. His favorability rating in the exit poll was 47 percent, with 50 percent of voters holding an unfavorable view. As a result of this "empathy gap," he'd lost what many thought a winnable election.

Because Romney had failed to activate enough public emotional motivation, when they cast their ballots, people chose the can-

2   Kranish, Michael. "The Story behind Mitt Romney's Loss in the Presidential Campaign to President Obama." Boston.com. December 22, 2012.

didate they liked—the one who made them feel understood, the one they identified with, the one who seemed to empathize with their problems. The *other* one.

EMOTION'S ROLE AT THE POLLING BOOTH

Put yourself in Romney's shoes. Imagine staring at yourself in the bathroom mirror the morning after the election, trying to make sense of your loss. You've been highly successful in your business career, you were the popular seventieth governor of Massachusetts, you have a wealth of experience, you love your country, and you know you can lead. Why didn't voters see that?

To paraphrase former President Bill Clinton's advisor James Carville, "It's the emotions, stupid."

I have always been puzzled as to why some candidates believe they can win primarily by making a strictly rational appeal to voters and directing them to their website or book to examine their detailed policy platform. Does anyone really go there, except journalists?

Yes, candidates need to have attractive policy positions and be competent leaders—that's obvious. Having enough money is important too. However, there is an equally vital requirement to achieving political victory, one that, surprisingly, too often gets relegated to the bottom of the list of campaign priorities: *a candidate needs to create an emotional platform—one that continuously makes an emotional connection with voters.*

The act of voting itself is usually driven by emotions.[3] We saw this in the 2018 midterm elections when voters' emotions were inflamed on both sides because of President Donald Trump's polarizing policy positions and mercurial leadership style. Citizens flocked to the polls and voter turnout hit an all-time high.[4] Make no mistake: when voters' emotions are aroused, they get themselves to the polling booths.

How do we know voting is driven by emotions? Because *every* decision is driven by emotions—even the smallest decision. The famous neuroscientist Dr. Antonio Damasio discovered this fact while studying patients who experienced damage in the area of the brain associated with emotions. To Damasio's surprise, these patients struggled to make even the most basic of decisions. They couldn't even choose what to eat for breakfast, what shoes to wear, or what show to watch on TV.[5]

With damaged *emotions* came damaged *decision-making*.[6] Damasio concluded that every decision—whether we want to admit it or not—has emotion at its root.

Neuroscientists know that for humans to make any type of decision, our 86 billion brain neurons need to gather evidence for each option available to us. A decision is made when one group of neurons accumulates enough evidence that exceeds a certain threshold. Some of this evidence comes from our sensory

3   Searles, Kathleen, and Travis N. Ridout. "The Use and Consequences of Emotions in Politics." Emotion Researcher. February 2017.

4   Vesoulis, Abby. "Donald Trump Drove Record 2018 Midterm Election Turnout." Time. November 12, 2018.

5   Antonio Damasio, *The Strange Order of Things*, New York: Random House, 2018.

6   Camp, Jim. "Decisions Are Emotional, Not Logical: The Neuroscience behind Decision-making." *Big Think*. June 11, 2012.

world outside, and some evidence comes from our emotional gut instinct. In his research measuring brain wave activity and free will, American physiologist Benjamin Libet concluded that the brain shows signs of a decision even before a person acts. Incredibly, according to Libet, "the brain's wheels start turning before the person even consciously intends to do something. Suddenly, people's choices—even a basic finger tap—appeared to be determined by something outside of their own perceived volition."[7]

What do these neuroscience findings mean for candidates? Although a voter's decision to choose one candidate over another may have some predetermined basis, the choice is largely informed by his or her emotions. As a candidate, you must emotionally resonate with voters. If you want them to vote for you, you need to make them *like* you and believe you understand them.

The candidate who has the best ten-point plan (or, in Mitt's case, a fifty-nine-point plan) is not necessarily the one who wins the most votes on Election Day. Candidates who have the best ground game or the most money also don't automatically win. Granted, those help—but our finance team raised over a billion dollars. Lack of money was not what lost Romney the election.

Today, voters are mainly looking for three emotion-based qualities when they're deciding whom to vote for:

1. This candidate likes me
2. This candidate understands me
3. I trust this candidate

---

7   Gholipour, Bahar. "A Famous Argument Against Free Will Has Been Debunked." *The Atlantic*. September 10, 2019.

If you dare to overlook these three key qualities, you risk losing your election. Unfortunately, too many candidates and campaigns don't pay enough attention to the power of what I call *emotional optics*.

Your first impression, nonverbal cues, facial cues, appearance, and word choices are some of the major elements of your optics that make voters either like you, feel understood by you, or distrust you. They want to know: are you friend or foe?

I observed firsthand that Mitt Romney—as a spouse and father—knew how to establish warmth, trust, and care. But, as a political candidate, he and his handlers failed to apply these skills to his campaign.

Many successful candidates instinctively use the building blocks of making an emotional connection—but not all. If you want to win, you must *learn* how to articulate a consistent authentic vision that plugs into the voter's gut and aligns with their needs.

I dedicated two and a half years of my life to getting Governor Romney elected. Because of my own PRSD (Post-Romney Stress Disorder), I don't want you to commit the same campaign emotional malpractice as Romney and his team. I've written this book to help you strengthen your presence through scientifically proven strategies that will help emotionally connect you with voters.

Research studies on likeability and brain activity support the power of all these factors which make up an emotional connection. Neuroscience shows us that the way you speak can synchronize voters' brain waves with yours. You can literally get voters to think like you. Other studies show that content which is emotional lights up a specific area of the brain five times more than just sharing simple facts. When you arouse voters' empathy, you'll activate the "love" hormone oxytocin, a neurotransmitter which bonds people to you and makes them feel warm and trusting.

Although I can't guarantee you will win your election, this book will arm you with tested tips based in cutting-edge neuroscience, cognitive and social psychology, and my years of coaching candidates. Critical to your success is making each voter feel that you understand and value *them*. Follow the tools and techniques I describe, and you will be a better candidate (that I *can* guarantee).

THE CANDIDATE'S DEADLY SINS

I've always been interested in how and why people do what they do. I earned a PhD in psychology from Boston College and spent forty years as an academic and clinical psychologist. Even though I started my career working with individuals, couples, and families, I also found myself intrigued and confused as to why certain political candidates won or lost. What were the victors doing right? What were the defeated candidates doing wrong?

My years as a practicing psychologist and my media experience on television, radio, and as a syndicated newspaper columnist made me realize that winning and losing had a lot to do with a candidate's relational presence and presentation style. I discovered the key factors that explain *how* candidates' emotional optics affected their runs for office.

Over decades of compiling research, conducting surveys and coaching candidates who ran for local, state, and national office, I've refined my recommendations and believe I understand better now what works and what doesn't.

Even to this day, I find myself watching a candidate on TV and calling out instructions like a baseball fan watching the post-season division series: "play it this way, not that way!" Sometimes, I'd be at a campaign rally, mentally coaching the candidates from backstage: "Move this way, not that way! Make me *feel* this way, not that way!"

When candidates embodied qualities of *strength* and *warmth*, they hit it out of the park with voters. Candidates struck out when they failed to project these qualities. If they did something that made them look uninformed, they seemed weak and incompetent. If they failed to appear warm and personable, they came across as unlikable.

For example, the 2008 vice president candidate and governor of Alaska, Sarah Palin, looked naive and uninformed when she tried to claim that Alaska's proximity to Russia equated to foreign policy experience. In 2016, Democratic Presidential nominee Hillary Clinton, at a Manhattan fundraiser for wealthy donors, described her opponent Trump's supporters as a "basket of deplorables," and she instantly sealed her impression as being unlikeable.

Campaign moments like these are emotional-optics killers. When political candidates misstep in their relationship with voters, they commit what I call the *Candidate's 7 Deadly Sins.*

But, don't despair! You can learn to transform these vices into virtues. Let's examine the Candidate's 7 Deadly Sins, along with the virtues that give voters an impression of strength, followed by the virtues that make you seem warm and likable.

WEAKNESS SINS VERSUS STRENGTH VIRTUES:

1.   **Don't be Pessimistic—be Optimistic.** Think of Jimmy Carter's 1979 "malaise" speech versus Ronald Reagan's slogan, "It's Morning Again in America!" Voters want aspirational leaders who offer hope and will guide them to a better tomorrow.

2.   **Don't be Tentative—be Decisive.** Example: John Kerry was seen as a tentative "flip-flopper" which largely doomed his presidential campaign against George W. Bush. Compare Kerry's tentative decision-making with a moment like John F. Kennedy's decisive "moon shot" address to Congress in May 1961: "Now it is time to take longer strides—time for a great new American enterprise—time for this nation to take a clearly leading role in space achievement."[8] Decisiveness implies strength, confidence, and clear-headed leadership.

3.   **Don't be Reactive—be Deliberate.** Think of famous gaffes, like President George H.W. Bush checking his watch during a Town Hall presidential debate, versus Bill Clinton's measured, thoughtful, and engaged responses to questioners. Deliberateness demonstrates a leader who is prudent and won't be thrown off by surprises or emergencies.

---

8   NASA. Accessed January 15, 2019. https://er.jsc.nasa.gov/seh/ricetalk.htm.

4. **Don't be Canned—be Authentic.** Remember the broken-record performance Senator Marco Rubio delivered in the 2016 Republican Presidential debate: when challenged by Governor Chris Christie, Rubio defaulted to the comfort of a well-rehearsed stump speech and repeated the same memorized line three times. That's canned. Consider former President Barack Obama's warmth, jokes, and affectionate relationship with his wife and daughters—that's authentic. Authenticity shows voters that you're relatable, trustworthy, and likable.

5. **Don't be Cerebral—be Empathic.** Think of candidates who obsess over policy plans (boring), versus candidates who tell stories (engaging and relatable). Empathic candidates show voters that they care about everyday Americans.

6. **Don't be Arrogant—be Humble.** Example: Vice President Al Gore's eye rolls and sighs during a presidential debate, versus George W. Bush's folksy affability. Voters want a candidate who will share the credit for America's success with them, not someone who wants to pump themselves up and not share credit.

7. **Don't be Rigid—be Agile.** When candidates get stuck on a tough question like a deer caught in the headlights, that's rigid. When they can think on their feet, that's agile. Agile candidates can appeal to a wide variety of audiences by discussing their experience in different ways. Agile candidates also excel at explaining why they have changed a position.

MAKE THE CONNECTION, OR LOSE THE ELECTION

I've been on the inside of over twenty campaigns. I've coached candidates, Democrats and Republicans, that have both won and lost. Without fail, the candidates who won ensured there was an emotional connection with voters. They avoided the deadly sins, and they practiced the virtues.

From my experiences working with candidates on the campaign trail, I've developed techniques that can help you win. Along with the vices and the virtues, this book will show you how to:

- Nail your first impression with voters
- Communicate to maximum effect so voters listen to you and like you
- Manage voters' emotions by activating the right neuro-networks in their brains
- Avoid the campaign sins and practice the campaign virtues
- Establish a personal "master narrative" that will help you emotionally connect with voters

We live in hyper-partisan times. Many voters will not look at candidates beyond the "Rep" or "Dem" listed next to their names. However, with so many elections won or lost on the margins, courting the independent voter becomes critical to swinging the election your way. Voters will take a closer look at you, *if the emotional connection you make is strong and clear.*

If you're a candidate who doesn't have as much financial backing or grassroots ground game, you can still use emotional optics to get a needed leg up on your competition. The candidate who tells stories, discusses their upbringing, makes personal contact with voters, finds commonalities with them, and demonstrates confidence and warmth—*that's* the candidate who will swing a close election their way.

The political battlefield is littered with those who fell on their swords by failing to connect emotionally with their voters. Instead of having to pull out a white flag of surrender, let me help you raise a flag of victory.

CHAPTER ONE

NAILING YOUR FIRST IMPRESSION

"People forget what you said. People forget what you did. But people will never forget how you made them feel."

—MAYA ANGELOU

Heading into the nation's first-ever live presidential debate in 1960, the odds were stacked against him. It wasn't his youth or inexperience that mainly worried Americans—it was his religion. Voters feared that John F. Kennedy, a Catholic, would take his orders directly from the Pope.

Given the country's state of mind back then, this was amongst their major concerns. The US was embroiled in the Cold War, there was growing social unrest, and the Civil Rights movement had exposed deep divisions within the country. Rationally speaking, the best candidate for the country's next president was obvious: "Nixon's the One."

As a former candidate for governor of California, US Congressman and Senator, and the current vice president under Eisenhower, Richard Nixon brought seasoned leadership to the table. He also had foreign policy experience that far outweighed Kennedy's.

But the power of personality and appearance was about to hold sway.

Kennedy—warm, handsome, magnetic, and perpetually-tanned—knew his image worked to his advantage. He also knew that he had a golden opportunity to sell that image via television to millions of Americans.

During that nationally televised presidential debate—viewed by over 70 million people—Kennedy capitalized on every opportunity to create a positive connection with voters. His handlers chose a dark blue suit that highlighted his tan and helped him stand out against the gray backdrop. He wore makeup and looked well-rested. When answering the moderator's debate questions, he looked right into the camera. Viewers felt he was speaking directly to them. For a public that knew very little about Kennedy, he came across as trustworthy and likeable.

Nixon got the "stagecraft"—a term coined by Josh King, Bill Clinton's advance man and author of *Off Script*—entirely wrong. Prior to the debate, he'd campaigned all day and was still recovering from the flu. He had recently undergone knee surgery and looked gaunt after losing twenty pounds in the hospital. Worse, when getting out of his car at the debate studio, the door banged against his newly operated-upon knee.

As opposed to Kennedy's youthful look and permanent tan, Nixon had a perpetual five-o'clock shadow. Studio artists tried to cover it up with shave stick, but when he began sweating under the hot lights, the glycerin-based product made perspiration bead on his forehead. His gray suit almost disappeared into the matching background and made his face look ashen. He looked haggard.

When responding to questions, Nixon looked at the moderator, not the camera, as if he was avoiding viewers. As a result, he gave the impression that he was somewhat shifty and untrustworthy—not a great optic from someone already nicknamed "Tricky Dick."

Despite feeling tired and ill, Nixon had no trouble competing with Kennedy on substance. He highlighted his superior experience and record in the White House, speaking clearly and effectively.

A small survey of radio listeners concluded that Nixon had won the debate. However, a majority of television viewers came away with a different opinion. One commentator noted, "Kennedy's style advantage over Nixon wound up being far greater than Nixon's substance advantage over Kennedy."[9]

Prior to the first debate, a Gallup poll showed Nixon only slightly leading, 47 percent to 46 percent. After the fourth and final debate, Kennedy edged Nixon by 49 percent to 46 percent. A survey conducted after all four debates were completed showed that of the 4 million undecided voters, 3 million of those voters ended up casting their ballot for Kennedy.[10]

9   History.com Editors. "The Kennedy-Nixon Debates." HISTORY. September 21, 2010.

10   "Campaign of 1960," *John F. Kennedy Presidential Library and Museum.*

Overnight, Kennedy changed Americans' skeptical view of him from an inexperienced, immature junior Senator to a knowledgeable and capable future president. Although Nixon rallied for the subsequent televised debates and vastly improved his visual optics, he couldn't recover from that disastrous first appearance.

Kennedy had won the first impression—and, as this chapter explains, people's first impression of you is immediate and lasting.

WHAT THEY SEE IS WHAT YOU GET

How did Kennedy do it? On September 26, 1960, many viewers had turned on their televisions with preconceived notions about him. They assumed he was too young, too inexperienced, too Catholic. Somehow, though, he was able to flip this assessment.

How did Kennedy change voters' perceptions? Mainly through nonverbal emotional optics—the way he dressed, his posture, the direction of his gaze—Kennedy gave the public a positive way to reconsider choosing him. He convinced people that he was trustworthy and that he understood them. Ultimately, JFK made voters *like* him.

Why was Kennedy's style so powerful? Why does likability override qualities like experience or expertise?

Here's why: when people punch or bubble-in your name on the ballot, they not only form a relationship with you, they also make a *commitment* to you with their vote. You don't need a marriage counselor to know that trust is essential for commitment. And, if your likability index isn't high enough, voters will be reluctant to support you.

This chapter focuses on the importance of Emotional Optics in making a first impression: What they see is what you get. If you want to get votes, make sure voters see something they like about you. As Emory University psychologist Dr. Drew Westen says, politics deals in the "marketplace of emotions."[11]

HOW EMOTIONS WIN ELECTIONS

How do you know if a campaign speech is truly engaging and convincing the audience?

Several neurological studies have sought to measure what excites our brains when we listen.[12] Participants were outfitted with special caps that record what content arouses brain activity and what content quiets the brain.

Subjects were shown stimuli like a James Bond movie or a politician's speech. Simultaneously, researchers use a procedure called functional magnetic resonance imaging (fMRI) to observe increased blood flow to the brain. They then measure the specific neurological brain wave illumination that follows the blood flow. It turns out that the way we communicate has a major impact on what lights up in listener's brains.

Messages targeted towards participants' rational brains (logic)

11   Ibid., Westen.

12   Sim, Yanchuan, Brice D. L. Acree, Justin H. Gross, and Noah A. Smith. "Measuring Ideological Proportions in Political Speeches." *Association for Computational Linguistics*. October, 2013.

make for dim illumination. But when the messaging target is emotional, the brain starts to look more like a Rolling Stones concert. When communication is powerful and effective, more parts of the brain light up. These brain areas show increased electrical activity. What's remarkable is that when an entire audience is engaged—as when we are at the movies or at a political rally— brains light up in unison.

THE BLUE COASTS AND RED CENTER OF THE BRAIN

"Blue coasts and a red center" often is the way our nation's electoral map is described—but it's also a description of how we think, according to Dr. Westen.[13]

Part of the brain called the ventromedial prefrontal cortex, which processes risk and fear, is our gut decision maker. This area is also involved in:

- All emotional experience
- Social and emotional intelligence
- Moral functioning

So the same part of our brain that determines our moral choices also connects to our emotional gut. Westen colors this region of the brain red on brain maps. It's located front and center, where neurological connections are densely gathered.

Surrounding this ventromedial prefrontal cortex are the areas of the brain associated with judgment, logic, and philosophical

---

13 Westen, Drew. *The Political Brain: The Role of Emotion in Deciding the Fate of the Nation*. New York: PublicAffairs, 2016.

ideas. We can think of these areas as the "coasts" of the cortex. They're much smaller than the "red center," and Westen colors those blue.

Conveniently, these brain areas reflect the same geographical regions of our country's politics. Democrats—concentrated on the coasts of the United States—usually approach voters by appealing to those blue coasts in the brain. They primarily use dispassionate logic to argue their points. Republicans, on the other hand, traditionally appeal to voters more via that red center: they try to arouse voters' emotions.

In the last several decades, political victories have been won on the battlefield of that red center. When Democrats have stuck with logical argument, they have generally done poorly in elections. When Republicans stoked anger and emotion, such as during the Tea Party wave starting in 2009, they usually reaped victory.

The reverse has been true when Democrats stepped away from the narrow "coasts of the cortex" and whipped up emotion in their base. Barack Obama was carried to victory in 2008 via an emotional campaign promising "hope and change." The same was true for Bill Clinton, the "Man from Hope" in 1992. During other elections, Democrats have stirred up fear in voters by issuing doomsday warnings that Republican leaders would take away their healthcare and Social Security.

Consistently, it's *emotion* that drives voters' enthusiasm, engagement, and preferences. The knowledge that emotion heavily influences our behavior should prompt a strategic breakthrough for candidates and campaign managers! Westen explains neurologically why candidates should make every attempt to appeal to voters' emotions:

> You can flog it out for those few millimeters of cerebral turf [i.e. "the coasts"] that process facts, figures, and policy statements, or you can take your campaign to the broader neural electorate, [i.e. "the red center"]...targeting different emotional states with messages designed to maximize their appeal.[14]

Westen believes that candidates need to target voters' emotional states with messages that will resonate. It's much less effective to appeal to people's ideas than to their feelings.

The 2016 presidential election provides a perfect example of what can happen when the "blue coasts" of the brain are targeted yet the emotional "red center" is ignored. Hillary Clinton's cerebral appeal to voters' logic fell short of an Electoral College victory. Donald Trump, on the other hand, was savvy. His rhetoric hit voters in their gut by fomenting resentment at the "swamp" in DC. Additionally, he aroused Americans' fear of terrorism and proposed building a wall on the southern border to keep out illegal immigrants, whom he claimed would take American workers' jobs away. And he won.

Though there were many additional factors at work in Trump's campaign, what ultimately carried him to victory was his emotional connection with anxious, angry, disillusioned, and disenfranchised voters.

---

14 Westen, Drew. *The Political Brain: The Role of Emotion in Deciding the Fate of the Nation.* New York: PublicAffairs, 2016.

When people see and listen to you at a campaign rally, or watch your televised ad, they're drawing conclusions about whether they like you. Eventually, those impressions turn into action— either they'll vote for you, or they won't. What they see is what you get.

HIT VOTERS IN THE FEELS

According to Dr. Nathan Hollinsaid of Tufts University, "Emotional appeal has the potential to play a powerful role in politics."[15] Hollinsaid studies the reasons why we vote and whom we vote for. He's especially interested in how Trump won and what there was about his "personality, campaign and candidacy" that was able to grab a bigger piece of the Republican vote among men, whites, Evangelical Christians, and Catholics than previous Republican candidates.

Hollinsaid writes, "Both positive and negative emotions play a crucial role in voter behavior. They influence whom we decide to vote for, affect our willingness to participate in the political process, and shape our attitudes about politicians."

Hollinsaid points to research by Dr. Nicholas Valentino and his colleagues to show it's the specific emotions of anger, enthusiasm, and anxiety that could be more important in motivating voters.[16]

1. **Anger:** Valentino and his colleagues found that anger has the most potent emotional effect on voters' behavior. Angry

15   Hollinsaid, Nathan. "The Emotions of Elections." *Tufts University*. February 22, 2018.

16   Valentino, Nicholas, et al. "Election Night's Alright for Fighting: The Role of Emotions in Political Participation." *The Journal of Politics*. 2011. 73(1): 156–170.

voters are more apt to turn out to vote, attend campaign rallies, volunteer for political campaigns, and blame others for their current economic situation. Angry voters also are more attracted to news which confirms their existing beliefs and are less inclined to seek out contrary information.

2. **Enthusiasm:** Being enthusiastic will increase participation in the political process. Enthusiastic voters are more likely to attend campaign events and go to the polls to vote. They watch more news, televised political events, and the party conventions. Enthusiastic voters are more tribal and partisan and are consistent in voting for the same party candidates.

3. **Anxiety:** Interestingly, anxiety does not increase voter participation. However, it causes voters to change their preferences and beliefs more. When voters feel anxious about their economic security, they look to policies that address immigration, national security, and taxes. Anxious voters don't like incumbency or tribalism. They'd rather vote for challengers or political newcomers.

The upshot: candidates who understand the important role these emotions play can target them through their speeches, ads, music, imagery, and optics!

We're driven by our emotions because our brains are biologically built to operate this way. In his book *Just Listen: Discover the Secret to Getting Through to Absolutely Anyone*, Dr. Mark Goulston, who has worked with FBI agents and Fortune 500 CEOs, says:

You have not one, but three brains laid on top of one another. There's the outer layer—the neocortex, which we usually think of as our brain. It's the most recent, most evolved part that controls our higher-order functions, all the intellectual brilliance and impeccable manners we like to show the world. But there are two other, much older parts wrapped around each other below the neocortex: the reptilian, or lizard brain which triggers our survival instincts and fear responses; and the mammalian brain, our emotional center, the seat of all feelings and moods, and also memory.[17]

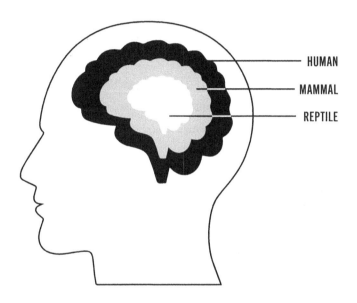

The more political candidates understand how the emotions of anger, enthusiasm, and anxiety govern voters' behavior, the more effectively they can connect with them. For example, when a constituent is in the grip of a powerful emotion—feeling strongly about a social or economic issue—they literally have no brain ability to process a candidate's logical message. The constituent

17   Goulston, Mark. *Just Listen: Discover the Secret to Getting Through to Absolutely Anyone.* New York: Amacom, 2015.

is running on raw emotion and base impulses. They can't think—so don't try to persuade them.

The candidate's goal in this instance is to recognize the constituent's block and, as Goulston says, "move people from lizard to mammalian brain back to human brain before trying to deliver your message."[18]

VOTES ARE DRIVEN BY SURVIVAL INSTINCTS

We're hardwired to make instant assessments about other people, using our limbic system's gut instinct. Damasio calls the gut "the first brain"[19]—and for good reason.

The deeply ingrained roots that form first impressions are throwbacks to our earliest ancestors. These primitive humans were better off listening to their guts than their brains. Why? Because their lives depended on it. When confronting a rival tribe or a savage beast, there wasn't time to debate a list of pros and cons. Surviving required snap judgments: fight or flight? Friend or foe?

Today is no different. When we feel our survival is threatened, we're much safer reacting from visceral instinct than wasting valuable time pondering a cerebral exit strategy.

Although our instincts were biologically created through evolution millennia ago, they are still very much active in our decision making. The political positions of candidates who appear on an election ballot feel connected to survival. Think of the emotions

---

18   Ibid.

19   Antonio Damasio, *The Strange Order of Things*, New York: Random House, 2018.

aroused by discussion of *Roe v. Wade*, healthcare, education, the Green New Deal, gun control, nuclear proliferation, immigration, climate change, the border wall, or the economy. We care about these issues because we believe they have a direct impact on our protection and safety.

CULTIVATING STRENGTH AND WARMTH

Voters want to see *strength and warmth* in their leaders because those two qualities seem to best guarantee a voter's well-being.

Psychologist Dr. Amy Cuddy, a Harvard researcher and popular TED speaker, found that people's first impressions primarily look to answer two questions:

- Can I trust this person? [Warmth]
- Can I respect this person? [Strength]

Cuddy found that people looked for answers to these questions, in that order—once again, because of primal survival instincts. A gifted leader is no good to you if you perceive him as a threat. Therefore, in forming any relationship, we look to establish trust first.[20]

The combination of these two qualities is key. Warmth assures us that we can trust them. Strength assures us of a leader's competence and capability. As humans we desire to have our needs met. We want to feel safe and secure because that ensures our survival.

---

20 "Harvard Psychologist: People's First Impression of You Is Based on 2 Basic Criteria..." *Birn Partners*. January 27, 2016.

Ultimately, voters choose the candidate they like: the one they trust, the one they feel understands someone like them. You've got to make the emotional connection because it's the positive emotional feeling voters are left with that will cement their bond with you.

If a voter decides she wants to vote for you for rational reasons, she may change her mind as soon as the incoming emotional data changes. One bad gaffe or false move, and you may lose her vote.

But if that same voter *likes* you, she'll be inclined to forgive you for any number of sins.

However, forgiveness has limits. A ridiculous and unrealistic example of this forgiveness fantasy—overlooking anything a candidate will say or do—took place at a campaign stop in Sioux City, Iowa, during the 2016 presidential campaign. Candidate Donald J. Trump controversially bragged, "You know what else they say about my people? The polls, they say I have the most loyal people. Did you ever see that? Where I could stand in the middle of Fifth Avenue and shoot somebody and I wouldn't lose any voters, okay? It's like incredible."[21]

How much time will you get before voters have concluded whether they like you, trust you, and feel you understand them? Surprisingly, only a few seconds.[22]

---

21   "Trump: I Could Stand in the Middle of Fifth Avenue and Shoot Somebody and I Wouldn't Lose Any Voters." *RealClear Politics*. January 23, 2016.

22   Baer, Drake. "Science Says People Decide These 9 Things within Seconds of Meeting You." *Business Insider*. September 05, 2018.

THE SCIENCE OF FIRST IMPRESSIONS

Imagine you're walking down the street, and you see someone approaching you at a distance. Your first impression is that it's a homeless person with a cart. They look hunched, and it sounds like they're mumbling. Your limbic system automatically fires up and without even consciously admitting it to yourself, you draw snap conclusions: "Homeless. Crazy. Avoid."

As the figure gets closer, however, the data changes. The limbic system calms down as the rational brain takes over: it's a mother, pushing a stroller. The apparent hunch is a backpack, and the mumbling is baby talk, spoken to her child. You relax, and your conclusions change: "Mother. Harmless. Cute child. Smile."

Our brains are hardwired to identify rapidly whether we can trust another person.[23] The psychological term for this snap judgment is called "thin-slicing." People take in quickly only the thinnest slice of someone else's behavior, speech, mannerisms, and appearance to decide whether they like or trust that person.

A thin-slice is not a rational decision—it's an instinctive gut reaction. Despite our speedy conclusions, first impressions have been found to be largely on target. One study asked students to rate professors after seeing a ten-second silent film clip of them. At the end of the semester, they were asked to rate the professors again. Amazingly, the evaluations lined up. Students took less

---

23   "Even Fact Will Not Change First Impressions." *ScienceDaily*. February 14, 2014.

than ten seconds to predict accurately whether these teachers would be good, or bad—"friend, or foe."[24]

As the saying goes, "you never get a second chance to make a first impression." First impressions are enormously difficult to change, and it's not surprising that when provided contradictory information that should logically change a person's impression of someone, first impressions stay fixed.[25]

Because a first impression is sealed so fast, it is paramount to immediately secure a positive emotional connection with voters. Emotion is processed in the brain much more quickly than information. The candidate's personality traits and optics are what provoke emotional reactions first in voters, followed by a discussion of the issues. What's most important is how the candidate presents themselves personally, and *then* how they present their plans.

Unsuccessful candidates can easily miss the mark. They incessantly talk policy and cite statistics rather than acknowledging voters' anger and frustration. Or they inadvertently insult the identity of a demographic instead of stoking their pride.

Strategies which target the rational brain have much less clout than strategies that aim at the gut. As a candidate, Trump knew this technique. Bill Clinton and Obama understood this method. Romney—as well as too many other candidates—failed to grasp

---

24   Ambady, Nalini, and Robert Rosenthal. "Half a Minute: Predicting Teacher Evaluations From Thin Slices of Nonverbal Behavior and Physical Attractiveness." *Journal of Personality and Social Psychology*. Vol. 64, no. 3 (1993): 431-441.

25   Nauert, Rick, PhD. "Why First Impressions Are Difficult to Change: Study." Live Science. January 19, 2011.

that winning requires an appeal to emotions to gain the voter's trust. Their survival is at stake, remember?

WE FEEL, THEN RATIONALIZE

Almost unknowingly, voters try hard to seek information that confirms their initial impression. Psychologists call this "confirmation bias." Essentially, we look only for facts that reinforce what we already believe, searching out media and content that is lopsided in favor of our current position.

The confirmation bias is constantly at work in our lives. You might be in the supermarket when you spot a woman whose child is throwing items off the shelves. If the mother ignores her child's behavior rather than showing signs of correcting him, you'd assume she has very little parental control. The thin slices you've observed have determined a firm first impression.

Your confirmation bias will now fight to seal that negative impression. Even if you were to have an enjoyable conversation with this woman in the checkout line later, after watching her behavior she would be hard-pressed to convince you that she could control her child.

Voters will extend the same confirmation bias either in your favor or against you. For all the voters you initially impressed, the confirmation bias will help you. They will look to give you the benefit of the doubt and cheer on your successes.

Voters who may be undecided or critical of you will be scanning for your every misstep and expect you to falter. And some will tend to gloat about it. As voters encounter repeated exposure to your candidacy, their impression of you will be reinforced—either positively or negatively.

And how is that impression reinforced? The rational brain finally steps in!

Emotion precedes reason, but reason doesn't want to be left out. We feel first and form our confirmation bias—and then rationalize. Our conscious brain collects reasons to justify the emotional reaction.

Psychologist Dr. Eyal Winter, author of *Feeling Smart: Why Our Emotions Are More Rational Than We Think,* writes, "There is a thin border between our emotional and analytical/cognitive internal system."[26] The "thin border" Winter talks about means there's very little separating the gut and the brain—they're inclined to agree with each other.

If your gut tells you that a certain candidate is likable, your brain internalizes that message cognitively and finds reasons to support that gut impression of likability: "Well, he's funny. He seems down-to-earth. And he created lots of jobs while he was governor." We may assume we're making a rational decision, when it's actually emotionally based.

Still, you need to give voters reasons to support you. Winter notes, "Emotions need to be credible, at least at some minimal

---

26   Winter, Eyal. *Feeling Smart: Why Our Emotions Are More Rational Than We Think.* New York: PublicAffairs, 2014.

level, if they're to serve us in creating credible commitment."[27] In other words, a candidate may successfully clinch a good first impression with voters, but it can't stop there. If you want voters to *commit* to you, you need to provide them with credible reasons to back up their positive impression.

Many voters will have their confirmation bias in place—either for you or against you—as soon as they read your party affiliation. Under these circumstances, you may not be able to sway them in either direction.

However, today, most close elections are decided by Non-Party Affiliates (NPAs): independent voters who do their best to evaluate candidates objectively. It's possible that NPAs may disagree with you on some of your policies but still ultimately decide they like you and give you their vote. For these independent and persuadable swing voters, it is critical to establish a positive emotional connection and reinforce it by providing them reasons to establish an authentic bond.

HOW TO CREATE CURB APPEAL

We now know that first impressions are crucial. Houses on the real estate market are often evaluated on their "curb appeal." Likewise, voters use drive-by "thin slices" of nonverbal cues to determine whether they like a candidate. And what exactly are the features they look for?

---

27   Ibid.

SMILE!

Your nonverbal cues are significant tip-offs to voters, as these cues form the first impression voters get of you. Consider the following:

- Fifty-five percent of what you communicate to people is accomplished visually, through your appearance and body language.[28]
- Thirty-eight percent comes from the impression you give vocally—your tone, volume, and cadence.
- Merely 7 percent of what we communicate to others comes through what we say. Remember, some research shows these first impressions are formed within a mere fraction of a second.

Smile! According to a study in the *Journal of Nonverbal Behavior* by Dr. Susanne Quadflieg of the University of Bristol, people whose smile appeared to be authentic (with wrinkles around one's eyes) were judged to be more intelligent than those whose smiles were deemed to be fake. She attributes this finding to the idea that our judgments are driven by hunches. Quadflieg says of her test subjects, "If they have a spontaneously favorable impression of a person—and authentic smiles can elicit a rapid favorable response—they tend to judge other characteristics, like intelligence of the person, also more positively. An authentic smile tends to enhance attractiveness."[29]

Harvard neuropsychologist Dr. Tali Sharot, author of *The Opti-*

---

28   Steib, Mike. *The Career Manifesto: Discover Your Calling and Create an Extraordinary Life*. New York: TarcherPerigee Book, 2018.

29   Fields, Lisa. "13 Easy (and Scientifically Proven!) Ways to Look Smarter." *Reader's Digest*. October 13, 2019.

mism Bias: A Tour of the Irrationally Positive Brain, says that optimism is hardwired into our cognitive processing.[30] If a candidate looks stern and tough, a voter feels threatened. They go on the defensive rather than moving towards a candidate.

UCLA neuroscientist Dr. Marco Iacoboni believes our brains are wired for sociability. His studies have found that if one person watches another person smile, mirror neurons in that person's brain will light up as if he were smiling himself.[31]

Robin Dreeke, founder of People Formula and former chief of the FBI's Counterintelligence Behavioral Analysis Program, says, "When you walk into a room with a bunch of strangers, are you naturally drawn to those who look angry and upset or those with smiles and laughing? Smiling is the number one nonverbal technique you should utilize to look more accommodating."[32]

Through social-cognitive studies, we know that our minds create snap judgments of character based on facial appearances. Within a split second of seeing a candidate's face, we unconsciously build opinions about their overall personality.[33] Voters instantly decide whether the candidate is strict, kind, honest, or competent based solely on how they appear. Even a photo posted on social media can communicate to voters an impression of a candidate's fitness for office.[34] When you create positive nonverbal emotional optics

30 Sharot, Tali. *The Optimism Bias: A Tour of the Irrationally Positive Brain.* New York: Vintage Books, 2012.

31 Colagrossi, Mike. "How Mirror Neurons Allow Us to Send Other People 'Good Vibes.'" *Big Think.* August 28, 2019.

32 Dreeke, Robin. *It's Not All about "Me": The Top Ten Techniques for Building Quick Rapport with Anyone.* People Formula. November 13, 2013.

33 Barr, Neta and Linz. "Very First Impressions." *Emotion.* Vol. 6 no. 2, (2006): 269–278.

34 Cafferty, Jack. "What If Voters Choose Candidates Based on Their Looks?" *CNN.* October 27, 2010.

cues with your facial expressions, you'll communicate warmth and strength to voters' unconscious minds.

During the 2012 Presidential election, Kasia Wezowski, co-director of the Center for Body Language, conducted an online study. She had 1,000 Democrats and Republicans view two-minute video clips of Mitt Romney and Barack Obama delivering neutral and emotional content at various campaign events. She recorded participants' facial expressions by webcam and looked for six key emotions: happy, surprised, afraid, disgusted, angry, and sad, coding for the "tenor of the emotion (positive or negative)" and how strongly it was expressed.[35] President Obama produced stronger emotional reactions with fewer negative feelings. Interestingly, 16 percent of Republicans had negative reactions to Governor Romney. When the candidate's body language was analyzed, researchers found that Obama displayed more "open, positive, confident positions congruent with his speech." By contrast, Romney "often gave out negative symbols, diminishing his message with contradictory and distracting facial expressions and movement."

USE POSITIVE BODY LANGUAGE

You'll be more self-assured if you can alter your physical stance—a nonverbal technique which may be helpful when you're fighting nerves backstage at a campaign rally! Amy Cuddy discovered that our basic body positioning can raise either our testosterone level (the hormone connected with confidence) or our cortisol levels (the hormone connected with stress).

---

35 Wezowski, Kasia. "6 Ways to Look More Confident During a Presentation." *Harvard Business Review.* April 6, 2017.

After observing the behavior of animals, Cuddy noticed that when these animals wanted to intimidate or dominate, they made themselves bigger. Some chimps raised their arms, bared teeth, and screeched. Birds puffed their feathers and spread their wings. The opposite happened when the chimps wanted to hide or flee: they made themselves smaller. What might happen when humans change their bodies in similar ways?

Cuddy conducted a test to study what hormonal changes occurred in humans after they spent time in either a "power pose," where their bodies were made larger (i.e., in a Wonder Woman stance), versus a "submissive" pose, where they made their bodies smaller—hunched over, or curled up, like a person bent over a cell phone.

Cuddy's results were remarkable. She found that testosterone levels consistently went up after test subjects spent just two minutes in one of her power poses. On the other hand, participants who'd held the submissive pose had an uptick in their stress hormone, cortisol.

Even more fascinating, Dr. Cuddy found that these hormonal changes were visible to strangers. She then examined how participants were perceived in an interview setting. The test subjects who had spent time in the "power poses" before being interviewed were consistently graded as more competent, charismatic, and capable by an unbiased panel of other participants.[36]

Cuddy's rallying cry to those hearing about her research is "Fake it 'til you become it!" By simply making your body larger in your

36   Cuddy, Amy. "Your Body Language May Shape Who You Are | Amy Cuddy." *YouTube*. October 1, 2012.

posture and stance, you can literally change your brain chemistry. You will authentically feel and be perceived as more confident and capable.

Pay attention to your posture as you interact with voters. If you walk with your shoulders scrunched, you will appear weak and untrustworthy. If you make yourself look too stern and imposing, you might make some people feel threatened. Adopt a posture that is relaxed and upright, and you'll portray warmth and openness.

Using hand gestures as you speak can help articulate your point—think of Bill Clinton or JFK, who both pointed their index fingers to punctuate specific ideas in their speeches—but it's important to keep your hand gestures somewhat contained. Three recent major Democratic candidates, Bernie Sanders, Beto O'Rourke, and Elizabeth Warren, use flailing hand gestures in their campaign appearances, and the effect is distracting. Sanders' gesticulations, which would normally be considered annoying, are often overlooked because people agree with him philosophically. O'Rourke, however, moves all over the place like a kung fu master, and his restless gestures make him appear scattered. Warren's hands never stop talking.

Limit the amount of hand gestures you use as you verbalize your ideas. According to Kasia Wezowski:

> Early in Bill Clinton's political career he would punctuate his speeches with big, wide gestures that made him appear untrustworthy. To help him keep his body language under control, his advisors taught him to manage a box in front of his chest and belly

and contain his hand movements within it. Since then, the 'Clinton box' has become a popular term in the field.[37]

Picture a box around your torso that extends from your shoulders to the bottom of your waist: your gestures should be contained within this space. By making sure your gestures accent—rather than detract from—your message, you give your audience an opportunity to connect with you. They'll be able to listen to your words instead of trying to follow your call to arms.

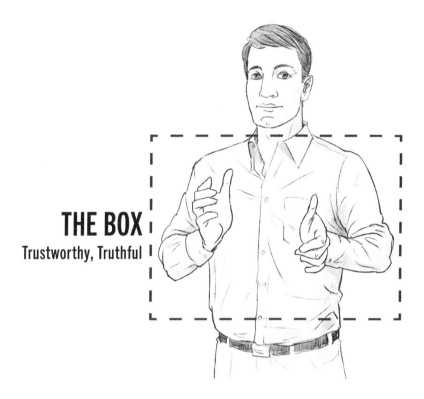

THE BOX
Trustworthy, Truthful

SIMILARITY CREATES LIKING

Presenting yourself as someone whom voters can relate to is

---

37   Ibid, Wezowski.

key. Have you ever seen a couple that looked physically similar—almost as though they could be brother and sister? These couples hint at a neurologically proven fact: we like people who are like us. Our survival is better assured if someone is like us. Today's political tribalism is based on this principle.

Despite evolution, we are still on constant alert for physical attacks from foes. In modern-day life, our philosophical differences can feel threatening and dangerous—our survival instincts are triggered and play out on the political battlefield. But when we know someone agrees with us, they no longer feel like a danger. *Similarity* creates *liking*. And we determine whether another person is like us within milliseconds of a first impression.

Psychological research has examined how much we assume we are like others from first impressions alone. In one study, participants inventoried their own personality traits. Then, they were shown silent video clips of politicians they didn't know. After watching the videos, they inventoried the politicians' personalities, based on nonverbal cues, using the same scale. Finally, participants were asked: would you vote for this candidate? Consistently, participants said they would vote for candidates who seemed most similar to themselves.[38]

This study concluded that we use our own personalities as a reference point for judging others. As a candidate, you should know that the more voters can personally relate to you, the more likely they are to vote for you. When you "mirror" voters—use similar phrasing, dress like them, walk like them—they will, even if not

---

38 Koppensteiner, Markus, and Pia Stephan. "Voting for a Personality: Do First Impressions and Self-evaluations Affect Voting Decisions?" *Journal of Research in Personality* 51 (2014): 62-68.

consciously aware of it, think, "Hey! He's just like me." And *similarity* creates *liking*.

When you're backstage at a campaign rally, peek through the curtain. Examine the hats: do they have work logos? If so, what kind of logos? Is this a working-class crowd? What's written on the t-shirts? Are there many people wearing sports paraphernalia? What are the relative ages? What's written on the signs? You can pick up a wealth of information just by scanning the audience, which can indicate who people are and what they may care about.

When you walk onstage, speak to those needs. If you can, adjust your appearance to better match your audience. If they're casually dressed, roll up your sleeves. If you saw a hat with "City Electric" emblazoned on it, you can say, "To my friends out there who are electricians or plumbers, or work for a living in trades—" then, speak to the issues that concern them. You can establish a tight bond by highlighting similarities between yourself and the audience.

You can enhance your approach to an audience of voters by doing some homework ahead of time. Be a savvy candidate. Have campaign volunteers collect questions from the crowd to find out their main concerns. The volunteers can pick up snippets of conversations and additional clues by mingling with the attendees, and they can pass all that information on to you.

LISTEN UP

Don't just watch your audience of voters; listen to them, too. Emphasize that every candidate and politician should be, according to speaker and performance coach Akash Karia, more *interested* to be *interesting*.[39] To draw interest from voters, you'll need to demonstrate your interest in them. Ask voters to tell you about themselves.

In her book *Small Talk Hacks,* Karia describes how two Harvard University psychologists found that when a person talks about themselves, their brain releases dopamine, a chemical neurotransmitter that activates the same pleasure center in the brain as food does. Karia says, "People would forgo money in order to talk about themselves." Use this research to your advantage as a candidate by learning to listen.

Don't hog the conversation to impress voters or be what Tim Herrara calls a "conversation bully." Be willing to hear voters' perspectives and acknowledge or even solicit opinions that oppose your own. If you make a declarative statement like "I believe in Second Amendment rights to possess a gun," also say, "That's my opinion; what do you think?"

Wired into our DNA is the need to feel understood by others. As a candidate you need to stop talking and start listening so you can diagnose a voter's raw emotions.

According to Elitsa Dermendzhiyska, because voter emotions are raw, their feelings need to be taken seriously.[40] Make sure voters know you feel their issues are important and matter to you. "The key, counterintuitively, is to show that you empathize

39   Karia, Akash. *Small Talk Hacks.* AkashKaria.com, 2015.

40   Dermendzhiyska, Elitsa. "What World-Class Communicators Do Differently: 3 Lessons from Neuroscience." *Medium.* April 24, 2017.

by acknowledging their negative emotions," Dermendzhiyska says. That way, you pull the other person towards you instead of pushing them away. Dig deeper into their frustration. Don't interrupt, even if you feel attacked. When you understand and acknowledge their stance, you'll be able to better get through to them with your ideas.

Dermendzhiyska says to avoid a rookie mistake of speaking too soon, keep quiet and encourage your voter to keep digging deeper into how they feel about an issue. "Remember, this is just another person's subjective experience of the situation. You don't need to agree with their story, you just need to hear it out. Think about saving the relationship versus winning the argument."

CONVEY STRENGTH AND WARMTH

This chapter focused on helping you create a *positive first impression*. That favorable "gut connection" will create a confirmation bias that will work in your favor.

And what else? Surely, if it were that simple, candidates wouldn't politically sin as often as they do. Political candidates slip up in any number of ways, especially if they don't make voters' emotions a top priority.

The success of a first impression comes down to *strength* and *warmth*. Think of the memorable politicians who have lost major elections in recent years. Many of them, unfortunately, can be summed up in one critical word: Hillary Clinton, untrustworthy. Sarah Palin, uninformed. John Kerry, flip-flopper. Mitt Romney, not relatable.

Despite being very accomplished leaders, these candidates failed to impress voters because they were seen to be lacking either *strength* or *warmth*. They were deemed either weak or unlikable. For candidates, specific traits matter. The emotional optics of your personality traits will make or break a campaign.

Most candidates tend to be more gifted in one category than another. John F. Kennedy, George W. Bush, Ronald Reagan, Bill Clinton, and Barack Obama were easily likable candidates, but they had to prove their strength and competence to be President.

Richard Nixon, Hillary Clinton, George H. W. Bush, and Al Gore were all unquestionably qualified to be President but struggled to communicate warmth and affability to voters. The smart candidates were those who worked to overcome their deficits. The candidates who failed to be emotionally mindful of their shortcomings—and take corrective action—lost elections.

As we get into the chapters devoted to the seven political sins and virtues, take stock of yourself. Are you smart, capable, with plenty of experience to discuss? Then work on marketing your likability. Your strength virtues will already be obvious. Are you charismatic, warm, and personable? If so, work on marketing your strength as a leader. Your charm will already be evident.

The rest of this book aims to address specific ways that candidates will "sin" politically. Each sin is paired with a virtue—for example, biblically the deadly sin of envy is paired with the corrective virtue of gratitude.

I've identified seven deadly political "sins" that turn off voters.

Each chapter discusses a campaign sin and how it destroys your chances of connecting emotionally with your constituents.

With the right training and deliberate practice, you can transform each sin into a virtue.

CHAPTER TWO

FROM PESSIMISTIC
TO OPTIMISTIC

"An optimist sees an opportunity in every calamity; a pessimist sees a calamity in every opportunity."

—SIR WINSTON CHURCHILL

"Malaise" is a word which implies a general feeling of uneasiness. It's the sense of weakness your body experiences before coming down with a cold, or several cloudy days without sun. "The Malaise Speech" was the title assigned by the media to President Jimmy Carter's famous televised address, given on July 15, 1979, during the third year of his presidency.

As Carter neared the end of his final year in office, the American public became increasingly agitated. Drivers waited for hours in mile-long lines to get gas, and interest rates were at a staggering 18 percent. The country appeared to be floundering and was still divided by Watergate and the Iran hostage crisis. The July 4 celebration at the White House had been canceled due to rain, and the President's expected national address had been likewise postponed. Carter decided that, rather than speak yet again about the energy crisis, he would discuss the deeper issue he felt plagued the American people. After ten days of soul searching, he arrived at his diagnosis: "A crisis of confidence."[41]

Carter felt in command of the issues. He began his speech well, identifying himself as a leader who desired to listen to the people and feel their pain. But then his message abruptly took a pessimistic turn.

While staring directly into the lens of the TV camera, Jimmy Carter complained that the "erosion of confidence in the future is threatening to destroy the social and political fabric of America." His emotional optics and physical gestures resembled that of a scolding father. Carter was asking the people of America to rise to a higher moral calling. He summoned his fellow Americans to discard their "worship" of "self-indulgence and consumption," and choose instead confidence and purpose.

Initially, the address was received positively. Carter appeared to persuade Americans that they could rise above the "crisis of confidence" he'd identified. But at Carter's first misstep—firing several Cabinet members shortly after the speech—Americans swung the other way. The public mood, along with his poll numbers, plummeted.

Rather than take personal responsibility for the moral crisis facing America, citizens concluded it must be the fault of their leader. It

41   Carter, Jimmy. Top 100 Speeches of the 20th Century - American Rhetoric. Accessed January 08, 2019.

was Carter who was failing to lead them. It was Carter who was responsible for the gas shortages and bad economy—Carter, who was weak and failing to inspire.

At the polls in the 1980 election, the American people made their disappointment in the thirty-ninth president clear. Carter was trounced by Republican challenger Ronald Reagan, who won forty-four states and 489 electoral votes—or 90.9 percent of those votes. This was the most lopsided presidential win ever for a first-time president. In voters' eyes, Jimmy Carter himself was their personal "crisis of confidence." To them, he was no longer a strong or capable leader.

What was Carter's chief sin, which convinced the American people he was no longer fit to hold office? His pessimism.

THE SIN OF PESSIMISM

Pessimism doesn't work politically. Voters want aspirational leaders who will orient them towards a brighter future. If you don't seem capable of envisioning a better tomorrow, how could you possibly lead?

Harvard professor Tali Sharot, author of *The Optimism Bias,* says, "To make progress, we need to be able to imagine alternative realities—and not just any old reality, but a better one. And we need to believe we can achieve it."[42] We rely on our leaders to construct those new realities for us and show us the way to move forward.

No wonder the American people's "crisis of confidence" was

42   Sharot, Tali. *The Optimism Bias: A Tour of the Irrationally Positive Brain.* New York: Vintage Books, 2012.

pinned on Carter. The prevailing opinion became that he didn't know how to rally his fellow citizens. Americans concluded he couldn't step up and exude optimism.

Citizens wanted Carter to listen to them, and he listened well—he correctly identified the prevailing mood in the country. However, Carter didn't balance the "malaise" with a message of hope, optimism, and action. In failing to inspire, he was branded an unacceptably weak leader.

Politicians certainly *should* acknowledge the emotional state and personal challenges of their constituents. But if they don't counter these negative feelings with their own message of optimism, they'll, like Carter, also be viewed as incompetent. Consider, once again, how this relates to our survival: in times of crisis, is a person better off following a leader who is negative and not forward-looking, or one that is positive and solution-oriented?

Americans view pessimism as a profound attitude weakness when times are most dire. They desire a candidate who serves as a cheerleader to rally them out of frustration and fear; one who says, "Follow me, I know the way. Don't give up. You can do it!"

In the Republican presidential primary of 2016, the sixteen candidates competing for the nomination often seemed like squabbling children. Perhaps the feeding frenzy was to be expected: attacks beget counterattacks. If they failed to counterattack, criticized candidates assumed—probably rightly—that viewers would see them as weak. Unfortunately, the free-for-all pummeling and scorched-earth tactics continued throughout the four debates—and beyond.

Potential nominees' jabs, insults, interruptions, and rounds of incivility made for great entertainment but did little to inspire hope or confidence in the American people.

Democrats, likewise, have failed to project optimism in recent years. Their 2016 frontrunner, Hillary, had a decisive "anti-message" that was echoed by many of her fellow Democrats in other races. However, those candidates, including Hillary, were roundly criticized for failing to articulate their own positive platform of how they would lead the country to a better future.

IF THERE'S NO OPTIMISM—THERE'S NO IMPRESSION OF STRENGTH

Professor Robert F. Bruner, Dean Emeritus of the University of Virginia's Darden School of Business, researched what makes a good leader. His work focused on US presidents, and he used a combination of literary studies and social science to analyze the role of optimism in leadership.[43] He conducted a "sentiment analysis" of post WWII presidents' writings to show indications of optimism. Bruner concluded—after extensive reading of presidents' biographies, memoirs, and State of the Union and inaugural speeches—that Dwight D. Eisenhower was the most optimistic of the post-WWII presidents.[44] Eisenhower's deliberate use of optimism was a "political posture" used as "emotional reinforcement"—even when he was feeling exhausted, fearful, and dejected.

---

43   Bruner, Robert F. "Better Angels of Our Nature: Optimism in Presidential Leadership." *Darden School of Business*. October 18, 2016.

44   Bruner, Robert F. "Optimism in Presidential Leadership: Case of Eisenhower's Smile." *Darden School of Business*. October 19, 2016.

Bruner believes that President Trump's election was an anomaly and exception to the previous findings that "nine out of ten times, the more optimistic candidate wins."

What about Trump?

How do we understand Donald J. Trump's appeal if it is the exception to the rule? Trump's campaign, Republican National Convention speech, and Inauguration speech were all famously negative.[45] And yet—he trounced his Republican rivals and garnered the necessary electoral votes to beat Hillary Clinton for the presidency. How did candidate Trump get away with running with his pessimism, where others haven't?

Unlike Jimmy Carter, Trump didn't end his speeches on a pessimistic note. He finished with the message that he adopted from Ronald Reagan's earlier presidential campaign phrase: "Make America Great Again." Millions of angry, anxious, disheartened, and disenfranchised voters found this slogan to be such an uplifting charge that hundreds of thousands flocked to his rallies and wore campaign hats with MAGA emblazoned on the front.

Additionally, any fallout from the public's impression of Trump's pessimism was largely absorbed by the story he told. Trump demagogued to ordinary people. His vitriol stirred up anxiety and anger, cast his opponents as convincing villains, and portrayed him as the hero who would restore America from its current state as a "hell hole" into greatness once again.[46]

---

45 Cook, Lindsey. "Donald Trump Is a Negative Nancy, and Republicans Positively Love It." U.S. News & World Report. February 23, 2016.

46 "Trump: 'This Country Is a Hell Hole, I Want to Make It Great Again'." Fox News. May 21, 2015.

In Donald J. Trump's story, he would ride, like Robin Hood, out from the woods of Central Park to "drain the DC swamp." He proclaimed, "I know the 'system'—and it is 'rigged.'" Trump loudly voiced that he was the only candidate with the know-how to help Americans who felt they had been ignored.

When he campaigned, Trump and his team swore they were not going to repeat Mitt Romney's 2012 mistakes. Trump did allow himself to be branded an "out-of-touch rich businessman," but he reversed the narrative by claiming he would take from the rich and give to the poor and middle-class.

Yes, Trump too was raised in a privileged family, and like Mitt, he was a highly successful businessman. Unlike Romney, who failed to proudly own his business wealth to promote his leadership skills, candidate Trump took the offensive by not allowing his opponents to use his mega-money as a weapon against him. Instead, he embraced and celebrated his billionaire status, boasting about it proudly as his way to sell hope to down-and-out Americans. It worked. Despite chronic bullying of his opponents and overwhelming the data monitors with boorish behavior and negative language, Trump still managed to come up with his own message of strength and optimism. Being true to his reality TV persona, Trump reportedly told his aides before taking office that they should think of every day as "an episode in a television show in which he vanquishes rivals."[47]

"I will fight for you" and "I alone can fix it," he promised the

---

[47] Poniewozik, James. "The Real Donald Trump Is a Character on TV." *The New York Times.* September 9, 2019.

American people—and enough voters bought his promise to vote him into office.[48]

TODAY'S POLITICAL MOOD: MALAISE

Candidates must exude optimism in today's culture.[49]

Polling shows Americans are more anxious, stressed, and forlorn than they've ever been. Frankly, we have never been more depressed.[50]

Over 50 percent of Americans feel lonely, with 40 percent saying they feel isolated, lack meaningful relationships, and lack companionship.[51] We're also more pessimistic.[52] For the first time, today's youth predict they'll be worse off than their parents.[53]

The Federal Reserve's 2017 Survey of Household Economics and Decision-Making shows that while economic security has marginally improved—for US citizens both inside and outside of the middle-class—Americans still feel in a position of "financial fragility." The report shows that one-third of American adults can't afford a $400 surplus expense, and some 6 percent can't

48   Schwartz, Ian. "Trump: "Clinton Campaign of Destruction" Will Ensure No Successful Person Will Run For Office Again." *RealClearPolitics*. October 14, 2016.

49   Thompson, Dennis. "More Americans Suffering from Stress, Anxiety and Depression, Study Finds." *CBS News*. April 17, 2017.

50   Thompson, Dennis. "More Americans Suffering from Stress, Anxiety and Depression, Study Finds." *CBS News*. April 17, 2017.

51   Jenkins, Aric. "Half of Americans Feel Lonely, Study Finds." *Fortune*. May 1, 2018.

52   Dann, Carrie. "America the Pessimistic: New Poll Shows Lackluster Views of the U.S." *NBCNews.com*. September 5, 2017.

53   Wieczner, Jen. "Most Millennials Think They'll Be Worse Off Than Their Parents." *Fortune*. March 1, 2016.

manage such an expense, even if they borrowed the money or sold something.[54]

We're also more divided philosophically, with partisan lines hardening and shared discourse shrinking.[55]

Today, Americans distrust politicians and increasingly distrust the political process.[56] And sadly, Americans' feelings of patriotism are on the decline. A Gallup poll released around the Fourth of July 2019 found that the percentage of Americans who felt "extremely proud" to identify as an American fell to the lowest level in the poll's eighteen-year history—just 47 percent, down from 70 percent in 2003. And a poll by the *Wall Street Journal* and NBC found recently that when broken out by age, the younger you are, the less likely you see patriotism as a "very important" value. Americans older than age fifty-five saw almost 80 percent agreement with the statement versus only 42 percent of those under age thirty-eight.[57] Is the ideal of American patriotism, as Samuel Johnson, the English man of letters said, reduced to "the last refuge of a scoundrel"?

Reports of Russian and Chinese troll farms infiltrating social media to sway public opinion and elections, fake news, deep fakes, and biometric technologies, along with reports of rogue FBI agents spying on political candidates, a two-tiered justice

54   "Report on the Economic Well-Being of US Households in 2017." *Federal Reserve Board*. May 2018.

55   Shepard, Steven, et al. "Study: Americans More Divided along Party Lines than Ever." *Politico*. October 5, 2017.

56   Montanaro, Domenico. "Here's Just How Little Confidence Americans Have In Political Institutions." *NPR*. January 17, 2018.

57   Adam Kirsch, "American Patriotism Is Worth Fighting For," *Wall Street Journal,* October 19, 2019.

system, and suspected voting fraud, now convince many Americans that the government system is stacked against them.

There's enormous distrust of the media as well. Culture wars rage. Identity politics, multiculturalism, and intersectionality dominate our public discourse. The Democrats are working tirelessly to impeach President Trump while slouching towards socialism, and the Republicans are moving toward populism—with each mainstream party racing as fast as they can towards their most extreme political position.

Perhaps—like Carter's 1980s Americans—we may be contributors to our culture of extreme ideology, division, and pessimism. But that doesn't mean we want to stay there.

General James Mattis, former Secretary of Defense under President Trump and former Supreme Allied Commander Transformation says in the *Wall Street Journal* that he is concerned that Americans today are too divisive.

> We are dividing into hostile tribes cheering against each other, fueled by emotion and mutual disdain that jeopardizes our future, instead of rediscovering our common ground and finding solutions. All Americans need to recognize that our democracy is an experiment—one that can be reversed. We all know that we're better than our current politics. Tribalism must not be allowed to destroy our experiment.[58]

We need office holders who can unify us, who can cross the aisle to work with the opposing party and get things done—rather than

58   Mattis, James. "Duty, Democracy and the Threat of Tribalism." *Wall Street Journal.* August 31, 2019.

line up opposite each other with ten-foot poles in their hands. Americans want leaders who will give them hope and bring them back together for the common good.

THE VIRTUE OF OPTIMISM

As the frustrated Americans in the eighties began to doubt Carter's leadership, another politician rose up with an inspiring message.

Former California governor Ronald Reagan's campaign narrative fit perfectly with America's yearning for change and a brighter future. Addressing Americans dealing with surging inflation, high unemployment, threat from the Soviet Union, an Iran hostage crisis, and spiking interest rates, Reagan asked, "Are you better off today than you were four years ago?"

Reagan's question formed a compelling narrative. The victims of anomie were the morale-depleted Americans. The villain was Carter. The hero was Ronald Reagan. His entire campaign was based upon a theme of restoring America's patriotism, pride, and spirit.

Reagan was naturally optimistic. Like Eisenhower before him, Reagan was fueled by his love of country and ran all his campaigns on optimism. Everything he did dripped with warmth, friendliness, and confidence. He wanted to revive the can-do enthusiasm in the country, and he did this by boosting the self-esteem of the American people. Ed Meese, Reagan's campaign manager said, "[Optimism] was just such a natural characteristic of Ronald Reagan that it was implicit in everything we did...He didn't come out and say, 'We should revive our spirits.' He did this subtly by his own manner, by the ideas he projected and by his talks in which he expressed his confidence in the American people."[59]

President Carter had complained that Americans lacked confidence. Referring to a speech in which Carter spoke of a crisis of confidence in America, Ed Meese said, "Ronald Reagan's idea was that the people aren't in a malaise, the leaders are in a malaise."

Reagan called his fellow Americans heroes. He said, "Heroism is a trait of ordinary people who are meeting the everyday challenges of their own lives and the country." The media nicknamed Reagan the "Great Communicator" for the skills he honed from his days in radio, as a movie actor and TV host of General Electric Theatre.

Reagan used his positivity and warmth, through his speaking and storytelling, to reassure the public that everything was going to be okay, so long as he was in charge. No wonder we put our faith in optimistic leaders who imply they will protect us and enhance our survival!

THE SCIENCE FOR OPTIMISM

Happy people attract us. This should come as no surprise—advertisers have been taking advantage of the optimism appeal for years. Unless you're watching a commercial for a migraine headache medication, most ads on TV feature people who are smiling.

59 White, Jason. "In Dark Times, Reagan Ran On Optimism." *NBCNews*. October 13, 2008.

Several research studies show that happier and more positive people are regarded as more energetic, more resilient, and more creative.[60] They are better liked and more wanted as friends.[61] And optimistic people are more likely to live longer and achieve "exceptional longevity"—living to age eighty-five or older.[62]

Upbeat people are also more sought-after as leaders. Political science research shows that citizens want their politicians to be optimistic—especially their candidates for president. One study examined the national convention acceptance speeches of presidential candidates after they had won their party's nomination, going back twenty-two election cycles. The study specifically looked at the level of optimism in each candidate's speech, compared to their opponent. In eighteen out of twenty-two elections, the more optimistic candidate went on to win the presidency.[63]

Furthermore, greater optimism led to a bigger win. The more positive the candidate was in projecting hope that America's problems were temporary and that they were going to set things right (relative to their opponent), the wider the margin of victory.[64] And the more optimistic the candidate, the more actively they were campaigning. Over the past thirty-five years, it appears that the most optimistic candidates won much of the time.

According to Dr. Sonya Lyubomirsky, a social psychologist and

60 Cohn, Michael A., et al. "Happiness Unpacked: Positive Emotions Increase Life Satisfaction by Building Resilience." *Emotion*. June 2009. 9(3): 361-368.

61 Achor, Shawn. *The Happiness Advantage*. New York: Broadway Books. 2010.

62 "New Evidence That Optimists Live Longer." *Boston University School of Medicine*. August 26, 2019.

63 Zullow, Harold M. and Martin E. P. Seligman. "Pessimistic Rumination Predicts Defeat of Presidential Candidates, 1900 to 1984," *Psychological Inquiry*, 1990, 1(1): 52-61.

64 Goleman, Daniel. "For Presidential Candidates, Optimism Appears a Winner." *New York Times*. May 8, 1988.

author of *The How of Happiness,* "Optimistic leaders are perceived to be more effective and happier people and even judged as more likely to go to heaven."[65]

Neuroscientist Dr. Tali Sharot makes the point that "Optimism may be so essential to our survival that it is hardwired into our most complex organ, the brain."[66] Sharot explains that pessimism is often paired with fear. When we feel pessimistic, our brain lights up the amygdala, an almond-shaped set of neurons located deep in the brain's medial temporal lobe. Part of the primitive limbic system that controls emotion, it's the same place that lights up when we sense we're in danger.

On the other hand, optimism activates the nucleus accumbens, the part of the brain associated with pleasure and happiness. Because we are biologically biased towards optimism, we have a built-in desire to feel happy.

The specific dangers humans have faced over the centuries may have decreased, but there's still plenty to be afraid of. A tanking economy, stock market crash, impending wars, attacks on our values—there's no shortage of perceived threats that make us feel uneasy. If all this neuroscience is correct, what we inherently seek is a political hero who will assure us that everything is going to be okay.

In fact, we rely on our leaders for this assurance. One survey conducted of 1,500 adults asked people the following on a seven-

---

65   Lyubomirsky, Sonya. "To Be Elected President, It Helps to Be an Optimist." *Psychology Today,* November 24, 2015.

66   Ibid, Sharot.

point scale: Generally speaking, how optimistic or pessimistic do you want your political leaders to be? They also asked participants to rate their own personal optimism.[67]

The results showed that people in the study wanted their leaders to be *more* optimistic than they themselves were. That preference for optimism held up across differences in gender, ideology, political parties, religion, and education. On the same survey, "pessimistic" and "overly pessimistic" were rated the least valued traits.

Conclusion: Americans want their political candidates and representatives to be positive. They'd rather have leaders err on the side of being overly rosy than be anything close to downbeat. Successful presidential candidates have played into this, offering optimistic visions for our country. In 1932, Franklin Delano Roosevelt campaigned with the slogan "Happy Days are Here Again." In 1984, Reagan's tagline was "It's Morning in America Again." In 2012 Obama's campaign ran on "Yes We Can."

For a candidate to win the hearts and minds of voters, he must be able to persuade these voters to imagine beyond the status quo. Inspirational figures are those who show us what that better idea might be—and how to get there.

THE SOCIAL FLOW STATE

To be a great and emotionally connected candidate, take the focus off yourself. Instead, focus on others. This will put you in

---

67   "Do US Voters Prefer Optimistic Politicians? Here's What We Found." *Washington Post*. August 1, 2016.

a "flow" state, where you can stop worrying about how others perceive you.[68]

Flow is a term used by University of Chicago psychologist Dr. Mihaly Csikszentmihalyi to describe the mental zone where you lose awareness of what you are doing. In a "flow" state, your prefrontal cortex, the self-critical part of the brain, shuts down.

You might be familiar with being in "flow." Have you ever been doing something, looked at your watch, and wondered whether it was broken because time had passed so quickly? That's being in a flow state.

As a candidate, when you are in a social flow state you feel your best and will come across as highly charismatic. The way to achieve that experience is to focus on the people you're talking to and look for what you can value in them.

Cheerfulness, an appreciation of others, confidence in a better future—these are captivating qualities to be around. And when a candidate delivers a speech that combines those assets, the payoff is usually emotionally compelling.

Imagine that you're a voter who has felt frustrated with the status quo or feels cheated that society has left you behind. Suddenly, a new political candidate comes on the scene who makes you feel understood and appreciated. This candidate is fun, funny, and upbeat—it's a joy to listen to them. What's more, this candidate lays out a vision for the future that, if carried out, would make your life noticeably better. When this candidate talks, you get

---

68 Csikszentmihalyi, Mihaly. *Flow*. New York: Harper Collins. July 1, 2008.

swept up in what they're saying. The candidate gets your juices flowing, inspires your enthusiasm and makes you want to spread their message to others.

Recall the brain science we've already covered. When listeners' emotions are evoked, their brains are alert and tuned in. Because of this arousal, charismatic candidates who are emotionally compelling are great at capturing people's attention and getting them to share in their vision.[69]

Dr. John Antonakis, a professor of organizational behavior at the University of Lausanne, says, "Basically put, charisma is all about signaling information in a symbolic, emotional and value-based manner. Thus, charisma signaling is all about using verbal—what you say—and non-verbal techniques."[70]

There are four general characteristics of charismatic people:[71]

1. They have a high degree of self-confidence.
2. They are good at expressing themselves and capture the attention of other people.
3. They are open to exploring new ideas and taking new (and sometimes risky) approaches to solve problems.
4. They are creative and establish new visions for how to accomplish goals.

Charismatic people can persuade through their words, encour-

69 Markman, Art, PhD. "Too Much Charisma Is Bad for Leadership." *Psychology Today*. March 26, 2018.

70 Clark, Bryan. "What Makes People Charismatic, and How You Can Be, Too." *New York Times*. August 15, 2019.

71 Ibid, Markman.

age with their optimism and confidence, and be assertive by using their understanding of emotions—both theirs and those of other people.

And, perhaps most importantly, charismatic people, according to Kevin Daum in an *Inc.* article, "connect empathically." He writes, "They genuinely and instinctively focus their eyes, ears, and soul on your being, not theirs. They make you laugh, they make you feel heard, they make you feel special or fascinated or safe or interesting. It isn't the same feeling in every case. But people connect and stay because they are having strong, positive emotions in the presence of someone truly charismatic."[72]

As a candidate, the last thing you want to do is to chase people or beg them to vote for you. Instead, you want others to pursue you. Charisma captivates people so they'll gravitate towards you naturally—and the biggest two components of projecting charisma are optimism and confidence.

CRAFTING A MESSAGE OF OPTIMISM

The specific words you speak and the way you structure your message can convey optimism or—if done badly—imply pessimism. Let's look at some specific forms of messaging that can help show that you possess an optimistic outlook.

USE POSITIVE MESSAGING

Optimistic candidates use words that are universally positive and nonpartisan. In Ronald Reagan's 1981 Inaugural Address, his

---

72 Ibid, Daum.

speech was peppered with words like "strong," "prosperous," and "new beginning."[73] Bill Clinton campaigned with the Fleetwood Mac song "Don't Stop," using the image of a new day to inspire voters. Think of Obama's slogan, "Yes We Can!" Or FDR's campaign words, "Happy Days Are Here Again." Choose messaging that is cheerful, forward-looking, and upbeat.

Reframe issues in a way that finds the positive slant. Whereas Jimmy Carter complained that Americans were experiencing a "crisis of confidence," Reagan told Americans that they were "everyday heroes." Reagan, like Carter, acknowledged Americans' struggle, but rather than criticizing them for contributing to their own troubles, he affirmed their heroic efforts at dealing with the challenges. That's positive reframing.

Americans need their values and standards affirmed. Your job is to explain how you'll help them move into a new and better future. We live in a country with an amazing history, and there's plenty to discuss about the ideals that will arouse voters' patriotism. Remind them: this is still, and has always been, the best place on the planet to live and fulfill the American dream.

Political Legerdemain: Answer the Question You Want

Candidates often find themselves faced with unpleasant questions, either about issues outside their current knowledge, gaps in their experience, or foibles from their past dug up through opposition research. It can be difficult to be cheerful in those moments. You can easily feel defensive and let anxiety or anger leak out. So, when under pressure, how do you maintain optimism?

73   Reagan, Ronald. "Inaugural Address." The American Presidency Project. January 20, 1981.

In those moments of pressure, I always advise candidates to answer the question they *wanted asked*, not the one they were asked. Some candidates do this clumsily, and their dodge is obvious. Some politicians, like former presidents Richard Nixon and Barack Obama, were masters at it. Telling a story can help you do this well.

Let's say the moderator asks, "What have you done or will do in your position as governor, commissioner, or mayor to address the shortage of affordable housing?" Maybe you don't like the question you've been given—let's say you haven't done much to address affordable housing. However, you have made *some* efforts to help improve business in your state, and you'd prefer to talk about that.

Gracefully shift the focus by telling a story that resonates with voters and ends optimistically. The story will pull your listeners' attention towards what you want them to focus on and can establish you as a likable candidate.

Former Florida governor and now US Senator Rick Scott became terrific at using the technique of answering the question he wanted asked. You can learn to use the same skill. When Scott lacked enough facts to answer a question about an issue, he wouldn't bluff an answer. Instead, he'd pivot and begin talking about his personal life story. He related how he grew up in public housing in the Midwest with an adoptive father who was a truck driver and a mother that was a store clerk. He was a latchkey kid from an early age.

As Scott spoke, you could see listeners were paying attention.

The crowd soon forgot the original question. He would then use his story to make an important point: he understood their frustration and fears about putting a roof over their head and food on the table, educating their children, and having enough money in retirement. He then told them what he could do to help: create jobs!

Beginning with a story such as the one Senator Scott told captures your audience's attention and shows you understand the challenge of living with less—you understand *them*. As voters listen to your story, their brains start producing oxytocin, which will bond them to you. If you don't have an empathic story from your own background, reference a story of someone you know and care about.

Start your answer by "feeling the pain" of the people who are represented by the moderator's question. When asked a question about the challenge of creating affordable housing, tell an empathic story like this: "I remember watching my mom sit at our kitchen table when I was a kid, staring at her checkbook. She usually had receipts piled around her. I remember once asking her if I could get a bike for Christmas, and she told me, 'Honey, I don't even know how I'm going to pay rent. I don't know how we're going to get you a bike.' So I get it. I've been there."

Whether you have held previous office or been an executive or worker with no prior political experience, you then need to shift from the empathic story towards optimism and hope. "It's incredibly important to me that we help the middle class. People like my mom and dad drive our economy. They shouldn't need to worry about being able to make a rent payment. That's why

I have worked to..." At that point, mention what programs you *have* put in place to raise worker's take-home pay and increase their living standards.

By the time you've told an empathic story and ended with a message of hope, voters will likely have forgotten the original question. Their main takeaway: you care for people like them and have a vision for how to improve their lives. And by answering the question that you wanted to all along, you'll be able to maintain your enthusiasm—rather than appear disingenuous or react negatively to a difficult question.

Speak Aspirationally and End with Optimism

The evening before the 1980 Presidential election, Ronald Reagan gave a televised speech. At one point, he said, "Americans...seek a vision of a better America, a vision of society that frees the energies and ingenuity of our people while it extends compassion to the lonely, the desperate, and the forgotten. I believe we can embark on a new age of reform in this country and an era of national renewal."[74]

Reagan's specific word choices conveyed his aspirations. As he spoke of "vision," "a new era," and "renewal," Ronald Reagan expressed hope and positive expectations about the future. His optimism inspired the American people to commit to his vision with their votes.

To speak aspirationally, you must recognize what Americans are currently experiencing and what they hope for going forward.

74   Reagan, Ronald. Election Eve Address A Vision for America. Accessed January 22, 2019.

Therefore, when you talk with voters, start by acknowledging the hard realities where they are starting from. Your recognition of people's struggles will establish you as a caring leader—someone to trust. If you can do this via a story, even better. The story will make your message personal, and you won't sound trite.

After acknowledging voters' challenges, bring the narrative to an inspiring conclusion. Address people's biggest hopes and dreams, and finish by talking about how you'll help them achieve those dreams.

Don't leave the narrative in a dark place, or you'll repeat the mistake that Jimmy Carter made in his "malaise" speech: the sin of pessimism. Imagine if, after Carter's strong, empathic start, he shifted to an inspiring tone. What if, after identifying the "crisis of confidence," he laid out a plan for restoring America's morale? Would Americans' perspective of him have changed if he'd been more encouraging, rather than admonishing them? History might have been different. Carter might have won a second term.

Voters want you to bring them the opportunity for happiness and renewed energy. They want to be shown the path that leads to a bright and exciting future. They want you to help them harness their positive energy. Most Americans are looking for you to provide opportunity, not outcome. When they don't receive this message from you, they won't vote for you—so speak aspirationally.

"REALISTIC OPTIMISM": BE INFORMED

There's a catch to blind optimism—voters don't want their politicians to be Pollyannas.

Eleanor Hodgman Porter's stories about a girl named Pollyanna featured a heroine who was eternally optimistic. As her circumstances got worse and worse, Pollyanna was determined to look on the bright side. The word today has come to be associated with obnoxious cheerfulness which ignores the seriousness of problems.

"Obnoxious" is not a word you want voters to associate with you.

Professor Robert F. Bruner advises candidates to have "realistic optimism."[75] Yes, you need to be optimistic. However, your optimistic view of the future should be grounded in facts and well-thought-out policies.

According to Tom Morris:

> The realistic optimist moves forward with eyes wide open, seeing obstacles, understanding challenges yet maintaining a determination to be creative in solving all problems. The realistic optimist never just hopes for the best, or blithely assumes the best, but works hard to make the best happen, in full realization that it may take longer than it should and be harder to accomplish than anyone could have imagined. But it's precisely the element of optimism that fuels as hopeful and persistent struggle forward.[76]

---

75 Hendrick, Dave. "Presidential Leadership and the Practice of 'Realistic Optimism'." The Darden Report. February 7, 2017.

76 Morris, Tom. "The Importance of Optimism." *TomMorris.com.* July 27, 2015.

Skeptics—many of whom work in journalistic professions or as media pundits—look at "Pollyanna" optimism as proof that you will be a risky leader. "This candidate," they'll complain, "is not realistic about the threats we face!" Rather than optimism working for you as a strength virtue, *uninformed* optimism could be viewed as a weakness that can lead to taking unnecessary chances and neglecting potential danger.

You can avoid this perception by making a list of all the potential threats your opponents may bring up when targeting you personally or your platform.

- What's the "scare factor" (on either side) with issues like gun control, climate change, the opioid crisis, and the issues unique to your target block of voters?
- What past baggage or mistakes have you made?
- Will your opponent try to raise your past or current personal life in debating you, in their effort to paint you as unlikeable?

Perhaps, if you're a Democrat advocating for universal healthcare, you might write out:

- Universal healthcare threat—Opponents will point out higher taxes, subpar medical care, and rationing

List those threats and get your team to help elaborate on what your opponent might argue.

And, if there is anything in your past that might be controversial, be transparent. A big mistake is to think a previous problem won't come out. Make it public before your opponent does.

Once you've come clean about your past or controversial positions you may have taken, form your rebuttals. How will your plans address those threats? For the example above, how will you address higher taxes and the fear of subpar care? Convert these "scare" points into a hopeful message. Back up your message with facts and solidify your inspirational vision through practice and role-plays.

Also, stay informed by reading a variety of news publications and watching cable news channels—those that agree with you *and* those that don't. Stay abreast of pop cultural developments. Stay current on social media platforms like Facebook, Twitter, and Instagram. As a bonus, being an informed candidate will help you project charisma.

When you have a handle on the facts of cultural and social issues, current events, and voters' local and national needs, then you can present a plan with an optimistic vision that people will believe in. Share specifically the ways that you're going to improve people's lives.

Trust Your Gut

Being informed enables you to trust your gut decisions. When candidates and elected politicians are ill-informed about the issues, they fall back on campaign staff to tell them what to do or say. They're not prepared for tough questions, which makes them look stupid or weak.

The Libertarian presidential nominee in 2016, Gary Johnson, learned the lesson of being uninformed the hard way. Many voters were looking to Johnson as an alternative to Hillary Clinton or Donald Trump. However, Johnson gaffed in an interview when he was asked what he would do about Aleppo, the city at the center of the Syrian refugee crisis. Tragic images of hospitalized children in Aleppo had been plastered all over the recent news pages and cable shows, but Johnson had to ask, "What is Aleppo?"[77]

That moment of ignorance killed his campaign. Voters had hope that Johnson would demonstrate enough strength to convincingly topple one of the two-party candidates. The Aleppo question was meant to provide Johnson with an opportunity to showcase his understanding of foreign affairs. He could have shown the American people he had a vision for how to resolve the complex Syrian war. Instead, he showed himself to be a man less informed than his constituents.

Remember, optimism is a strength virtue. But how can you convince people you can make their world better if you don't know what's happening in it?

Armed with knowledge about the complexities of an issue, you are better equipped to be spontaneous and trust your intuition. You're less likely to get machine-gunned down by an opponent or interviewer—or even sabotaged by an incompetent campaign manager. Instead, you can listen to your instincts and show yourself to be a confident, trustworthy leader.

Trust *your* vision. Let your enthusiasm for that vision brim over

---

77   MSNBC. "Gary Johnson Asks: 'What Is Aleppo?' | Morning Joe | MSNBC." *YouTube*. September 8, 2016.

with optimism and hope. Ground your plans to help people in facts and thoughtful policy. Inspire voters to let you lead.

CHAPTER THREE

FROM TENTATIVE TO DECISIVE

"Far better it is to dare mighty things, to win glorious triumphs, even though checkered by failure, than to take rank with those poor spirits who neither enjoy much nor suffer much, because they live in the gray twilight that knows neither victory nor defeat."

—THEODORE ROOSEVELT, *STRENUOUS LIFE*

In 1988, George H. W. Bush was locked in a campaign battle for the American presidency with Massachusetts governor Michael Dukakis.

Bush entered the nomination fight with high name recognition and high voter ratings for experience and competence. Bush held an impressive record: he'd returned from WWII as a combat-decorated veteran, served over two decades in Congress, and had been an ambassador to the United Nations and CIA director before being elected to serve eight years as the forty-third vice president under Ronald Reagan.

Despite these credentials, G. H. W. Bush had a flaw in his campaign that Democratic pollster Peter Hart summed up well at the time: "Fairly or unfairly, voters have a deep-rooted perception of him as a guy who takes direction, who's not a leader."[78] G. H. W. Bush had been labeled a "wimp."

At the 1988 GOP National Convention in New Orleans, Bush's goal was to separate himself from the popular Reagan, shake off what had become known as the "Wimp Factor," and appear strong, decisive, and confident.

Bush proclaimed to the gathered delegates.

> "I'm the one who will not raise taxes. My opponent now says he'll raise them as a last resort, or a third resort. But when a politician talks like that, you know that's one resort he'll be checking into. My opponent won't rule out raising taxes. But I will. And the Congress will push me to raise taxes and I'll say no. And they'll push, and I'll say no, and they'll push again, and I'll say, to them, 'Read my lips: no new taxes!'"

The audience rose to its feet and roared with approval.

This now-famous line from his speech had been planned and heavily debated by Bush's campaign team. Congressman Jack Kemp had originally suggested the line as the way to clearly define Bush's fiscally conservative stance. Speechwriter Peggy Noonan wrote the phrase into the initial draft of the speech; economic adviser Richard Darman crossed it out, calling the statement

---

78 Warner, Margaret Garrard. "Bush Battles the 'Wimp Factor.'" *Newsweek*. October 19, 1987.

"stupid and dangerous."[79] After all, if Bush were elected, he'd have to follow up on his bold promise. (Darman's critique was not only appropriate, but as we'll see, it would prove prophetic.)

Bush kept the words, following the guidance of other advisors who urged him to leverage the support of conservative voters. As he delivered his speech at the National Convention, Bush presented himself as strong and tough—a man of conviction.[80] Even though he initially trailed Dukakis by seventeen points, he rallied: the week after the convention, he'd already overtaken Dukakis in the polls. Ultimately, G. H. W. Bush was voted into office as our nation's forty-first president by a landslide.

And then, in what has been called one of the most famous broken promises in political history, George Herbert Walker Bush relented. He raised taxes.

In 1990, under pressure to strike a budget deal, Bush compromised with the Democrat-controlled congress to hike taxes. Bush deemed his decision to be in the best interest of the country. But the public felt betrayed. Reagan White House Press Secretary Marlin Fitzwater described Bush's backtrack as the "single biggest mistake of the administration,"[81] while Republican pollster Richard Wirthlin went so far as to call Bush's "read my lips, no new taxes" promise "the six most destructive words in the history of presidential politics."[82] Citizens now believed that Bush

---

79   Greene, John Robert. *The Presidency of George Bush.* Lawrence, Kansas: University Press of Kansas, 2000.

80   THNKR. "1988: When Bush Said Read My Lips." YouTube. August 27, 2012.

81   Barilleaux, Ryan J. and Mark J. Rozell. *Power and Prudence.* College Station, Texas: Texas A&M University Press, 2004.

82   Mackenzie, Colin. "How Bush Blew It." *The Globe and Mail.* November 4, 1992.

couldn't be trusted to keep his word. He was labeled indecisive and untrustworthy. And, if you're seen by voters as an untrustworthy politician—that's the kiss of death.

When G. H. W. Bush went back on the campaign trail in 1992 seeking a second term, his opponent was former governor of Arkansas Bill Clinton. Clinton and his team bludgeoned Bush repeatedly with Bush's broken promise of "no new taxes."

On November 3, 1992, Bill Clinton was voted into office with 43 percent of the popular vote, and G. H. W. Bush went into the history books as a one-term president.

THE SIN OF TENTATIVENESS

My belief is that all political candidates should be Mirandized prior to starting a campaign: "You have the right to remain silent. Anything you say can and will be used against you..."

We live in an era with cell phone cameras, Twitter streams, numerous media platforms, and countless ways to dialogue on the internet. Expect that your every word will be recorded. What you say—especially the mean-spirited and stupid stuff—can, and will, be used against you.

Even the boldest candidate should hesitate before they speak. But there's the rub: in the end, voters want confident, decisive candidates who aren't afraid to speak their minds or take a stand. "Be candid and bold! But also—don't ever say anything that anyone could take the wrong way!"

It's a catch-22. (The second half of this chapter will help you resolve this dilemma.)

Candidates who are direct, transparent, and open with definite policy positions come across as strong leaders. They appear *trustworthy*. However, if those same candidates break a campaign pledge, their initial show of strength quickly weakens and is seen as fake. They are no longer believable. They're forced to make excuses to defend themselves, which makes them seem faltering, unsure, tentative—weak.

Will a tentative leader help you survive? Will you trust a leader to guide you to a better future if they seem anxious, untrustworthy, or indecisive?

No. That's why tentativeness appears such a sin, and decisiveness appears as a virtue.

There are several ways politicians act tentatively. Breaking a promise will make voters doubt your reliability. Acting aloof, soft-spoken, hesitant or foolish will also raise red flags with voters.

Let's look at the most common ways candidates stumble into the sin of tentativeness.

PASSIVITY

Pushover might be the word that comes to mind when you think about behavior that is "passive." You don't define a strong leader as someone you can manipulate or push around.

When you're unable to convince voters that you'll defend their interests vigorously, you are coming across as passive. Not taking charge of your branding permits others to define you, which in turn makes you appear passive. Being vague about how you would handle important issues—that's passive.

All candidates need to be vague at some point, because no one has a handle on the specifics of every issue. However, your method of answering voters' questions can still make you come across as decisive or—if done badly—passive.

Don't ramble. Don't try to fashion a policy statement out of thin air. Don't vaguely defend a position using fluff details—you'll only seem uninformed.

Try a reply like this:

> Thank you for that question. I don't have all the facts on that issue, and I'd like to learn more about it before I lay out my position. My priorities in this campaign are [these cornerstone issues]. However, I recognize the impact this issue may have on you and many Americans, which is why I'd like to assemble a good team to research it.

The above response starts with courteousness, moves to personal recognition of the issue's importance to this voter and others, goes to honesty, reminds voters of what you stand for, and indicates you're going to get a good handle on it. That's confident. That's decisive. Also, using words like "defend," "first priorities," and "assemble a good team" shows that you're thinking like a leader.

Be honest with voters. Telegraph clearly that their concern is your concern and one you want to learn more about. That way, voters can't hold your lack of knowledge against you. Remind voters what your cornerstone policy platform ideas are and highlight those issues as your main priorities.

Voters don't expect you to know everything. But they do want to see an attitude of conviction and confidence, even when you're acknowledging that you don't know something.

FENDING OFF ATTACKS

If you accept an opponent's attack without fighting back, you'll come across as passive. In the CNN Republican debates of 2016, unconventional candidate Donald J. Trump unleashed zinger after zinger. Trump threw this comeback at Rand Paul: "I never attacked him or his looks and believe me there's plenty of subject matter right there."

Trump delivered another quip during the February 2016 GOP debate. Marco Rubio hit Trump with a seemingly rehearsed line: "if he builds the wall the way he built Trump Towers he'll be using illegal immigrant labor to do it." Trump's reply: "So cute. Such a cute sound bite." Trump's retort undercut the brunt of Rubio's line.[83]

When hit by these zingers and others, most of Trump's GOP presidential opponents laughed nervously, as if they weren't bothered by the sting of his bites. Some tried, and failed, to interrupt him. Some shook their heads in silent protest. Generally, most of the candidates got nicknamed and bulldozed. As world champion

83   Diamond, Jeremy. "Donald Trump's 6 Debate Tactics." *CNN Politics.* September 26, 2016.

ex-boxer Mike Tyson so famously said, "Everybody has a plan until they get punched in the mouth."

Responding to others' attacks is hard to get right. You can return the mudslinging and dirty your own principled image, or you take the attack without fighting back and look like a wimp.

Carly Fiorina, the former CEO of Hewlett Packard, was the only woman GOP presidential candidate on the 2016 debate stage. She was considered by viewer polls to be the winner of that first debate—though she'd entered the contest with the least name recognition of those vying for the nomination. Part of her strength was the image she projected to viewers through her strong response to the truculence onstage.

When a debate moderator asked Fiorina to respond to Trump's insulting comment about her face—something he later said was meant to refer to her "persona"—Fiorina was invited to state what she thought of Trump's persona. Fiorina paused, smiled, and then said, "I think women all over this country heard very clearly what Mr. Trump said."[84]

Fiorina didn't take the bait or engage Trump in battle. Instead, she gave a measured, assertive response that showed she could hold her own. Her comment turned the focus back on the rudeness of Trump's comment and kept her unscathed.

Passivity in the face of pressure, attacks, or challenging questions

---

84 Mashable. "Carly Fiorina's Most Memorable Moments from the Republican Debate | Mashable News." *YouTube.* September 17, 2015.

will make you seem weak. Own your convictions and be prepared to stand your ground—nicely.

FLIP-FLOPPING

During the 2004 Presidential campaign, George W. Bush produced a campaign ad against Massachusetts Senator John Kerry, his opponent. The ad featured grainy footage of John Kerry windsurfing. Descriptions of Kerry's inconsistent decisions were described in a voiceover, and every time Kerry was said to have changed political positions, the footage cut to the sail in a different position. The ad ended with "John Kerry: whichever way the wind blows."[85]

The ad showed Kerry to be a solid windsurfer but also ruthlessly exposed his history as a flip-flopper. Americans decided they couldn't trust him to keep his word.

When Kerry was asked to address his inconsistent voting record about the Iraq war, he supplied a weak explanation: "I actually did vote for the 87 billion, before I voted against it."[86] The Bush team pounced on Kerry's statement as confirmation of his waffling.

Despite Kerry's cringe-worthy sound bite, politicians sometimes need to course correct on an issue. To move legislation forward, compromises often need to be made—as G. H. W. Bush discovered. Sometimes, policy proposals are packaged in such a way that one part may appeal to your voters, while other points are deal-breakers. Candidate Kerry found himself in a conun-

---

85   Maviglio. "Historical Campaign Ad: Windsurfing (Bush-Cheney '04)." *YouTube*. May 2, 2006.

86   Roselli, Mike. "Kerry Discusses $87 Billion Comment." *CNN*. September 30, 2004.

drum: instead of explaining his shifts with stories and context, he summed up his dilemma with a statement that became his Achilles' heel.

Here's how you can avoid being labeled a flip-flopper: give more context. Help voters understand what steps you took to arrive at your decision. Storytelling can save you. If you convey your change of heart within the context of a story, you're less likely to produce a disastrous, oversimplified sound bite.

Later, trying to moonwalk away from his own disastrous sound bite about "voting for it, before voting against it," Kerry gave a few more details, described on CNN:

> After the remark became controversial, Kerry explained that he had supported an earlier Democratic measure that would have paid for the $87 billion in war funding by reducing Bush's tax cuts. After it was defeated, he said he voted against final passage of the bill to voice his displeasure with the president's Iraq policy. Kerry told ABC on Wednesday that the comment 'reflects the truth of the position, which is I thought to have the wealthiest people in America share the burden of paying for that war.'[87]

Kerry's voting record made sense when he included adequate context about tax cuts. However, after his initial ambivalent quote, no one was the least bit interested in his follow-up explanation. The Bush campaign made sure no potential voter forgot Kerry's inconsistency in his decision-making.

Flip-flopping implies that the candidate has little conviction and

---

87 Ibid.

will be easily persuaded. The recommendations I list at the end of this chapter will help you better develop your stance on issues—which is the best way to avoid being viewed as inconsistent in your beliefs.

WEAKNESS

In the first presidential contest without an incumbent since 1968, fifty-four-year-old Massachusetts governor Michael Dukakis was running against George H. W. Bush. Dukakis wanted to impress voters with his grasp of national defense issues by portraying a strong image of himself as a ready-made Commander in Chief. In his book *Off Script,* Josh King says, "In campaigns, if you're not creating the message, the message is created for you."[88] In Dukakis' case, his message was created for him by his campaign team. Dukakis overrode his gut instincts to not follow along with the plan his handlers had constructed. As you will see, rather than appearing as a strong commander, the resulting stunt made him come across as awkward and tentative.

On September 13, 1988, Dukakis arrived at the General Dynamics Land Systems facility in Sterling Heights, Michigan. His advance campaign team, led by Matt Bennett, arranged a media photo-op for him to take a test ride in a decommissioned sixty-eight-ton MIAI Abrams tank. Nicknamed "Whispering Death," the tank was powered by two 750 horsepower diesel engines that could propel it up to forty-five miles per hour.

Dukakis pulled on a pair of grey protective coveralls. On his head he donned a tank commander's helmet with a white sticker about

---

88 King, Josh. *Off Script*. New York: St. Martin's Press. April 26, 2016.

an inch and a half high with "Mike Dukakis" stenciled in black across the top. The plan was for Dukakis to mount the tank. Then the bay doors would open, and the tank would race out to face the waiting press corps. The tank would do several maneuvers and then head back in.

Following the tank ride, Dukakis would climb onto the stage and give a speech with the theme "tough on defense."

Dukakis climbed into the twenty-six-foot long, twelve-foot wide tank and took the commander's position, His head and torso stuck twelve feet in the air from the turret. Dukakis—all of five feet eight inches—looked absurd. Even though he was hesitant to wear the helmet with his name emblazoned on it, he did anyway.

With his big, bushy black eyebrows, red tie, and button-down shirt, Dukakis settled in and began to write his political obituary. He placed his hands on the machine gun, the hanger doors opened, and the tank came forward. At the first pass, the tank made some slow turns past the press corps and then headed to the far end of the field. Then, suddenly, the tank began to move at high speed directly at the press corp. It went left, then right. It zigged and zagged towards the onlookers. As the tank picked up speed, photographers snapped pictures. A close-up photo showed Dukakis giving a toothy grin beneath a ridiculous helmet.[89]

Photographer Arthur Grace said that Dukakis looked unwell, as if he was on the final turns of a massive rollercoaster ride. Matt Bennet wrote that "The governor, who was controlling the turret, almost wiped 'em all out."

---

89 Politico. "Dukakis and the Tank: The Making of a Political Disaster." *YouTube*. December 3, 2013.

Once he began to disembark the tank, Dukakis became unsteady and needed help climbing down the stairs.

The local and national reporters gathered were supposed to be impressed. Instead, they doubled over laughing. The late-night comedy and daytime radio shows parodied the ride. The Bush campaign quickly put out ads making Dukakis look like a buffoon.

Some political pundits call Dukakis's campaign tank incident the greatest American political candidate fiasco in history. According to Josh King in *Off Script*, Dukakis ushered in the political "Age of Optics."[90] Post-Dukakis, both voters and candidates, as judge and jury, now realize how important optics have become to the world of politics.

The image of Dukakis in an out-of-control tank projected weakness—no question. But Dukakis's willingness to wear the helmet and go along with the photo-op in the first place also exposed his tentativeness. He had initially voiced concern and been against the tank ride idea, but he succumbed to the will of campaign handlers. This failure to go with his gut and stand up to his principal strategists showed weakness and resulted in disastrous optics that caused his image and poll numbers to plummet. He lost the election.

Rule number one: Don't be photographed or filmed in a goofy hat.

Rule number two: Remember that you're the person who steers your campaign. Voters want to see you have the strength to be boss of their city, district, state, or country. You might feel

90 Ibid, King.

tempted to listen to your advisors over your instincts—maybe that feels like the wise thing to do. But if you're not *decisive* as a leader, you're not leading.

Voters are looking for you to be strong. Demonstrations of weakness on your part will make them feel disillusioned and unsafe. Remember: *you* are the boss!

THE VIRTUE OF DECISIVENESS

The men and women who fought for our country during World War II are remembered as the "Greatest Generation." These brave soldiers looked to two outstanding leaders for inspiration and strength: Franklin Delano Roosevelt and Britain's Prime Minister, Winston Churchill. Both men were decisive and resolute in their leadership during the chaos of World War II.

When Churchill delivered his first speech as Prime Minister in May of 1940, Hitler's armies were moving across Europe, battling to occupy France. Churchill began his leadership with a speech about Britain's stance against Hitler:

> You ask, what is our aim? I can answer in one word: Victory. Victory at all costs—Victory in spite of all terror—Victory, however long and hard the road may be, for without victory there is no survival.[91]

One month later, France capitulated to Hitler. The situation in Europe seemed dire. Britain was Hitler's next target on his path to world domination. Yet Churchill did not bend in his resolution to fight on. His decisiveness to stay the course inspired and ral-

91   Dockter, Warren. "Winston Churchill's 10 Most Important Speeches." *The Telegraph.* January 29, 2015.

lied the British people. In what many consider his most famous speech, Churchill said:

> If we can stand up to him, all Europe may be free, and the life of the world may move forward into broad, sunlit uplands. But if we fail, then the whole world, including the United States, including all that we have known and cared for, will sink into the abyss of a new Dark Age made more sinister, and perhaps more protracted, by the lights of perverted science. Let us therefore brace ourselves to our duties, and so bear ourselves that, if the British Empire and its Commonwealth last for a thousand years, men will still say, "This was their finest hour."[92]

Across the Atlantic, Franklin Delano Roosevelt (FDR) held back from committing the US military to the war in Europe. However, when America was bombed by Japan in a sneak attack at Pearl Harbor on December 7, 1941, Roosevelt did not flinch. He responded with resolute conviction in his famous "A Day that Will Live in Infamy" speech.[93]

Three days later, Germany declared war on the US after the United States declared war on Japan. Upon FDR's recommendation, the United States Congress and Senate jointly voted unanimously to declare war on Germany.

These World War II years in both Britain and the United States are remembered as a time of incredible unity. Why were the countries so united? Because they were led by decisive, strong leaders who spoke with great conviction against a great evil. Roosevelt

---

92 Ibid.

93 Chan, Melissa. "Franklin Roosevelt Infamy Speech: Pearl Harbor Transcript." *Time.* December 7, 2016.

and Churchill naturally recognized the power of connection and forged deep emotional bonds with their citizens.

CONNECTOR-IN-CHIEF

In the 1930s, before the advent of TV, about 90 percent of Americans owned a radio. Seizing upon the potential of radio for reaching the masses, FDR began to use this medium to communicate intimately and directly to the public throughout his presidency. He began a series of addresses that became known as "fireside chats" (though he was seated at a microphone-covered desk in the White House when he delivered his speeches).

The topics that FDR talked about ranged from economic policies and domestic issues, drought, and unemployment to the battle Europe faced against the Fascists and Nazis in World War II. In several of his chats, he would evoke memories of the Founding Fathers, Abraham Lincoln, and other inspirational Americans. After most chats ended, "The Star-Spangled Banner" was played. FDR always appealed to Providence or God at the completion of a chat, asking every American to face the challenges the country was experiencing with faith, patience, and understanding.

The fireside chats were intended to connect emotionally with the public and boost their confidence and optimism that events affecting the country would work out positively. Undoubtedly, it also boosted his favorability. Historian David Kennedy described FDR's fireside chats as "cultivated yet familiar, commanding yet avuncular, masterful yet intimate." Following the first chat, the White House received overwhelming response from the public, receiving about 500,000 letters. Americans wrote about their appreciation for FDR's comforting reassurance. The White House mail room quickly went from one full-time employee to seventy.

According to Dr. Russell Razzaque, "FDR's capacity to connect in this way didn't come about by accident" but through his own personal experience overcoming extreme hardship. At age thirty-nine, FDR was diagnosed with infantile paralysis, or polio. He was fully paralyzed for a time, and even after regaining control of his limbs, he was confined to leg braces or a wheelchair. Razzaque contends, "His struggle with polio had a profound effect on his emotional makeup and the way he saw and interacted with the people he came across."[94]

Doris Kearns Goodwin, author of a biography of FDR, described his demeanor after contracting polio this way:

> He seemed less arrogant, less smug, less superficial. Far more intensely than before, he reached out to know [the public], to understand them, to pick up their emotions, to put himself in their shoes. No longer belonging to his old world in the same way, he came to empathize with the poor and the underprivileged, to people whom fate had dealt a difficult hand.[95]

FDR's ability to connect emotionally with people showed his high Emotional intelligence (EQ). He was always flexible in looking for solutions. He kept experimenting till he found an answer, whether self-derived or gotten from others.

Dr. Razzaque says that when FDR died, the public was so grief-

94 Razzaque, Russell. "FDR Was the Connector-in-Chief." *Political Influence*. April 3, 2012.

95 Goodwin, Doris Kearns. *No Ordinary Time*. New York: Simon & Schuster, 2013.

stricken that a journalist he met told him the story of a citizen he came upon who was crying so hard that the journalist asked him if he knew FDR personally. "'No,' said the man, 'but he knew me.'"[96]

FDR used his personal pain and suffering to identify with ordinary citizens who were themselves mired in adversity. He wanted to ease their anxiety and fear, and famously told the nation, "The only thing we have to fear is fear itself." FDR used his emotional bond with the American public as a vehicle to guide the country through troubled times. His radio chats helped calm people's fears and raise their optimism.

Decisive leadership and emotional connection, like that displayed by FDR and Churchill, shows that you can be trusted and relied upon. Voters who are making decisions connected to their survival want to feel safe and secure. If you show clear decisiveness, voters see you as a person who will stand up to protect and defend them. This was especially critical for both leaders to get their countries to rally around them.

Decisiveness is the ability to be authoritative—even when you're not sure you have all the facts. You may not possess all the information, but you still must act decisively. If it's the wrong decision, you'll quickly figure it out and correct your course. But if you don't decide, there are only a few outcomes: Things will stay the same or get worse. So to not decide is to decide.

---

96   Ibid, Razzaque.

RELATIONSHIP BETWEEN DECISIVENESS AND TRUSTWORTHINESS

Just what quality enables some politicians to be seen as decisive and strong? What was it for Churchill? What was it for Roosevelt?

For both great World War II leaders, their decisiveness arose directly from their strong moral convictions. Churchill believed it was England's sacred duty to fight the evil represented by the Nazi regime. Roosevelt strongly believed in the values and rights that America stood for and must defend at all costs.

Because strong moral conviction and determination often go hand in hand, decisiveness is the strength virtue that is largely responsible for showing your *trustworthiness*. People look for you to demonstrate trustworthiness even before they examine your competence. If they don't trust you, they won't vote for you.

If you are decisive, voters see you as taking a stand for something you believe in. That's appealing! Even if people disagree with your position, you'll still appear strong and confident in your convictions. When a leader appears confident, people feel safer. That safety factor then ushers in trust.

Reliability and Truthfulness—A Cautionary Tale

Tell people the truth. Be transparent. Don't hide anything. Demonstrate your reliability with voters by being honest.

History is replete with examples of politicians who get into trouble when they attempt to cover things up. However, you can build trust with voters when you honestly level with them. Credibility is established over time. You need to develop a track record of being truthful and real with voters.

Several political candidates have gone to great lengths to get elected, including exaggerating or even making up stories of their experiences to impress voters. In a notable example, Joe Biden initially ran for president in 1988 but was forced to drop out of the race after he was accused of plagiarizing then-British Labour Party leader Neal Kinnock's phrases. Biden even adopted parts of Kinnock's biography as his own. Clips of speeches by Biden and Kinnock were put side-by-side, and the copying was evident for all challengers to see.[97]

This incident, which Biden called "a tempest in a teapot," has followed Biden through subsequent campaigns. In 2015, then-GOP-candidate Donald Trump said about facing Biden if he was nominated, "I think I'd match up great. I'm a job producer. I've had a great record. I haven't been involved in plagiarism."

Biden is now in the running for a 2020 presidential spot against Trump, and when asked about any potential liabilities of his campaign, Biden replied, "I am a gaffe machine...but my God, what a wonderful thing compared to a guy who can't tell the truth."

Let's look at another cautionary tale: the true story of a disgraced legislature candidate shows why you should never embellish facts or fake details on your resume.

In many ways, "KP" (not his real initials) was the ideal candidate running for a local political office in 2012. He was articulate,

---

97   O'Neil, Luke. "'I Am a Gaffe Machine': A History of Joe Biden's Biggest Blunders." *The Guardian.* June 2019.

smart, photogenic, involved with local charities, well-liked, and capable. However, shortly after he announced his candidacy and secured the backing of local donors, his opponent's opposition research unearthed a discrepancy in his resume. He claimed to have a college degree from a leading university. He didn't. It was a lie.

A state news outlet reported that he had attended that university from August 1984 to May 1988 but did not graduate. KP initially denied the allegation that he had faked his resume.

Not so fortunate for him, his opponent flagged the lie, and the ploy quickly fell apart.

Finally, this candidate owned up to his deceit. He admitted that he lied and officially dropped out of the race.

In forging the diploma, not only did KP damage his public image and get exposed as a liar—he also committed fraud. He was publicly shamed and sentenced to one hundred hours of community service. In the end, he buried what might have been a promising political career.

If the opposition brings up a detail you feel insecure about, find a way to spin it differently. For example, if someone said, "I notice that you don't have a college education," the candidate who faked his degree could have acknowledged the truth. He might have said, "I came very close but had to drop out just shy of graduation because of family difficulties. There are a lot of successful people out there without college degrees, and I'm one of them."

Speak confidently, give a brief explanation, and you can end the conversation there. As history has shown with many political scandals, including Watergate, it's the cover-up that gets people in trouble. When you come clean, you minimize any trust that can be lost with voters, and you demonstrate authenticity and truthfulness. When you're trying to get elected or re-elected, show voters that they can trust you. If you're caught in a lie, that's not going to serve you well. Save yourself some time, embarrassment, and pain by telling the truth from the start!

Keep Your Word

"Let's get to work!" Rick Scott called out during his 2010 Florida gubernatorial campaign. Scott campaigned on the need to produce jobs, cut taxes, and produce a budget surplus—pivotal issues at that time for many voters. It was the Great Recession, and the state's unemployment rate was over 11 percent. Scott promised to generate 700,000 new jobs in Florida.

At the end of Governor Scott's eight-year term, he had largely kept his campaign promises. Florida's economic growth had outpaced the nation's in seventy-nine out of the past eighty months, with the one-month exception being when Hurricane Irma hit. The unemployment rate had dropped to 3.3 percent.[98] Scott created 1.7 million new jobs and paid down $10 billion in state debt. You can bet that impression of trustworthiness and decisiveness made the difference for Scott in 2018, when he eked out a narrow victory for a seat in the US Senate over the eighteen-year sitting senator Bill Nelson.

---

98   Turner, Jim. "Gov. Rick Scott Leaving Office with Low Unemployment Rate - 8 Points Lower than When He Was Sworn in." *Sun-Sentinel.com*. December 21, 2018.

Scott's passion for jobs isn't just a political strategy. It's his personal passion. His moral conviction is that if people are willing to work hard, they deserve opportunity. Scott's belief comes from his own experience, which he passionately discussed in stories regularly on the campaign trail. Scott's message to voters is that he understands what it's like to live from hand to mouth, with no safety net. But Scott's philosophy is that that doesn't have to stop you from becoming successful. You just need opportunity—and he's going to get it for you.

Governor Scott believed in his message, and he worked hard to make good on his promise once he was elected. When he succeeded, voters knew they'd been right to trust him. The voters of Florida dispatched a long-term familiar popular incumbent who had served Florida since Richard Nixon was president. Rick Scott was justly rewarded with a new title of US Senator and a continued role in the state's leadership.

Voters look for leaders they can depend on. They want people who say what they mean and then do it!

Avoid campaign hyperbole—that's a recipe for a broken promise. During the 2016 campaign, Donald Trump famously promised he would get Mexico to pay for an enormous wall covering the entirety of the southern border. Trump might have initially been able to get funding for the wall passed through legislation. However, after the Democrats took back the House in the 2018 midterms, he had no chance. Trump's exaggerated claims fired up his base in the beginning, but he ultimately had to backtrack on his pledge. After a prolonged government shutdown ended—when Trump finally gave up the fight for congressional wall funding—his approval ratings dropped to their lowest ever. Most telling, it was the unkept promise of the border wall, and the related economic hit of the shutdown, that finally cracked Trump's base.[99] His approval ratings with his core constituent demographics slipped across the board.

So: no campaign hyperbole. Keep your promises aspirational, but realistic.

If you do have to break your word, remember to address voters' emotions when you explain why you've changed your mind or couldn't get a campaign pledge accomplished. Remember, emotion drove voters to pick your name in the first place, so you need to keep emotion front and center when you deliver news that may let them down. Use storytelling and context to make sure they understand the full picture that led you to make your decision.

DEVELOPING THE VIRTUE OF DECISIVENESS

When you identify your core issues, you take an important step in developing the virtue of decisiveness. Your core issues should be points you feel strongly about on a personal level, which you can back up with your professional record of experience.

Bob Dole, the Republican Presidential nominee in 1996 and long-time US Senator from Kansas, failed to do this. He was, in many ways, a textbook example of candidate tentativeness. *The New York Times*, in analyzing Dole's loss to Bill Clinton, noted many weaknesses of his campaign: he was indecisive, spoke haltingly, often rambled off-topic, and didn't assume authority of his cam-

---

99   Graham, David A. "The Shutdown Leaves Trump's Base Cracked." *The Atlantic*. January 26, 2019.

paign until its final days.[100] But possibly his biggest problem was his failure to determine his core message:

> Lacking any other unifying theme, Mr. Dole bounced through the fall, experimenting by the week with different messages: That Mr. Clinton was responsible for an increase in teenage drug use. That he was a liberal. That he could not be trusted. That he was unethical. One result of these quicksilver changes, in the view of some of his own aides, was that Mr. Dole undermined his description of himself as steady and dependable.[101]

Finally, Bob Dole tried to focus his campaign on tax cuts. For Dole's entire career, he'd worked to reduce the budget deficit. But his chief platform policy went against his own moral convictions and professional record. He didn't believe in his message, and voters didn't believe in him.

In developing the virtue of decisiveness, avoid Bob Dole's mistake: determine your core issues, stick to them, and make sure you know them, inside and out.

CORE VALUES EXERCISE

You can choose your core issues in brainstorming meetings, or after looking at polls, but I recommend an old-fashioned method: write them down. Typing or writing them out will help your points to crystallize in your head. Research facts and evidence and get members of your team to help you reinforce the points through

---

100 Nagourney, Adam, and Elizabeth Kolbert. "How Bob Dole's Dream Was Dashed." *The New York Times*. November 8, 1996.

101 Ibid.

role play debates. Choose issues that matter to you personally, so that your genuine emotional conviction comes through. Consider creating a table on paper with the following columns—conveniently, there are seven.

Column 1: Major Campaign Topics

Make a list of the topics you'll most likely be asked during the campaign. Your list might look like this:

1. Healthcare and coverage for pre-existing conditions
2. Gun control
3. Jobs
4. Immigration

Make the list as lengthy as you need to cover the issues you'll probably be questioned about.

Column 2: Your Views

Next to each campaign topic, write out your views. Provide the supporting evidence you want to explain your rationale. If you're going to take on both the small and big topics, your responsibility is to know the facts.

You need to articulate a plan for what you will specifically do about these concerns if you're elected. How will you deal with hot-button issues like immigration? What's your plan for increasing healthcare access? Get a realistic plan in place so you can convince voters—and more importantly, yourself—that you care and can be trusted to get the job done.

Column 3: Rate the Strength of Your Views on Each Issue

As you identify the issues and write out your views, you might realize that your passion is high for some, but for others, not so much. Pay attention to your feelings and then start ranking the issues in order of their importance.

Next to each issue, write a number between one and ten, noting how strongly you feel about your position. A "ten" on an issue means you're rock solid and can't be budged. A "one" on an issue means you could change your mind with almost no provocation.

Do this honestly and personally. Pay attention to your gut and your own history of voting. Don't give high rankings to issues just because you know they are emotionally popular with voters but haven't been historically important to you. Voters will be able to look at your record and spot inconsistency. Then you may be accused, like John Kerry, of heading "whichever way the wind blows."

Once your policy issues are ranked, your platform will begin to take shape. The issues marked with the highest numbers become your cornerstone priorities—the points you'll be able to speak to with the most conviction. Those issues will define your candidacy. Stick with these, regardless of polling, regardless of pundits, regardless of lobbyists. Hold to your core beliefs and present yourself as the strong, decisive leader your voters want.

The issues ranked with middle scores have more flexibility. If one concern is popular with voters, but you feel less strongly about it, you might be able to incorporate it into your platform. However, if your ranking number is less than a six—you won't be able to speak with enough emotional conviction. Some of these lower-ranked issues are areas where you can signal a willingness to compromise.

Issues ranked below a three or four will not form the major focus of your campaign. However, they do highlight a great opportunity: talk to voters about these topics. You'll do your best listening around these lower-ranked concerns, because you'll genuinely want to.

Regardless of what the polls say week to week, down deep voters want a strong, decisive candidate who is clear about what they believe. Putting these rankings down on paper helps you reinforce their emotional importance and allows you to better stick to your guns when the pressure's on.

Column 4: Your Opponent's Views

In your next column, write out what your opponent's arguments might be. What is their supporting evidence? What is their rationale? What questions will they ask you? Watch videos of your opponent's speeches and make notes on their lines of reasoning.

You need to do your homework to feel confident that you have a full and complete understanding of your opponent's arguments. You'll debate your own position better if you do. Having command of the facts will make you seem confident and decisive. You're less likely to appear anxious when your opponent is making their case, because you will have anticipated their stance.

Column 5: Possible Challenges to Your Views

Now try to predict what your opponent will say to challenge *your* policies. What negatives will they raise to put down your plans? Anticipate their comebacks and have a ready response.

Will your proposals cost too much? Will some voters complain a policy is socially unequal or unfair? How will your tax cuts be paid for? For each potential predicted challenge, write out your opponent's argument, and then write out your rebuttal.

Again, adapt this exercise according to the strength of your ranking numbers. Your rebuttals to others should be strong, definite, emphatic, and center on your core issues.

You'll give a different rebuttal for issues with middle or low rankings. With these issues, you can reach some agreement with your opponent. I strongly suggest you share a story that a voter has related to you on the campaign trail—and demonstrate yourself as a caring listener.

In completing the "Column 5" exercise, be sure to fully consider each side of the argument. When you win your election, you're going to be in a different position than when you ran: representing *all* the people, not just the constituency that voted for you. By entertaining multiple points of view on a given issue, you will be a better debater, and a better leader.

Column 6: Construct Your Emotional Platform

After sorting your views and your opponent's, too, you can begin to construct your emotional platform—how you will *relate* to the voter on each of these issues. Remember: voters vote with their gut, not their brain. Establishing a plan for making an emotional connection is critical!

Brainstorm the stories you'll tell that connect to each issue. Through storytelling, you establish that emotional bond with voters. What anecdotes do you have? What examples can you share about real people?

Your emotional platform is crucial. You may be smarter than your opponent, but they can certainly out-emotion you! And typically, it's the more emotionally available candidate who takes the win on Election Day.

Column 7: Identify Common Ground with the Opposition

Finally, identify the common ground you share with any opposing viewpoints. If you want to change someone's mind to align with your ideas, you must reframe issues so that they line up with voters' existing beliefs. Here, you need to identify common ground.

For example, if you strongly believe in Second Amendment rights and your opponent is all for stronger gun restrictions, don't stand your ground but find the common ground. You both might want responsible gun ownership. You both value safety. If you're addressing an audience with a variety of opinions on gun control, aim for discussing that common ground first. Get everyone on the same page. *Then* start targeting your stance.

Finding the common ground allows you to discuss voter issues in an empathic way, which shows nuance and understanding—*without* making you seem inconsistent in your views or weak.

Assembling the information in each of the columns I've outlined will help you avoid the sins of being tentative, passive, inconsistent, and weak. You will know your platform thoroughly and be able to logically and emotionally defend your positions with confidence.

There are additional points to consider when projecting the virtue of decisiveness. These fall outside of your campaign platform.

BELIEVE IN YOUR MESSAGE

Candidates who inspire demonstrate strength, decisiveness, optimism, and trustworthiness. *That's* what voters want on an emotional level from their candidates.

Be clear and thoughtful. Be deliberate—even courageous. Have a conviction about something important to you and believe it wholeheartedly.

Decisive leadership is a critical strength virtue. The best way to demonstrate conviction is by developing a platform you genuinely believe in. Take a lesson from Churchill, Roosevelt, Florida governor Ron DeSantis, or even Bernie Sanders: *believe* in your message and take the voters with you.

CHAPTER FOUR

FROM REACTIVE TO DELIBERATE

"When a resolute young fellow steps up to the great bully, the world, and takes him boldly by the beard, he is often surprised to find it comes off in his hand, and that it was only tied on to scare away the timid adventurers."

—RALPH WALDO EMERSON

Sarah Palin, John McCain's vice-presidential running mate in the 2008 election, was picked to appeal to Americans through her folksiness. "I'm a hockey mom!" the then-governor of Alaska proclaimed. She was warm, personable, and wore her Alaska-frontier identity with pride.

Palin was also one of the most prolific gaffers of all time.

One campaign interview typified her lack of awareness and ended with disastrous optics. Palin filmed a scene pardoning a

Thanksgiving turkey. She described herself as being a "friend to all creatures, great and small!" Immediately afterwards, the camera panned to her standing fifteen feet away from turkeys being fed into a slaughtering machine.

Her interview was completely upstaged by the sound of the fighting, flapping turkeys behind her, and the sight of the hatchery worker who stared at Palin's back, seemingly incredulous that she would be filming so close to his butchery.

When NBC News contacted Palin's office for a comment, they were told that a photographer had asked Palin if she wanted the turkey slaughtering as a backdrop. Her response: "No worries!"[102]

Yes, worries.

Palin's series of gaffes ultimately made her seem like an uninformed, imprudent, and foolish candidate. McCain's skeptics and supporters grew increasingly anxious at the thought of Palin being "a heartbeat away from the presidency." His choice of Palin as running mate was viewed as irrational and a chief reason McCain lost to the Obama-Biden ticket.

As Reuters noted, analysts determined the choice of Sarah Palin made many Americans question McCain's judgment.[103] Although Palin still had a devoted following of conservative fans, one 2010 study by Stanford researchers estimated that the

---

102 Heathr456. "Countdown: Sarah Palin's Turkey Pardoning Fiasco." *YouTube.* November 20, 2008. Accessed January 31, 2019.

103 Mason, Jeff. "Why John McCain Lost the White House." *Reuters.* November 5, 2008.

choice of the little-known Alaska governor as his running mate cost McCain roughly 2 million votes.[104]

Lack of awareness, being uninformed, making an impulsive statement or thoughtless action—all these gaffe-worthy conditions point to the sin of being reactive.

Reactive candidates and politicians often behave without being deliberate, prudent, or mindful. They shoot first and aim later, which is defensive. They react to criticism with thin-skinned sensitivity, like Donald Trump. They can be condescending, as when Hillary Clinton insulted her opponent's supporters as "deplorables." Or when Mitt Romney said he thought 47 percent of the population desired to live on handouts. They can be tone-deaf and impulsive. Most of all, they demonstrate a jaw-dropping lack of awareness about themselves and their voters. This lack of awareness can be summed up as poor emotional quotient (EQ) or intelligence. EQ, popularized by psychologist Dr. Daniel Goleman, is the ability to identify and manage one's emotions as well as the emotions of others.[105] According to an article that researchers published in *Psychology Today*:

> Emotional intelligence is generally said to include at least three skills: emotional awareness, or the ability to identify and name one's own emotions; the ability to harness those emotions and apply them to tasks like thinking and problem solving; and the ability

---

104 Bump, Philip. "How Sarah Palin's Endorsement of Trump Could Do More Harm than Good." *The Independent*. January 20, 2016.

105 Goleman, Daniel. *Emotional Intelligence*. New York: Bantam, 1995.

to manage emotions, which includes both regulating one's own emotions when necessary and helping others to do the same.[106]

Reactiveness, or lack of self-regulation, emanates chiefly through gaffes—embarrassing moments like Palin's that can threaten a campaign's viability. Voters see gaffes as glimpses into what candidates really believe. They don't assume these moments are the exception to the well-crafted speeches more often heard on the campaign trail. Instead, voters believe the gaffes betray the truth. As the late American journalist and political commentator Michael Kinsley famously said, "A gaffe is when a politician tells the truth—some obvious truth he isn't supposed to say."[107]

Gaffing may or may not reveal the truth about a candidate's beliefs. What it *does* reveal is a lack of focus and EQ. When politicians go on autopilot and stop being mindful of themselves or their surroundings—that's when they are most likely to transmit bad emotional optics. They forget facts or previous campaign incidents, fall back on canned speeches, don't think before they speak or react, fail to understand their moods, abilities, or motivations, don't express themselves appropriately, and do not spend enough time interacting with their specific audience. As a result, they can easily be caught off guard by something unexpected, and then—they react automatically, not deliberately.

A GAFFE MACHINE

After months of speculation, former vice president Joe Biden has

---

106 Winch, Guy. "Test Your Practical Emotional Intelligence." *Psychology Today*. November 1, 2013.

107 Mahnken, Kevin. "Why Do Republicans Keep Committing the 'Kinsley Gaffe'?" *The New Republic*. April 25, 2016.

officially announced his candidacy for the democratic nomination in the 2020 presidential race. Although Biden is currently under scrutiny for allegedly using his influence when vice-president to garner his son Hunter lucrative consulting contracts with Ukraine and China, recent polls show him to be the favorite in a crowded field of over twenty others vying for the nomination. Unlike some of his younger rivals, Biden has been in the public eye for decades as a US Senator from Delaware and a Vice-President for eight years. But he has a problem: Joe Biden is a master gaffer. Syndicated columnist Dana Milbank calls Biden the "Lamborghini of political gaffes."

Gaffing is a symptom of a politician not being mindful, and with this trait Biden is legendary. He gaffes so frequently that it's almost a personality trait. It's just "Joe being Joe"—at least to Democrats, who tend to see even his outrageous missteps as a charming quirk. The public has grown accustomed to Biden's ways and somewhat desensitized to his gaffes. Will their goodwill last?

In 2010 at a St Patrick's Day reception for Irish prime minister Brian Cowen, Biden got confused over which of Cowen's parents had passed away. "His mom lived in Long Island for ten years or so, God rest her soul," he said, before catching his mistake. "Although she's, wait. Your mom's still alive. It was your dad that passed. God bless her soul. I gotta get this straight."[108]

On a 2008 campaign stop in Missouri when running for vice-president, Biden called out Senator Chuck Graham to stand up for a round of applause. Graham is a paraplegic since the age of

---

108 O'Neil, Luke. "'I Am a Gaffe Machine': A History of Joe Biden's Biggest Blunders." *The Guardian.* June 2019.

sixteen. "Stand up, Chuck. Let them see you," chortled Biden. "Oh, God luv ya, what am I talking about," said Biden. "I'll tell you what, you're making everyone else stand up, though pal," he said. "You can tell I'm new."

In a major gaffe during his 2007 run for the democratic presidential nomination, Biden said of future president Barack Obama, "I mean you've got the first mainstream African American who is articulate and bright and clean and a nice-looking guy," Biden said, implying that being "bright," "clean," and "nice-looking" set Obama apart from other African Americans.

On the Daily Show with John Stewart, Biden tried to explain away his comments about Obama. "What I meant was that he's got new ideas, he's a new guy on the block." Stewart looked on skeptically until Biden realized he was digging himself into a bigger hole and finished with, "It's not working, right?"

And recently while campaigning in Iowa, he told his audience that "Poor kids are just as bright and just as talented as white kids."[109] Biden claimed in a 2012 speech in Detroit, "I've known eight presidents, three of them intimately. I'd rather be at home making love to my wife while my children are asleep."[110]

Politicians like Joe Biden may always gaffe naturally. It's part of who they are. The misspeaking is not intended to be mean-spirited. Many candidates drive on autopilot because they get tired. The campaign trail is exhausting. You can't prevent the need to turn on the cruise control—but you need emotional

---

[109] Stevens, Matt. "Joe Biden Says 'Poor Kids' Are Just as Bright as 'White Kids'." *New York Times*. August 9, 2019.

[110] Halper, Daniel. "Biden: I've Known 8 Presidents, 3 'Intimately'." *Weekly Standard*. August 22, 2012.

intelligence to minimize it. You can prevent the urge to take your hands off the steering wheel by building personal awareness, and using Deliberate Practice, which we'll discuss in the second half of this chapter.

First, let's take a closer look at what's behind a candidate's reactive behavior.

THE SIN OF BEING REACTIVE

Reactiveness can give the impression that someone is up against the ropes. They're confused, defensive, they're desperate—they seem worried about their survival. Americans are not impressed with anxious, fearful candidates.

Most forms of reactiveness reduce to one common denominator: a critical lack of awareness. Not being mindful of your environment or aware of how you'll be perceived by others can only lead to trouble. Think of the people you're talking to and think about the context. When you're mindful of others first, you are less at risk for committing some of the sins listed below.

IMPULSIVE

George W. Bush was roundly criticized when, at an international summit in 2006, he gave German Chancellor Angela Merkel a brief shoulder massage. Although Bush apparently intended the shoulder squeeze as a friendly greeting, his spur-of-the-moment action was viewed by millions around the world and seen as impulsive and inappropriate.

Impulsivity implies thoughtlessness. Voters perceive that you're not considering the consequences of your actions—a big sign of weakness in a leader.

One study mapped out different types of impulsivity.[111] One is called **Non-Planning Impulsivity,** which refers to actions that are more concerned with the present than the future. When a candidate makes an off-the-cuff statement without thinking about the ramifications, that's Non-Planning Impulsivity.

Attentional Impulsivity is when you struggle to maintain focus. Candidates commit Attentional Impulsivity when they're distracted by fatigue, anxiety, or circumstances. They stop being mindful.

Motor Impulsivity occurs when you're acting physically without thinking. When candidates show physical signs of nervousness or irritation—like twitches, sweating, sighs, eye rolls, or compulsively drinking water—that's Motor Impulsivity.

Acting impulsively can be triggered by stress and anxiety—something candidates often feel on the campaign trail.

But there is a type of impulsivity called **Functional Impulsivity,** which is the ability to think quickly on your feet and take advantage of unexpected opportunities. People who operate with this type of impulsivity can respond quickly and are still able to self-monitor and maintain control. Every candidate and politician should aim to develop this type.

---

111 Huang S., et al. "Trait Impulsivity Components Correlate Differently with Proactive and Reactive Control." *PLoS One.* April 19, 2017.

"The Dean Scream" is one of politics' most memorable gaffes. In 2003, former Vermont governor Howard Dean was a front-runner for the 2004 Democratic Presidential nomination. After a strong showing in Iowa, Dean began a stump speech by rattling off the states he intended to win. As he named these states, his voice got louder and louder, the TV camera panned in closer and closer, and he ended the list of states with a giant cowboy scream: "yaaah!"[112]

Magnified partly by the way the camera displayed his physical optics, voters immediately got the impression that Dean was unhinged. Dean himself later wrote in a *New York Times* op-ed, "Even well-known candidates can damage themselves with gaffes if they appear to confirm things about the candidate that voters worry about."[113]

In Howard Dean's case, voters worried that he didn't possess the calm temperament needed to effectively lead the country as president. His primal scream seemed to confirm their fears. Ultimately, the Democratic Presidential nomination went to Senator John Kerry, someone who presented himself as calmer and more collected.

Letting your emotions hijack the steering wheel—whether it be through excitement, anger, or pessimism—will leave the impression that you're driving your campaign recklessly and that you

---

112 CNN. "2004: The Scream That Doomed Howard Dean." YouTube. July 31, 2013. Accessed January 31, 2019.

113 Dean, Howard. "Gaffes on the Campaign Trail." *The New York Times*. September 22, 2016. Accessed January 31, 2019.

have no self-control. We'll address how to practice self-discipline so you can be more in charge later in the chapter.

UNINFORMED

Another famous gaffe by VP candidate Sarah Palin came when she boasted of Alaska's proximity to Russia as evidence of her foreign policy experience. In a 2008 campaign trail interview with *ABC News*, Charles Gibson asked Palin whether her home state's proximity to Russia afforded her insights on US-Russian relations. Palin replied, "They're our next-door neighbors, and you can actually see Russia from land here in Alaska, from an island in Alaska."[114]

Her statement to Gibson was lampooned on *Saturday Night Live*, when actress Tina Fey impersonated Palin, saying, "I can see Russia from my house!"[115]

Fey deliberately distorted Palin's words to make her look naïve and uninformed. However, it is true—on a clear day, you can stand on the Alaskan island of Little Diomede and see the Russian island of Big Diomede, roughly two and a half miles away.

Although Palin herself never delivered the famous "I can see Russia" line, she still was punished severely by being mocked and made to look stupid and foolish.

---

114 "Full Transcript: Charlie Gibson Interviews GOP Vice Presidential Candidate Sarah Palin." *ABC News.* November 23, 2009.

115 *Saturday Night Live.* "Sarah Palin and Hillary Clinton Address the Nation - SNL." *YouTube.* September 23, 2013.

The consequence of making what might seem like an innocent, or even true, statement is that others can twist your remark to make you look weak. Voters need reassurance that their leaders have the knowledge necessary to lead. Be careful not to set yourself up. If you react with hesitance, confusion, or vagueness, you won't seem like a confident or strong leader.

TONE-DEAF

After 9/11, George W. Bush involved the US in the Iraq war. The war was controversial and based largely on suspicions that Iraqi president Saddam Hussein possessed "WMDs"—weapons of mass destruction.

The war's controversial nature should have given Bush pause when discussing it publicly. However, he displayed a lack of EQ when making several mistakes in emotional optics that came across as insensitive to the electorate.

The *Boston Globe* describes one of them:

> In May 2003, President George W. Bush stood on an aircraft carrier under a giant 'Mission Accomplished' banner and declared that 'major combat operations in Iraq have ended'—just six weeks after the invasion. But the war dragged on for many years after that and the banner became a symbol of U.S. misjudgments and mistakes in the long and costly conflict. Bush was heavily criticized for the move.[116]

---

116 Lucey, Catherine. "Bush Was Haunted by His Own 'Mission Accomplished.'" *BostonGlobe.com*. April 14, 2018.

Yes, Bush had acknowledged in his speech that there were more dangerous battles to come, but the words he used couldn't compete with the emotional optics of the banner. The banner came to symbolize Bush's insensitivity to the casualties of the war, and his misjudgment about how long it would take to actually "accomplish" the mission.

In 2004, Bush made another tone-deaf gaffe at the White House Correspondents' Dinner. Pictures on a slide show were projected to the attendees, featuring Bush looking under various items of furniture in his office. Bush narrated, "Where are those WMDs? They've got to be here somewhere..."

Those attending, alongside other viewers, were livid. Bush's joke, which was intended to mock himself, was called tasteless, childish, and appalling. John Kerry—Bush's future opponent in the presidential race—issued a scathing statement: "if George Bush thinks his deceptive rationale for going to war is a laughing matter, then he's even more out of touch than we thought."[117]

While it's true that Bush won re-election, these gaffes did him no favors. His seeming emotional insensitivities portrayed him to many as a leader who was oblivious to the feelings of his voters and ignorant about the consequences of his administration's policies.

To avoid appearing tone-deaf, listen to what other people are saying. Watch news items from a variety of sources. Find out what accusations are being leveled against you, and why. Without

---

117 Teather, David. "Bush Jokes about Search for WMD, but It's No Laughing Matter for Critics." *The Guardian*. March 26, 2004.

that information, you risk making a remark that comes across as thoughtless and insensitive.

DISTRACTED

Candidates can commit the sin of reactiveness when they're distracted. Distractions come from a variety of sources. Maybe your opponent is baiting you, or a transitory event or challenge grabs your attention. Often, candidates are distracted by their own emotions.

In 2013, Florida Senator Marco Rubio was chosen to make the Republicans' response to Obama's State of the Union speech. Understandably, Rubio was a little nervous. This would be an address to millions of viewers across America. During the speech, Rubio began sweating and his mouth became dry. Someone had placed a water bottle just out of the camera frame. Rubio suddenly moved out of camera view, stooped, and reached for the water. *The New Yorker* describes the comical moment:

> [Rubio] made a gamble and reached for a water bottle off-screen: he lurched down to his left and fumbled a bit, making a terrifyingly intimate moment of eye contact with the audience before taking a quick sip from an unfortunately tiny bottle and then ducking to put it back. He quickly returned to his speech and spun out the final few minutes. But, by then, those eyes had turned faintly sad; while continuing to perform the words, Rubio looked as though he knew he'd made a mistake, and that all anyone would remember in the morning would be the image of him stooped to the edge of the

frame, sheepishly grasping for the smallest plastic bottle of water in the District of Columbia.[118]

Rubio, a great retail politician, was able to neutralize the innocent gaffe by poking fun at himself on late night television by entering onstage with a bottle of water in hand, and acknowledging, "God has a funny way of reminding us that we're human."[119] Despite his mostly successful damage control, most people remembered only one thing from his speech: the water bottle moment.

Rubio's incident highlights the challenge every candidate might face: your mind can distract you and your body may betray you. How do you control for that?

Don't get agitated and don't get irritable. Politicians get bombarded daily with plenty of criticism, much of it unfair—it's easy to get annoyed by the complaints. You need to rise above the fray and not react defensively. Stay the course with your message and stay plugged into the voter's gut.

CONDESCENDING

When voters choose you as their candidate, they're making a commitment. However, when voters feel criticized by a candidate, their willingness to commit dissolves in a hurry.

Mitt Romney made a condescending comment at a Boca Raton closed-to-the-press fundraiser, where he thought he was safe among supporters. The bartender, Scott Prouty, a past resident

---

118 Crouch, Ian. "Marco Rubio's Water-Bottle Moment." *The New Yorker*. February 13, 2013.

119 Ibid.

of Massachusetts, put his cell phone on the bar and secretly recorded Romney's speech. Prouty later leaked a copy of the recording to the Mother Jones media outlet. Prouty told MSNBC, "The guy was running for the presidency, and these were his core beliefs. And I think everybody can judge whether that's appropriate or not or whether they believe the same way he does...I felt an obligation to expose the things he was saying."[120] The secretive nature of the clip made voters conclude that this must be what Romney *actually* believed, when he could let his guard down behind closed doors.

And what did Mitt say? "Forty-seven percent [of Americans are] dependent on the government, believe that they are victims... believe the government has a responsibility to care for them..."[121] The words that Romney used, describing nearly half of America's voters as welfare victims, may not have been what he actually felt or wanted to say in that way—but the phone camera recorded his every word. Ironically, when the 2012 presidential election results were tallied, Romney got 47 percent of the popular vote.

Remember to be emotionally aware—anything you say can and will be used against you!

When candidates or politicians are condescending, they come across as elitist and unkind. It's understandable that you have your personal biases—most people do. But if you continue to nurture your inclinations, you'll eventually let a comment slip like Hillary and Mitt did and offend key constituents.

---

120 Johnson, Luke. "Mitt Romney On 47 Percent Remark: 'Actually, I Didn't Say That' About Personal Responsibility." *MSNBC.* July 29, 2013.

121 David Corn, "The Story Behind the 47 Percent Video," *Mother Jones,* December 31, 2012.

Cultivate this nonjudgmental attitude by paying close attention to the feelings of the voters—*all* voters, those who support you and those who don't. Genuinely try to get in their shoes. Perhaps if Romney had personally spoken to more voters who experienced rough economic times growing up or were unemployed with no source of income for long periods, he would have shown a more empathic view of those he was seemingly putting down.

THE VIRTUE OF BEING DELIBERATE

Ronald Reagan was a model of thoughtful and prudent deliberateness. His philosophy of the world and the role of government was clear. His message was focused, and persuasive. As an actor, he was highly attuned to his outward behavior and over many years developed enormous discipline. He memorized many of the speeches he gave—even ones ninety minutes long. He presented himself as strong and capable.

Reagan was known as the Great Communicator. He earned that nickname, in large part, by maintaining high EQ—the acute awareness of his surroundings, where he was, what he was doing, and the tone of his words. According to James Poniewozik, chief television critic of the *New York Times*:

> Actors need to believe deeply in the authenticity and interiority of people besides themselves—so deeply that they can subordinate their personalities to 'people' who are merely lines on a script. Acting, Reagan told his biographer Lou Cannon, had taught him "to understand the feelings and motivations of others."[122]

---

122 Ibid, Poniewozik.

He was laser-focused on his vision and carrying out his goals. His keen awareness enabled him to ingratiate himself to almost anyone. Even when people didn't agree with him, he was still liked.

National political campaign operative Michael Gagnon, chief executive office of the Maine Heritage Policy Center, says:

> Reagan's best strength was in understanding his audience and relating to them in what felt like a genuine, authentic way. He understood people, and how to command a room. In particular, his use of warmth and humor to engender trust and positive feelings of connection were both unique among his colleagues, and effective. Reagan's sunny positive style seems a relic when compared to the caustic and often acrimonious communications of today's politicians. It was very hard to dislike Reagan for his personality. He had a knack for the inspirational, a pitch perfect delivery and a real sense of the moment.[123]

These personality traits and highly developed speaking skills enabled Reagan to work across the aisle. Reagan's relationship with the late Massachusetts congressman Tip O'Neill, who became Speaker of the House following the 1980 election, exemplifies this skill. As Reagan noted in his memoirs, the two were friends after 6pm—O'Neill noted that "before 6pm it's all politics." Even so, O'Neill's son Thomas reflected that they collaborated well:

> While neither man embraced the other's worldview, each respected the other's right to hold it. Each respected the other as a man. What

---

123 Gagnon, Matthew. "How Would You Rank the Last Ten Presidents (Trump-LBJ) in Terms of Speaking Style?" *Quora*. October 28, 2019.

both men deplored more than the other's political philosophy was stalemate in a country that was so polarized by ideology and party politics that it could not move forward. These were tough words and important disagreements over everything from taxation to Medicare and military spending. But yet there was a stronger commitment to getting things done.[124]

Politics are certainly as divisive today as they were for Reagan and O'Neill, and Reagan's ability to embrace the partisan differences and opinions of others allowed him to collaborate and respond deliberately, rather than reactively.

It would be easy to dismiss Reagan's gifts as a politician by saying they're innate. How could you possibly emulate someone so naturally talented?

But that's an injustice to Reagan. His strengths as a politician came from his famous discipline. Even his campaign strategist, John Sears, said, "Discipline is nine tenths of politics."[125]

The virtue of being deliberate is a discipline you can learn and put into practice.

HOW DO YOU BECOME DELIBERATE?

"Mindfulness" is a booming industry these days. There are mindfulness coloring books, mindful diets, and soundtracks to listen to. Businesses offer meditation sessions and mindfulness seminars. Even schools guide students through mindfulness breaks.

---

124 O'Neill, Thomas P. "Frenemies: A Love Story." *The New York Times.* October 5, 2012.

125 Troy, Tevi. "History Is Clear: It's Discipline that Wins Presidential Races," *The Observer,* November 20, 2011.

Mindfulness is a useful skill which should be cultivated. However, it's also limited in scope. The focus of being mindful is mainly cerebral—it's a meditation technique.

A MINDFUL POLITICIAN

Tim Ryan, a Democrat congressman from Ohio and former 2020 presidential candidate, practices mindfulness daily. When asked in an interview, "Has mindfulness helped you in not getting as triggered as you might by a fear-based approach to politics?" Ryan replied:

> The enemy today in America is division and what feeds the division is fear, and there's plenty of fearmongering going on, at the highest levels. It's very difficult not to react because it's so obnoxious sometimes, so hurtful, and demeaning to other people that you get angry, but you need to be able to walk yourself back from some of that stuff or let it go and try to focus on what the real issues are, because if you're caught up in the Washington fear and anxiety, you're forgetting about the fear and anxiety that your constituents are feeling every day around economic insecurity, healthcare insecurity, and retirement insecurity. And your job is really to focus on their fear and pain, not yours.[126]

Ryan has been called the "Rustbelt Yogi" and holds nonpartisan mindfulness sessions in Congress open to all. He feels that mindfulness practice is relevant to today's politics:

> I'm hoping we can get people on both sides of the aisle to move away from the turbulence that is dominating the surface of our

126 Boyce, Barry. "The Mindful Politician." *Mindful*. April 3, 2019.

politics, and the media covering our politics. Let's get to a little bit of a deeper place where we can reconnect to some better values, American values. Values grounded in the Constitution and the founding documents: providing for the general welfare, providing for the common defense—these are the values in our country that we need to get back to.

For action-oriented people, like a typical political candidate, it may be more helpful to take the "mindfulness" concepts of presence and focus that Tim Ryan advocates one step further. Below you'll find strategies, actions, and new habits that you can cultivate. They boil down to three main steps: Be aware. Be deliberate. And practice!

BE AWARE INTERNALLY

To combat gaffes, reactiveness, and impulsivity, candidates need to build their awareness—both internally and externally. When Sarah Palin was filmed in front of turkeys being slaughtered, she was not concentrating on the optics of what was happening around her. But lacking internal awareness can be even more problematic for candidates.

Do you know who you are? That's what we're talking about with internal self-awareness. Do you know your strengths and weaknesses? Do you know your defense mechanisms and your coping strategies? What are your personal biases? Are you aware of what trips off your emotions? When does your behavior impact others positively, and when does it turn them off to you?

When you're self-aware, you know your values, your vision, your passions and aspirations—and *that* is what you must emotionally relate to the voter.

Values

Get a firm grasp of your moral code and values. Obama was highly respected for demonstrating personal integrity as a husband and family man. Because he projected warmth and devotion to his family, Americans perceived him as a man of ethics and truthfulness, even if they didn't like his politics.

Bill Clinton, on the other hand—although a master retail politician—was undermined by his own lapses in integrity. Although he too portrayed himself as a committed family man, accusations of sexual misconduct plagued him, and he ultimately was caught lying about sex under oath to a grand jury—for which he was impeached. Clinton's problem was not that he was a serial cheater—it's that he campaigned with values that were later shown to be inconsistent and hypocritical with how he lived.

Donald Trump has had multiple marriages and countless affairs, along with accusations of sexual assault. However, Americans haven't punished him for that perceived misconduct the way they did Clinton, because Trump's identity as a playboy was already well-known. The values he projected weren't attached to being primarily a devoted husband and father—they were connected to him being a winner and successful billionaire businessman.

Get a firm handle on your own moral code, values, and vision. Make sure you live out those values in your personal and public life. Present a vision to voters that reflects what you genuinely believe in.

Eurich's Three Steps for Insight

There are excellent resources available to help build self-awareness. I recommend Dr. Tasha Eurich's book, *Insight*.[127] Eurich includes an Insight quiz that helps determine your self-awareness and how others perceive you. Her book and workbook provide exercises to help increase self-awareness in seven areas: values, passions, aspirations, fit within your environment, patterns, reactions, and impact on others. It's practical and informative.

Eurich advocates a three-step method to increase your self-awareness. First, **decide you want to know the truth.** Politicians have a bad habit of surrounding themselves with "yes people" who don't level with them. Make the decision to know the truth about yourself and how others perceive you.

Second, in the spirit of seeking the truth, **ask for feedback from a "loving critic."** You'll have plenty of feedback from harsh critics if you go into politics, but a loving critic will be able to speak objectively while maintaining kindness. In a later section where we discuss Deliberate Practice, we'll talk more about who is best equipped to give you that needed feedback.

Third, **ask what, not why.** If I'm practicing my golf at the driving range and I hit a slice, it makes little sense to ask, "Why did I do that?" It makes more sense to ask, "*What* should I have done differently with my hands and body?"

Similarly, when you're analyzing your performance as a candi-

---

127 Eurich, Tasha. *Insight: The Surprising Truth about How Others See Us, How We See Ourselves, and Why the Answers Matter More than We Think.* New York: Currency, 2018.

date, start by asking the question, "What *should* I have said to that voter? What did I say that I shouldn't have said, and how can I say it differently next time?" The "what" question will guide you into practical problem-solving and will be more productive than just asking "why."

One caveat: If you notice a pattern of responding to a certain type of question in a negative way, *that's* when you should start digging deeper with "why." What buttons in you are being pushed by others? Why do those questions spark such strong reactions from you and them?

Study Your Vulnerabilities

When I was a kid growing up, my mother parented with the assumption that everyone was guilty until proven innocent. That's how she was raised. I was sometimes punished first, and only later would I be asked if I did it. As an adult, I've had to work hard to not react defensively when I feel I'm being blamed for something I didn't do.

We all carry a soundtrack that loops in our head. Certain messages pop up when we're faced with an emotionally triggering event. The triggers come from the experiences that we've had from the time we were young to now. The emotions connect to how we were raised, how we were treated, and what we were praised or punished for. These emotional triggers cause a psychological reaction, along with biological changes in our bodies.

Criticism is a big trigger of personal reactions—and as a political candidate, you're going to get ongoing criticism. Examine the way you react to negative feedback. Do you get angry or nasty? Hostile or depressed? Do you want to crawl into a hole and hide? Do you retreat? Do you sulk?

The reaction that gets activated likely helped you cope when you were growing up. These reactions are defense mechanisms— they're what humans do mentally to protect themselves to survive.

Consider what your childhood experiences might teach you about how you react as an adult. If you identify the trigger of a reaction from your memories and are mindful of how you defend yourself, you often have the ammo you need to start "unlearning" that reaction—which will be a needed skill to avoid reacting badly!

Study Your Physicality

Pay close attention to what's happening physically in your body when you sense a bad reaction coming on. Marco Rubio gets dry mouth. Al Gore sighs. Donald Trump tweets. Some people sweat, some flush red, some people feel a tightening sensation in their chests—there are any number of physical reactions that can give us clues towards better self-awareness.

When you learn to notice these physical symptoms coming on, you can initiate techniques to calm yourself so you don't react badly. You can disguise your nervousness and develop strategies to mitigate a physical reaction that you anticipate might occur. For example, if you know you'll sweat in a certain situation, wear a shirt that won't show moisture. See if you can arrange a lower room temperature and keep a handkerchief close at hand. In some cases, you can joke about your physical reaction or find a way to spin it positively.

Nothing makes voter confidence plummet like seeing a candidate who's nervous. Voters are looking for strength, not signs of anxiety or fear. You'll sabotage yourself if you don't analyze the playing field—in this case, you. Decide to seek out the truth and come up with a game plan.

BE AWARE EXTERNALLY

Let's give her the benefit of the doubt. Let's say that Sarah Palin thought the turkey slaughtering interview might endear her to Americans. Perhaps she thought the up-close-and-personal-animal-encounter was quintessentially Alaskan and would add to her charm as a folksy, outdoorsy, pioneer-type.

Even if the interview optics were well-planned on Palin's part—that would still show poor external awareness. Why? Because Palin didn't have a true understanding of who her voters were. She was campaigning nationally for office, not locally. Most Americans really didn't want their Thanksgiving feast tainted with images of their main course's dying gasps. Or rather, gobbles.

As a political candidate, you need to be cognizant of your context, your political environment, your voters' emotions, and your voters' perception of you.

Be in the moment. Don't go on autopilot. Pay attention to your surroundings and the unique needs of the voters in front of you. We've discussed several times the importance of knowing your audience. Understanding their likes, dislikes, concerns, and culture will help you emotionally connect with each group of voters.

Political Environment

The political environment rapidly changes. You need to know where you stand on new issues that arise. Good politicians are constantly scanning their environment with an emotional periscope. Consider: What's going on around you? Where are people feeling disenfranchised? What's causing them to feel less enthusiastic? Are they concerned about healthcare, the environment, their jobs, or their welfare?

Your awareness of the political environment shouldn't *change* your values—but sharpen them.

How Others Perceive You

When Al Gore rolled his eyes and sighed in debates with George W. Bush, he assumed he was communicating his superior intelligence. But instead he looked rude and mean-spirited. If Gore had built more awareness of how voters perceived his reactions, he could have done a better job controlling his behavior.

Mitt Romney did not pay enough attention to voters' impression of his behavior. Had he been more attuned to people seeing him as out-of-touch and not relatable, he might have taken more opportunities to show himself as down-to-earth.

Instead, during one of the GOP presidential debates in Des Moines, Iowa, after Texas Governor Rick Perry claimed that Romney was attempting to cover up his past support for healthcare mandates, Romney challenged his rival to put some money where his mouth is. "Rick, I'll tell you what," Romney said, extending his hand. "Ten thousand bucks? Ten-thousand-dollar bet?" Perry declined: "I'm not in the betting business." By betting such a gross sum, Romney was suggesting that ten thousand dollars was pocket change to him. With that gaffe, Mitt instantly reinforced his opponent's negative branding that he was rich and out-of-touch. No doubt, this bet confirmed to the public his cluelessness about the lives of average Americans.

Building external self-awareness involves paying close attention to how the opposition negatively brands you. Make sure you contradict that branding early through your own positive messaging.

Your words and your nonverbal cues should reinforce the emotional message *you* want voters to carry with them. When you don't deliberately contradict the negative branding, you feed the enemy.

Keep your eyes on the polls, which shouldn't control you but inform you. Keep your eyes on the opposition's ads and how you're caricaturized in the media. Correct immediately voters' impressions through your own messaging, and work to improve deficits that the opposition constantly highlights.

Know your strengths, weaknesses, and what pushes your buttons. Most especially, you need to know how voters perceive you. Consciously and deliberately build your awareness of how you want to be perceived so you don't end up on the plate instead of on the menu.

DELIBERATE PRACTICE

Deliberate Practice, like mindfulness, is a cognitive technique.

Jason Shen, an expert in Deliberate Practice, defines it as "a planned, effortful series of activities designed to improve skill in a particular domain and guided by well-informed feedback."[128]

Essentially, Deliberate Practice is a way to practice a skill through mental rehearsal, followed by physical practice. Athletes who want to improve their skills work with a coach. Similarly, Deliberate Practice involves getting feedback and coaching. Let's go through this method step by step.

Focused Effort

First, **identify where you most need to improve.** For Romney, that was empathy and relatability. George W. Bush needed to work on discussing policy facts.

Remember your chief goals: you want to show voters you can understand someone like them. You want to be perceived as strong and warm, so you make an emotional connection with your constituents.

Ask yourself: What struggles do I have that are holding me back? Which of the seven deadly sins do I most need to improve?

Then, **get a mental representation of what this skill looks like when it's done well.** Watch videos of politicians who excelled in the areas where you struggle. Romney may not have liked this advice, but he could have learned about empathy from watching videos of Bill Clinton's interactions with voters or listening to FDR's fireside chats. Ronald Reagan and JFK are also excellent to

---

128 Shen, Jason. "The Complete Guide to Deliberate Practice – Better Humans." Better Humans. May 31, 2017.

watch. Both were masterful at maintaining focus, using amusing stories and jokes to deflect criticism, and connecting with voters by speaking with strength and warmth.

Choose well-defined goals towards improvement. When you want to learn a new skill, break that task into bite-sized chunks. Set clearly defined incremental goals, which will help you achieve mastery in the end.

If you're looking to improve your emotional connection with voters, maybe you tackle the goal of storytelling first. Here's an example of a list of clearly defined, step-by-step goals which could help you achieve that aim.

1. Identify a personal story that shows your core value of _____.
2. Practice telling the story in a way that highlights that value.
3. Improve the story by cutting out unnecessary details and strengthening elements like humor, emotion, rhetoric, etc.
4. Practice using the story to lead into a discussion of policy or a voter issue.

If you feel foolish in the beginning—that's good. It's a sign you're willing to be anxious and have the courage to try something new. Confronting areas of vulnerability for the first time will not be fun. Role playing with your campaign team, who are intentionally trying to bait you, will be irritating. When you practice telling a story of a time you failed or experienced tragedy—that might be emotionally painful.

But you'll be a much stronger candidate by learning not to be afraid.

Feedback & Coaching

If I go out to practice my golf swing, I could waste hours by taking swing after swing without knowing if it was good or bad. I might reinforce bad form or fail to make an easy correction. I'm too close to see my swing clearly. I need someone to give me feedback on how to improve—to help me break my swing into component parts and show what specifically to practice.

Candidates need honest and unafraid people around them to provide quality feedback as to where they can improve to connect emotionally with voters.

And who are these people? Probably not the ones who are most familiar to you in the campaign. They are already biased in your favor. The best source for objective feedback will come from an independent coach from outside your inner circle. Many campaigns hire political coaches, like me, or bring in professional actors who work with candidates to teach them to show emotion.

Ideally, your coach would have a psychological background. A political psychologist will coach candidates in mindfulness, focus, and exercises to build internal and external awareness. A psychologist can also diagnose a candidate's weaknesses where they fail to emotionally connect with voters. Then the coach teaches methods for relating better.

You'd also be wise to recruit outside feedback from the voters themselves. At various campaign stops, gather opinions from the audience. Have one of your campaign workers talk with a small group of voters to get their feedback about how you presented.

Remember Dr. Tasha Eurich's advice: you decide first that you want to know the truth. If you're not open to feedback, you can collect all the advice in the world and not benefit from any of it. You'll never improve if you're not genuinely willing to listen and apply recommendations.

Never Stop Pushing Yourself

Jason Shen writes, "Deliberate practice takes place outside one's comfort zone and requires a student to constantly try things that are just beyond his current abilities. Thus, it commands near maximal effort, which is generally not enjoyable."[129]

Your opponents and the media will try to trip you up. They will bait you and try to get a reaction. The exhaustion of the campaign trail will put you in a place of distraction, fatigue, and impulsivity.

To withstand these mental and physical challenges, remain mindful of your surroundings. Work at demonstrating your new skills in front of trusted people.

You can't be perfect, because you're human. You won't always react ideally or display the best emotional optics. But you can significantly strengthen your candidacy. Remember: *discipline* is nine tenths of politics.

---

129 Ibid.

CHAPTER FIVE

FROM CANNED TO AUTHENTIC

"Be yourself, everyone else is taken."

—OSCAR WILDE

Professional wrestling is staged. It features larger-than-life actors, and the winners and losers are fixed before the fights begin. So how did one of professional wrestling's biggest fakers become known as a uniquely real and authentic politician?

When Jesse Ventura ran for governor of Minnesota in 1998, he ran as a third-party candidate. His opponents, backed by the well-funded Republicans and Democrats, had a leg up on him—but Ventura had a better story.

Using his background as a Navy SEAL and professional wrestler, Ventura's message was simple, memorable, and perfectly suited to who he was. "I will fight for you!" he told Minnesota voters, billing himself as a reform candidate. His quirky campaign ads showed children playing with him as an action figure, miming

Ventura taking down corrupt politicians and special interest groups. He was able to assemble a powerful grassroots campaign and used the new platform of social media to reach out to voters. Ultimately, Ventura won the governorship.

Born James George Janos, Jesse "The Body" Ventura knew who he was and knew his brand. As a professional actor, he could play up his image. He was six foot four inches, he was hulking, and he was a fighter. His message of fighting for Minnesotans resonated with voters, because it was consistent with Jesse Ventura himself. Ironically, although he made his living in a pretend field playing a character—Ventura convinced voters that as a politician he was relatable and real.

Ventura's successful campaign reveals a little secret: there's an art to coming across as authentic. If you're not intentional in crafting your brand, as Ventura was, you can easily misrepresent yourself. When you shoot from the hip, you end up shooting yourself in the foot, and voters will get the wrong impression about who you are.

Mitt Romney certainly fell into this trap. As I've discussed, I know Governor Romney personally, and he is a great person. But he didn't take the necessary steps to show people "the real Mitt"—and as a result allowed his opponents to label him as inauthentic. They branded Mitt as staged, wooden, canned, and not relatable. As opposed to Ventura's likable message that he was changing up "politics as usual," Mitt seemed to *epitomize* politics as usual. Voters didn't take to that.

THE VIRTUE OF AUTHENTICITY

Authenticity is the first of the "warmth" virtues, because authenticity conveys to voters that they can *trust* you.

Matt Abrahams, professor at the Stanford Graduate School of Business and communications expert, says, "Research suggests authentic leaders are more trusted and believable. That trust builds up the leader's credibility and breeds confidence in her capability and intentions, which motivates greater engagement and effort from her audience members."[130]

Did you catch that? Authenticity leads to trust, which boosts your impression of strength! Your audience will want to *engage* with your campaign. Perhaps this is why authentic candidates are, more and more, seen as having the "it factor."[131]

Abrahams identifies four traits that are key to communicating authenticity:

1. **Audience-centric approach.** Abrahams reiterates the importance of knowing your audience and making efforts to connect with each unique group. An audience-centric approach shows that you honestly value the people in front of you.
2. **Openness.** Abrahams writes, "An authentic leader approaches her audience more openly, sharing her ideas and information through personal experience and stories."
3. **Warmth.** By communicating with empathy and optimism, you show an audience that you genuinely value them. When

---

130 Abrahams, Matt. "How Authentic Leaders Communicate." Communication Analytics Platform - Quantified Communications.

131 Thomas, Ken. "Authenticity Now the Attribute Craved by National Democrats." AP News. October 13, 2018.

they feel personally recognized by you, oxytocin gets released. This release then triggers an emotional response that makes people like you and bonds them to you. Remember that when people feel that you like them, they're more inclined to like you!

4. **Immediacy.** Abrahams explains, "Leaders [can] communicate in an immediate fashion by holding an open, balanced posture and using conversational language. These leaders might stumble and stutter or let out an occasional 'um,' but all of these convey an earnest honesty and presence in the moment."

No wonder Jesse Ventura impressed Minnesotans as being authentic. Videos of his speeches on the campaign trail show his demonstration of all four traits.[132] His public messages are filled with stories and anecdotes, his body language is relaxed, he affirms his audience and uses conversational language. In fact, he never once used notes during his campaign.

When voters don't feel like they can trust you, they will not feel safe in making a commitment to you with their votes. No trust, no commitment. It's as simple as that.

Authentic candidates present as being honest and heartfelt. Authenticity feels un-staged, and unforced. When George W. Bush was at Ground Zero shortly after 9/11, he stood up amongst the rubble on a truck with a bullhorn. As he began to address the crowd, one of the firemen called out, "Mr. President, we can't hear you!" Bush yelled back, "I can hear *you*! I can hear you, the rest of the world hears you, and the people who knocked these

132 RetaliateIn2012. "Jesse Ventura Victory Speech - Election Night 1998." YouTube. April 6, 2011.

buildings down will hear all of us soon!"[133] His voice was full of emotion. It was clear he was speaking from the heart.

That was an important moment for the American people. They believed their president understood their fear and pain, and their faith in Bush was reflected in the polls. Bush's approval ratings jumped from 51 percent to 86 percent after 9/11 and hovered between 80 and 90 percent in the four months after the attacks on the Twin Towers—the highest ever job approval rate for a president up to that time.[134]

To project authenticity, you need to be tuned into your own emotions. Acknowledging your feelings can feel scary for some candidates, many of whom love to be in control and are afraid to be real. They keep a closer eye on the polls than on their own hearts. However, candidates who are overly concerned with presenting a perfect image, rather than an authentic self, can commit a trifecta of sins: you come across as robotic, rote, and rehearsed.

AUTHENTICITY FOR MILLENNIALS

Authenticity is a necessary ingredient for any political candidate or politician. It's an especially critical trait to possess with today's millennials and other younger voters, who have now surpassed the baby boomers and Generation X in numbers.

Millennials, dot-commers, and younger voters don't want pretense. They've grown up with Facebook, Twitter, YouTube, other social media, and smartphones in hand. They know the ins and

---

133 AmericanRhetoric.com. "George W. Bush - 9/11 Bullhorn Speech." YouTube. April 3, 2009.

134 Gallup, Inc. "Bush Job Approval Highest in Gallup History." Gallup.com. September 24, 2001.

outs of crafting a public image and recognize inauthenticity in an instant. Rather than embrace the traditional way of doing business, these younger voters are more impressed with people who march to the beat of their own drum. They demand honesty.

In the 2016 Presidential campaign, Hillary Clinton struggled to win over these younger voters. Her sculpted presentation, along with accusations of a security-breach email scandal, made voters distrust her.

Millennials instead flocked to her primary challenger, Bernie Sanders. Sanders, old enough to be their grandfather, was disheveled, stooped, and had radical socialist policy ideas. But he presented as real. Millennials overlooked his age and physicality and were instead drawn to his passionate beliefs.

Studies show that millennials are less attached to traditional religion and traditional values. As a group, they're largely unclear about *what* they believe—but they do want to believe in something.[135] Millennials are more inclined than past generations to pin their hope and faith on a passionate leader with novel ideas, even if they don't understand all the ramifications of that political ideology.

For these millennial voters, an impressive resume is less important than an impression of authenticity.

Openness

A new level of openness is being demonstrated by younger-age

---

135 Smith, Kyle. "Millennials Are Totally Mixed up about What They Believe in." *New York Post*. September 5, 2016.

politicians via social media platforms like Facebook, Instagram, and Twitter. Alexandria Ocasio-Cortez—"AOC" as her millions of Twitter followers know her—did a live Instagram interview shortly after her 2018 election to Congress. While live-streaming the interview, she made macaroni and cheese in her Instant Pot.[136] The impression of authenticity she gives voters through moments like this have made her a social media superstar—with her own comic book—and a national figure with over 4 million Instagram followers.

Former three-term Texas Democratic Congressman Robert Francis "Beto" O'Rourke uses social media platforms to build a brand of authenticity. One article from The Hill notes, "O'Rourke has taken his supporters along with him on a trip to the dentist for a routine cleaning, shared diary-like entries about his life and talked of being in a 'funk' after leaving his job as a Texas congressman."[137] Like "AOC," O'Rourke has also amassed an enormous Twitter following and the endorsement of music superstars like Jay-Z and Beyoncé.

Even 2020 presidential Democrat candidate Senator Elizabeth Warren felt like she had to get into the authenticity act. She live-streamed drinking a beer in her kitchen with her husband present.

Why do live streaming, tweets, and social media stints connect with voters so powerfully? Has this largely replaced good old-fashioned campaign glad-handing?

136 Perry, David M. "Alexandria Ocasio-Cortez Has Mastered the Politics of Digital Intimacy." *Pacific Standard.* November 30, 2018.

137 Parnes, Amie. "O'Rourke's Strategy: Show Americans the Real Beto." *The Hill.* January 20, 2019.

When we can peer into the "real lives" of our elected representatives and political candidates—as "real" as a curated news feed can be—we perceive these people as open and transparent. A politician who's willing to flash his molars in the dentist's chair does not appear to be someone who's hiding skeletons in his closet.

Being personally transparent implies you're showing your authentic self to voters. That's key for voters who distrust politicians—as so many do. The "hypocritical politician" stereotype is someone who says one thing to voters but believes something else behind closed doors. If voters feel you're being open and honest with them, they'll trust that your decisions will be consistent with the person you've shown yourself to be. As legendary Indiana University basketball coach Bobby Knight once said, "Character is defined by what you do when no one is looking."

The message that comes through when you're being open and transparent with voters is simple: "This is who I am. This is what I believe. This is how I'm going to do things." That message should stay consistent whether you're having dinner with your family at home, talking to yourself in the bathroom mirror, posting on Twitter, or giving a speech on a debate stage.

THE SIN OF BEING CANNED

In the Republican primaries for the 2016 presidential election, the ante was raised for Marco Rubio. After doing well in several early primaries, many saw Rubio as the most likely seasoned candidate to beat Trump for the Republican nomination. Perhaps because the stakes were so high, Rubio overtrained ahead of the New Hampshire debate.

I know Marco personally, having worked on his campaigns. He's a gifted public speaker—he thinks well on his feet, he's naturally upbeat and optimistic, and he knows how to be emotionally compelling. But he went into that debate with the expectation that he needed to be *perfect*. Wanting to be fully prepared and knowing how much was on the line, he memorized answers—something that I advised him not to do when he called me from Los Angeles prior to the debate. I told him to be himself, tell his compelling story, and under no circumstances to "memorize lines."

Unfortunately, he *did* rehearse his lines. Voters could tell. During the debate, Rubio appeared canned and seemed to be following a blueprint. That was his undoing.

Chris Christie knew in advance about Rubio's tendency to memorize and script his performance. To distinguish himself against a crowded group of primary candidates, Christie lay in wait and then baited Marco, who was snared by Christie's trap. Like a broken record, Rubio repeated three times a variation of the same line, an attack on President Obama's policies. "Let's dispel this notion that Barack Obama doesn't know what he's doing. He knows exactly what he's doing," said Rubio repeatedly. "He is trying to change this country." Christie, who had called Rubio "scripted," called him out on his repetition as being robotic, saying that's what a DC politician does. "There it is, the memorized 25-second speech," Christie pointed out. "There it is everybody."[138]

The exchange went viral and Rubio's campaign momentum took

---

[138] Ben Jacobs and Sabrina Siddiqui, "Marco Rubio's Broken Record Blunder Costs Him New Hampshire Debate," *The Guardian*, February 7, 2016.

an immediate hit. Social media called him "Marcobot." Although he placed third in the Iowa caucuses and received several key endorsements, he failed to win the NH primary the next Tuesday and stepped out of the race soon after.

FINDING THE BALANCE

Rubio's mistake of trying to capture every point by rote is an obvious complication with striving for the virtue of authenticity. You must train, but not *over*train. You must be coached but appear authentic. How do you find the balance?

Marco Rubio needed to work on strategies for his tension—but not his speaking. He would have done well in that debate by not relying on rehearsed answers but speaking naturally and articulately, the way he normally does. But he tried to fix something that wasn't broken and memorized his lines. The result was a gaffe which made him appear robotic and canned.

Politics is not a game of perfection. You can gaffe and you can still win. The goal is to minimize the mistakes you make, and then transform your sins into virtues.

WHAT'S YOUR EXCUSE?

"We were outspent."

"The districts are gerrymandered."

"Bad voter turnout."

Defeated campaign teams reach for many excuses to explain the loss. Here's the one I think is the most painful—in part, because it's the excuse which resonated most when Mitt Romney was defeated: "Voters never knew him. If voters had only known him—we would have won."

Mitt Romney was afraid to be personally open and genuine on the campaign trail. Fear is one reason candidates don't project as authentic. Candidates may think, "If voters knew the real me, they might not like what they see." If voters don't feel they're seeing the *authentic* you, they won't *trust* you.

Ironically, by being himself, Romney failed to let voters get to know him. Mitt's Mormon religion discourages bragging about one's good deeds, and Romney's tendency was to keep quiet and underplay his accomplishments. In being overly modest, he felt he was being true to himself. Romney's scripted demeanor was repeatedly reinforced by his senior campaign strategist, Stuart Stevens, who overmanaged and overprotected him.

Stevens caused damage by wrongly assuming the campaign was about the policies, not about the person. Together, Stevens and Romney colluded to create a mutual protection strategy to hermetically seal Mitt against revealing more of his true individuality, or his "inner Mitt"—the candidate that the public yearned for and with whom he needed to establish that critical emotional connection.

I urged Stevens to fight the branding and put Mitt "out there" emotionally: "he needs to come off as more human." Knowing personally that Mitt loved to rake leaves, I told Stevens to film an ad. "Put a pair of Dungarees and a work shirt on him. Muss his hair up. Put him at his vacation home on Lake Winnipesaukee and get him into a pile of leaves with his grandchildren. Make him real."

Drawing on their arrogance that they knew better than anyone else, a short time later the campaign managers *did* shoot an ad with Mitt at Lake Winnipesaukee—but it wasn't Mitt rollicking in the leaves with his grandkids. To my chagrin, Romney instead was filmed riding a Jet Ski on the lake with his wife, Ann. How many people can relate to that? What do those emotional optics say?

The ad only served to reinforce the negative branding that already plagued his campaign. Mitt should have taken charge and worked with his team to find ways to contradict that negative image. Instead, he acquiesced, obeying his handlers like a passive choirboy. By not pushing back hard against how he was portrayed, Romney played right into the hands of his opposition.

Meanwhile, Romney's buttoned-up behavior came back to bite him. By withholding himself, he opened the door for the opposition to negatively brand him and never offered a counterargument. He failed to correct their message with the truth about who he really was. Ultimately, by committing many unforced verbal gaffes, Mitt ended up with the tongue lashing.

At the end of the day, you can't just blame a poorly run campaign on a bad campaign manager or strategist. You can't blame the media for misrepresenting you. The media is like an unthinking shark, attacking whenever it smells blood. If voters didn't get to know you—whose fault was that? The buck always stops with *you*—the candidate.

Remember: you are the boss! Your campaign is about your vision, your candidacy, your story and values. Your job is to make sure those qualities resonate. The second half of this chapter offers strategies to help you successfully demonstrate the virtue of authenticity.

THE ART OF AUTHENTICITY

The classic 1957 movie *A Face in the Crowd* is about a manufactured political candidate. Andy Griffith plays a no-name carnival barker named Larry "Lonesome" Rhodes, a country-and-western singer who's discovered by a talent scout in an Arkansas jail. Rhodes is given a radio show and then a TV show and becomes an overnight media sensation. Audiences are captured by his folksy humility. He quickly becomes one of the country's top influencers. However, as he becomes more famous, his initial humility gives way to Machiavellian self-importance. His undoing comes when a live microphone captures, unbeknownst to him, his blistering criticism of the public as "idiots" who believe every word he says.

The chilling award-winning drama makes one point clear: some candidates may be excellent at portraying authenticity—but might be phonies.

And the converse is also true: some candidates may be terrible at "playing" at authenticity, like George H. W. Bush or Mitt Romney—but they're great leaders and terrific human beings.

In 2016, Donald J. Trump was a billionaire presidential candidate who bragged about his comeback from massive debt, failed real estate deals, bankruptcy, and divorce. Voters who had also experienced setbacks in life saw a similar vulnerability to theirs. To them, Trump was not the stereotypical politician. In their book *The Great Revolt*, *Washington Examiner* syndicated columnist Salena Zito and Brad Todd of OnMessage, Inc., say,

> Unlike the perfectly coiffed, family-portrait, groomed-from-childhood-to-be-president Mitt Romney or the image-conscious, guarded, lifetime political calculator Hillary Clinton, Trump was perfectly imperfect to a wide swath of the electorate. For all his braggadocio, he was vulnerable in a way neither Romney nor Clinton could be. His coarseness and profanity on the campaign trail reinforced his authenticity to them.[139]

There's an *art* to conveying authenticity. Like any of these virtues, there are strategies you can work at to successfully build your brand.

If you don't understand your strengths, weaknesses, fears, hopes, and values, then you might end up as just another Lonesome Rhodes: a candidate who is easily manufactured by other people but ultimately revealed as inauthentic.

Second: Employ strategies to effectively *communicate* your authentic self. "Accidental" authenticity, like Mitt Romney's excessive modesty, might feel good and comfortable to you but deny voters access to some personality traits you're hiding that they might find attractive. You can also err in the other direction,

---

139 Zito, Salena and Brad Todd. *The Great Revolt: The Populist Coalition Reshaping American Politics*. New York: Crown Forum, 2018.

trying too hard to "show your brand." Then, you'll come across as theatrical instead of real—and turn voters off. Either way, you need to be thoughtful about the message you send. We will get back to this topic in the conclusion.

OWN YOUR STORY

Marco Rubio has a clear and powerful personal master narrative. In most of his campaign speeches, he shares early on, "My father was a bartender, and my mother a maid."

Sharing about his parents' humble professions shows voters that Rubio wasn't born with a silver spoon in his mouth. His parents were hard-working immigrants, and they passed their work ethic on to him. Rubio tells stories of his parents coming to America from Cuba with nothing, yet they still managed to raise a family and help him through college and law school. Now, he's a US senator. "I came from humble beginnings," he tells voters. "I understand what it means to struggle."

It's a compelling story. It's no surprise Rubio is eager to share it. But consider this: would Rubio have been as eager to share about his parents' jobs when he was a teenager? Maybe not.

At some point in Marco Rubio's life, something that may have once been a point of embarrassment became a hallmark of his success story. And the same is true for you.

Candidates often fail to own their story because they're embarrassed by some element of it. Recall the story of the candidate in the previous chapter, who lied about graduating from college.

Most everyone has aspects of their past that they'd rather not dwell on—but if you want to convey the virtue of authenticity, you need to own your story and embrace it.

Some candidates have been divorced several times. Some have declared bankruptcy. Some have an unimpressive education. You may not want to share regrets in your past, but you'll need to learn to discuss them. Opponents will use any mistake they dig up from your past against you, and you need to be prepared to discuss it in an open, honest, genuine way.

Several years ago, I was a regular weekly guest consulting psychologist on a prime-time morning Boston television show. There was a segment on marriage and divorce, and mid-interview, the host said to me, "Dr. Wish, you're divorced." It was true—and I hadn't been divorced long. The comment was surprising, and I think she expected to catch me off guard.

But I had nothing to hide. "Yes, I am," I responded. "It's unfortunate that I am, and I wouldn't recommend it to anyone. In fact, the only person I would ever put through it would be the Ayatollah. The process of getting divorced is like being held hostage." I tried to lighten the mood with a bit of humor. I didn't get defensive and I explained that my reason for giving advice was to help others avoid my same fate. Then, without missing a beat, I went on and spoke about the reasons why marriages break down.

In owning your story, you must first accept it. Whatever is in your past got you to where you are today. Most circumstances, good or bad, should be understood for what they taught you and how they strengthened you.

Reframe your story in a way that neutralizes any potential problem areas. In my case, I acknowledged the divorce, acknowledged the pain, and didn't let it get in the way of answering the question at hand. If you can respond openly, honestly, with tact and dignity, most people will identify with your struggle.

OWN YOUR STRENGTHS AND YES—YOUR WEAKNESSES

Weaknesses can help you seem more relatable to voters, when framed the right way. Don't discuss deficits that might prevent you from being effective. If you're terrible with managing money or working with other people—it's best not to highlight those. Instead, work on improving what you do best.

You can discuss weaknesses that you *used* to struggle with but have learned to overcome. Discussing a weakness can provide you an opportunity to discuss a newfound strength.

You can discuss weaknesses effectively when you acknowledge a disadvantage that is *irrelevant* to your job performance. This, too, can make you seem more human. Democrat Beto O'Rourke got widespread national attention when he almost beat Republican incumbent Ted Cruz in the 2018 Texas US Senate race. Cruz's near-loss to O'Rourke made people question whether historically "red" Texas might shape up to be a swing state in future years and stoked enthusiasm for a 2020 O'Rourke presidential run.

O'Rourke has been held up as the perfect example of authenticity among politicians, largely because of how open he has been on social media about his various highs and lows. Shortly after his defeat by Cruz, O'Rourke shared on the social media platform Medium that he'd felt "stuck" since losing the Senate race. "In and out of a funk," he acknowledged.

A man "born for the presidency," stuck in a funk? Such an admission wouldn't normally be made by politicians. But for many younger voters, his display of raw emotion is exactly why O'Rourke's statement held such popular appeal.[140]

An article from *The Hill,* which discussed O'Rourke's brand of authenticity, suggested his openness had legs: "Chris Lehane, a longtime strategist who worked in the Clinton White House, said the entry was effective because 'It shows he's human. That post in and of itself make himself not look like a politician and that's what people want,' Lehane said."[141]

No one is asking you to be perfect. Voters look to you to be trustworthy and capable. Show yourself as capable by owning your strengths. You can build trustworthiness by owning your weaknesses—provided you discuss them in the right way.

GET OUT OF YOUR COMFORT ZONE

O'Rourke had a novel strategy for revealing his values to the American people. He decided to go on a road trip. Explaining his rationale on Medium, he wrote, "Maybe if I get moving, on the road, meet people, learn about what's going on where they

---

140 Durkee, Alison. "Beto O'Rourke Officially Drops Out of the 2020 Race." *Vanity Fair.* November 1, 2019.

141 Parnes, Amie. "O'Rourke's Strategy: Show Americans the Real Beto." *The Hill.* January 20, 2019.

live, have some adventure, go where I don't know and I'm not known, it'll clear my head."[142]

O'Rourke intentionally drove out of his comfort zone with a mission in mind: he wanted to learn and be adventurous. Perhaps his motives were political, or perhaps they were personal. They might have been both—and that's probably why it worked for Beto. His road trip was authentic to his own personality and lifestyle.

This strategy wouldn't work for everyone—in fact, Hillary Clinton's effort at a road trip was largely seen as staged.[143] However, O'Rourke's posts from his trip accomplished what any candidate should aim for in demonstrating authenticity: he worked to let people know who he really was, sharing his observations, values, and ideas.

National political pollster Frank Luntz, author of *Words that Work,* notes that the best way to communicate authenticity is to "trigger personalization."[144] You want to help people see *themselves* in your message, in your stories, and in the experiences you share. Let voters see aspects of you that feel personal—those moments they will picture themselves in.

Sharing selfies from a road trip is one way to do that, but certainly not the only way. However, your choice to shift out of your comfort zone and trigger personalization should be unique to who you are.

---

142 Ibid.

143 Ibid.

144 Ibid, Luntz.

With white hair tufted on either side of his glasses, shoulders up near his ears, and his Brooklyn accent coming out in a growl, Bernie Sanders made crowds erupt as he roared, "We are going to start a revolution!"

Vermont senator Bernie Sanders could not be considered a polished politician like Bill Clinton. He did not have the gifts you would normally associate with a silver-tongued candidate. And yet, he amassed a cult following during the 2016 presidential primaries and is again vying for the Democratic nomination for president in 2020.

What is his appeal? His authenticity.

Bernie Sanders is out there. A self-proclaimed Democratic Socialist, Sanders does not shy away from putting forward a radical agenda that more moderate Democrats balk at. Yet he speaks his beliefs with such conviction that he convinced thousands of Americans to believe along with him.

He doesn't cater to polls. He is unapologetic about his message. Essentially, Sanders says, "This is what I believe in. If you like my message, then join me." He is true to himself. Not surprisingly, one of his largest demographics of supporters is young people who are naturally distrustful of politicians. To them, Bernie's unapologetic stance feels authentic and refreshing.

Sanders has looks more like a grandfather than JFK. (SNL's Larry David does a remarkable impression of him.) His supporters don't mind his rumpled professorial look, which adds to his image as a nonconformist. He doesn't have great posture. That too, became something crowds found endearing as they labeled Sanders "Uncle Bernie." Many of my recommendations in this book were totally disregarded by Bernie Sanders—but he got away with it. His authenticity and strength of conviction have carried him. Passion is the key to unlocking his authenticity.

As you develop your candidacy, be sure your platform and vision reflect your honest beliefs. Drop the pretense. Don't pander to the polls. Create a platform that you can own with passion. As you drive your message passionately, voters will come along for the ride.

EMOTIONAL OPTICS OF AUTHENTICITY

I need to acknowledge that the "authenticity effort" can backfire. Many a candidate has been ridiculed for trying to be authentic but coming across instead as staged. Remember, authenticity builds trust in voters. But when an attempt to seem genuine backfires, voters *distrust* you.

Optics matter. And the emotional optics of authenticity are slippery. Any attempt to show authenticity that isn't genuinely authentic *to you* will come across as—you guessed it—inauthentic.

When Alexandria Ocasio-Cortez was invited to give her colleagues in Congress some tips about using social media to connect with voters, she hit on this:

> "If you don't know what a meme is, don't post a meme," Ocasio-Cortez advised lawmakers during the session, according to ABC

News. "If you're an older woman, talk like an older woman talks... The top tip, I think, is really to be yourself and to really write your own tweets so that people know it's you talking," she said.[145]

One analyst examining O'Rourke and Ocasio-Cortez's social media strategies noted, "These tactics work for them because it's who they are and how they normally act and live. Other candidates can't just copy what they do but have to have a medium and a message that is authentic to them."[146]

What does it look like for *you* to be authentic? How do you appear to others, and how do you carry yourself? How do you behave, and speak, and function in the world as the real you? Think about ways you can let voters share those moments.

Anthony Scaramucci, the former Trump White House Communications Director, says in his book *Goodbye Gordon Gekko*, "Trying hard to be someone you're not is exhausting. John Kennedy once said of Richard Nixon...at each stop he has to decide which Nixon he is at the moment, which must be very exhausting...Remember, the best version of you is the way you define yourself when you are daydreaming—when your self-consciousness is low and your self-awareness is high."[147]

Authenticity is hard to fake. In the words of Oscar Wilde, "Be yourself! Everyone else is taken."

---

145 Ibid, Parnes.

146 Ibid.

147 Scaramucci, Anthony. *Goodbye Gordon Gekko*. New York: Wiley, 2010.

Here are some additional strategies to help you achieve the emotional optics of authenticity.

Personal Manifesto

Developing a personal manifesto can be an important step to guide your candidacy. When pressured by campaign strategists, pollsters, and politicos, it's easy to lose track of your authentic self. The personal manifesto is essentially your mission statement. It's an anchor. It should be a collection of sentences that answer these questions: Who are you? What do you believe in? What's important to you, and what specifically are you going to do about that?

I've described anecdotes about Rick Scott in this book already. As a Florida resident, I've gotten to know Scott as my governor, as a political candidate, as my senator and friend. If I were to draft a personal manifesto for Scott based on what I know about him, I might write something like this:

> I'm a guy who came from humble beginnings. I was raised in low-income housing and never really knew my biological father. I believe that anybody can succeed and that people need a good public education and work to feel good about themselves and help society. By creating jobs, I'm going to give people dignity and the opportunity to succeed, contribute, and feel safe.

The personal manifesto is part biography and part vision-casting. It's your narrative—your statement about hopes and dreams that you must never violate. Boil your candidacy down to the crux of what you're all about, and maintain your manifesto, even in the face of political pressure.

You will be accepted as an authentic, trustworthy candidate when you keep a firm grip on your deepest values.

Ten Words

Another helpful strategy to develop the optics of authenticity is to make a list of ten words that best define you. Identifying the best words will help clarify your branding and where you need to expand your emotional platform. If you've got four words that relate to intelligence, but no words that relate to emotional warmth—you've identified your first area to work on with Deliberate Practice!

Running for political office can wreak havoc on a person's sense of self and identity. You're being pushed and pulled in multiple directions. You'll be extolled by some and vilified by others. The polls can make you feel easily swayed. You may be in opposition to what polls show the public believes—so what do you do? What policies will you be flexible with? What areas are you determined to not bend?

Campaign strategists may urge you to win at all costs. "Do whatever it takes to appeal to voters!"

That strategy can backfire if voters detect inauthenticity.

Find the balance. You will need to adapt to the changing concerns of voters while being faithful to who you really are. If you demonstrate no core principles and beliefs of your own, you will be seen as unreliable.

Writing down ten key words that define your candidacy and

values will help you find that balance. You'll remember when you need to double-down on your principles and have more clarity on when you can bend.

Develop Your Emotional Platform

The personal manifesto and ten words help you strengthen your inner authenticity. Now, think about the outer optics of authenticity. How will you better *show* your voters who you are emotionally?

TV ads are one of the best methods voters get to know candidates. **Watch lots of TV political ads** with family and friends—especially children, who tend to be unfiltered and unbiased. Ask them, "what statements in the ads made you feel good about the candidate? When did you like their tone, posture, clothing, or setting? What made you dislike the candidate?" Collect feedback and use it to inform your ad development.

Pick out several TV clips from candidates you believe do a great job showing their authenticity. **Study the people who are doing it right.** Watch how they communicate. What do they do to emotionally connect with voters? What seems to be effective in their approach? Which of those methods could work for you?

Remember, at the end of the day, you need to do things your way. What works for one candidate won't work for you if you try to force it. Keep your personal manifesto and ten words in mind.

Then, study yourself. **Make audio and video recordings of yourself talking and play them back.** (You'll be introduced to voters on the radio and TV, so pay attention to how you personally project in both mediums.) Get feedback on your presentation optics. In the same way you examined the other TV ads for tone, style, setting, nonverbal cues, and statements, think about what works and doesn't work in your favor.

These recordings will function as your baseline. As you get more feedback, you'll find where you can improve or correct your approach. These initial recordings will help you measure future changes and are excellent material for practice and coaching.

Then, **role play to improve.** Give speeches to others and get feedback. Practice debates and get feedback. Do a model Town Hall and get feedback.

These role play exercises will help catch slip-ups: moments where you stumble, misrepresent yourself, lose focus, or appear condescending. After you identify your mistakes, consider how you could change your personal style so you still communicate your true self to voters.

Finally, **think about settings that convey the authentic you.** Where are you most relaxed? What do you do for fun? Where do you most enjoy connecting with people?

When political strategist and media consultant Mark McKinnon was working on George W. Bush's campaigns, he filmed him often in casual moments—when he was driving, interacting with voters, relaxing at a campaign stop. McKinnon explains his strategy for developing Bush's optics of authenticity:

Even though on all the issues people agreed with Gore and the

Democrats...what we discovered was that they liked the fact that [George W. Bush] was authentic...Maybe you didn't like exactly what his positions were, but you at least believed that he believed in what he was saying. So, most of what I did when I was filming him were documentary moments from the trail, or just candid interview moments that I would tease out of him, because it's really human... He had clear convictions, a strong moral component—it was just a really powerful, positive, emotional message.[148]

McKinnon identified what Bush's strengths were—his authenticity, his conviction, his moral values—and filmed Bush in the best settings to highlight those traits.

Don't film yourself at a desk—that's the wrong environment for a picture of authenticity, even if you do spend many hours a week there! You're looking for venues that have common appeal, that citizens can relate to and remain genuine to you. When Bill Clinton was running for President, he was filmed jogging in his shorts and then he stopped at a McDonald's for a burger and fries. It was humorous, likable, and real.

The best venues include children, family, animals, and charitable activities. Those settings are generally linked to positive emotions for people. They hold sentimental value and feel familiar, which triggers personalization (and releases oxytocin). Other settings hold that kind of emotional appeal as well—think coffee shops, Little League games, music concerts.

Unlike Jesse Ventura, your TV ads probably won't include an action figure that resembles you. The spots won't feature a jog

---

148 Ibid, Klein.

to McDonald's or include musings from a road trip, an Instant Pot macaroni and cheese dinner, a teeth cleaning at the dentist, or the Elizabeth Warren line "I'm gonna get me a beer."

Your ads will be unique to you. They'll be memorable, personal, and demonstrate to voters who you are and what you care about. They'll target voters' emotions and trigger personalization. Why?

Because you will have developed the virtue of authenticity.

CHAPTER SIX

FROM CEREBRAL TO EMPATHIC

"It's not hard to make decisions when you know what your values are."

—ROY DISNEY

In 2016, the debate stage in Los Angeles was jam-packed with sixteen Republican presidential primary candidates. Some were governors, and some were US senators. There were business leaders, a neurosurgeon, and a real estate developer turned popular reality TV star.

Each candidate competed for the public's attention and adoration, hungry for a moment in the sun where they could shine. Like a modern-day gladiator ring, the candidates were thrown in with the lions. Their survival depended on the public giving them a thumbs up or a thumbs down.

Donald J. Trump, at that point, seemed like a fringe candidate.

He had lottery-like odds of winning the nomination—much less the presidency—but Trump's acumen as a political candidate stemmed from his facility to stoke the audience's emotions.

Trump displayed his political gifts clearly when he was asked if there was a relationship between vaccinations and child autism. The neurosurgeon candidate, Dr. Ben Carson, gave a cerebral response to the question, citing studies and statistics that he felt disproved any connection between autism and vaccinations. His response was medically accurate—but it was far too academic and boring.

And, unfortunately for candidates who pride themselves on their intelligence, having all the facts, stats, and knowledge is worthless if you can't connect emotionally with voters.

Maverick political candidate Donald J. Trump, on the other hand, opted for a visceral, empathic response to the vaccine question. Instead of answering with data or statistics, Trump told a story—a simple anecdote of an employee he knew whose child became autistic after a medical treatment.

The story may have been apocryphal, but it certainly was emotional and memorable and resonated with the audience present—and the viewers at home. Rather than aim his shot at voters' heads, Trump fired directly at their gut. He targeted emotions repeatedly throughout his campaign—and, against incredible odds—achieved the greatest prize any modern-day gladiator could hope for: the American presidency.

Trump wasn't experienced as a public servant—but he *was* adept at public relations, sales, and as a reality TV star. James Poniewozik writes in his new book *Audience of One: Donald Trump, Television, and the Fracturing of America*, that Trump "achieved symbiosis with the medium. Its impulses were his impulses; its appetites were his appetites; its mentality was his mentality...He recognized intuitively what the televised debates were: an elimination-based reality show."[149]

Donald J. Trump understood the formula. He knew how to create drama, how to cast villains, how to posture as a hero, how to capture the audience's attention. Most importantly, he knew how to tap directly into the gut of the voters to sell himself.

Yet nothing that Trump did was rocket science—it was a learned formula that he had trained himself to excel in. The method he used to connect to voters' guts is the method I outline in this chapter. Just like a gladiator can be trained to throw a spear from a racing chariot, connecting emotionally with the voter is something you can also learn!

CEREBRAL EQUALS BORING

Not long after this presidential debate, I was at a cocktail party at my Congressman Vern Buchanan's home talking with Paul Ryan, Romney's 2012 vice-presidential running mate and Speaker of the House. I had spent time with Ryan before at one of our Romney campaign retreats in Utah, but now we were discussing the 2016 primaries. Paul asked me why I thought Jeb Bush, a successful and popular former governor of Florida and the favorite to win

---

149 Poniewozik, James. *Audience of One: Donald Trump, Television, and the Fracturing of America*. New York: Liveright. 2019.

because of his extensive endorsements and war chest he had raised early, hadn't secured the nomination.

"He's too cerebral. He's a policy wonk, Paul. Like you!" I joked. "Always the ten-point plan. Today, people don't want to hear a ten-point plan."

"I know," Paul agreed. "By the time you get to point two, their eyes glaze over."

I said, "You got it, that's right!"

Paul Ryan and Jeb Bush are enormously successful men and gifted politicians. They're intelligent, thoughtful, and they worked hard in their political careers to propose and implement policies they believed were in the public's best interest. However, they're also cerebral to a fault. They rely too heavily on their policy and data points. In response to questions, they lead with logic, statistics, facts, and plans.

None of those are necessarily bad traits. The government needs men and women who understand the fine print of how policies are enacted and promoted. Candidates *should* learn the data—but they shouldn't *campaign* with the data. Data is boring. If you're onstage with fifteen other opponents—or in a close race with just one—boring is your death knell.

After the Republican primaries were finished, winning over voters became a race between the Cerebral candidate, Hillary Clinton, and the Emotional candidate, Donald Trump. Hillary Clinton's political experience was far superior, but she often waded too deep into the weeds when discussing policy. Her campaign website had forty pages outlining policy positions, plus all the fact sheets for each of her proposals.[150] She eagerly referenced her multistep plans to prove she was ready to solve some of the nation's problems and repeatedly pointed to Trump's lack of any facts or plan.

But the American people weren't interested in any ten-point plan. Hillary's statistics and her unemotional, antiseptic approach to explain her policy positions didn't infect enough voters in the Midwest with enthusiasm. Ironically, Hillary kicked her campaign off with a "likability tour." However, she was famously guarded, rarely letting voters see "the real her." She struggled to shed her reputation as being untrustworthy and remote. According to Clare Bond Potter, Hillary "couldn't stop herself from voicing her own ambivalence about likeability as a qualification for office." [151]

"I think it's good to have a likable president," Hillary said. "But if I remember right, many people said they wanted to have a beer with George W. Bush. Maybe they should've left it at that." Perhaps, as the first woman running for President, she believed showing her emotions would brand her as weak.

In the 2008 New Hampshire primary Democratic debate against Barack Obama, the moderator asked Hillary how she would respond to New Hampshire voters who "like her resume" but just like "Obama more." Hillary deflected the question and quipped, "Well, that hurts my feelings."[152] She then commented that

---

150 Carroll, Lauren. "Hillary Clinton's Top 10 Campaign Promises." *Politifact.* July 22, 2016.

151 Potter, Claire Bond. "Men Invented 'Likeability.' Guess Who Benefits." *The New York Times.* May 4, 2019.

152 "The Nine Most Memorable Debate Moments." *RealClear Politics.* November 11, 2015.

Obama is "very likable." Obama turned her comment around and shot back, "you're likable enough, Hillary."

Hillary went on to win the New Hampshire primary, but, as we know, "likable enough" wasn't going to get her the nomination. Obama was more likable. Research supports the fact that women have a much more complicated road to travel when trying to pair "likability" with success.[153]

When there's no emotional connection with a candidate, voters don't feel a sense of trust. Especially given the many trust issues already present in Hillary's past—the private email server, Benghazi, questionable use of funds for the Clinton Foundation, Travelgate, the cattle futures controversy, and Whitewater, Hillary's inability to secure voters' trust was the deal-breaker. Voters struggled to form a likable connection with her. More importantly, her cerebral and detached manner didn't help voters feel she understood someone like them.

Trump is hardly the poster child for empathy. Do a quick Google search, and you'll find that pundits complain about his apparent *lack* of empathy. However, he is an expert at being able to read the emotions of his supporters and accurately reflect them back, a kind of empathy one author refers to as "cognitive empathy."[154]

Cognitive empathy is different than the empathy we usually think of, when one person genuinely feels compassion and care for another person. Rather, cognitive empathy is the ability to *detect*

---

153 Cooper, Marianne. "For Women Leaders, Likability and Success Hardly Go Hand-in-Hand." *Harvard Business Review*. August 7, 2014.

154 Willingham, Emily. "Yes, Donald Trump Is A Master Of Empathy." *Forbes*. November 3, 2016.

another person's emotions. Once the emotion is identified, a cognitively empathetic person can use their read of other people's emotions for their own gain—either for good, or bad. One *Forbes* columnist wrote critically (yet admiringly), "[Trump's] instinctive understanding of his fans' emotional states and his willingness to exploit them drive his success."[155]

The best candidates—the ones who endear themselves to voters, not just throughout the course of a campaign, but the course of history—possess both kinds of empathy. They *detect* voters' emotions and respond with *genuine compassion*. They see and feel.

EMPATHIC EXCHANGES

Presidents remembered fondly for their empathy, like Ronald Reagan, FDR, or Bill Clinton, established themselves as compassionate leaders through demonstrations of genuine care for others.

Think of Reagan's response to the tragic Challenger explosion in 1986. In one of his speeches, he mentioned by name the husband and children of a teacher who died onboard, saying he couldn't get them out of his head.[156]

Bill Clinton gave another example of empathy during the 1992 Town Hall debate against George H. W. Bush. During the debate, as he answered questions, Clinton walked directly up to the questioner, but Bush never got off his stool. He spoke slowly,

---

155 Ibid.

156 Grier, Peter. "Challenger Explosion: How President Reagan Responded." *The Christian Science Monitor.* January 28, 2011.

softly, and, at times, seemed distracted. At one point, as Clinton addressed an audience question about the economy, the camera caught Bush checking his watch. Just this glance was a thin-slice that signaled to Americans that President G. H. W. Bush was a blue-blooded Northeastern patrician who couldn't relate to real people.

Bush's decision to glance at his watch was consequential. Following this gaffe, he began an awkward exchange with another questioner. A young African American woman asked Bush how the national debt had affected him personally. Unfortunately, she confused the concepts of government debt and the economic recession. Bush began with an answer about interest rates. When the moderator attempted to clarify the question, Bush fumbled, became visibly flustered and chose to take his frustration out on the questioner. Bush's behavior became the perfect setup for Bill Clinton to look empathetic and down-to-earth as he stepped in to commiserate with the young woman's recession plight. He walked right up to the woman and engaged with her pain.

Clinton asked, "Tell me how it's affected you again...You know people who've lost their jobs and lost their homes?" The woman affirmed she had. Then he responded empathically, expressing emotion that affirmed the voter's struggle: "Well, I've been governor of a small state for 12 years...In my state, when people lose their jobs there's a good chance I'll know them by their names. When a factory closes, I know the people who ran it. When the businesses go bankrupt, I know them."[157]

With his empathic statements, Clinton plugged into her gut and

157 "October 15, 1992 Second Half Debate Transcript." Commission on Presidential Debates. October 16, 1992.

showed the woman he understood her and others like her. He validated her struggle. Through sharing his personal observations of a downtrodden economy, he demonstrated he understood the fear and anguish of those who had fallen on hard times.

Regardless of what failures or accomplishments may have defined the Clinton and Bush presidential legacies, moments like these were profoundly moving and memorable. They clearly showed the American people that they were deeply cared for.

Remember that casting a vote is participating in a personal relationship. In marking a ballot for you, the voter says, "I choose *you*. I trust *you*." That's why being empathic over cerebral is so crucial. When two or more people exchange empathy, oxytocin is released, a connection is established, and a positive relationship is forged. Ten-point plans don't form a relationship; emotion does.

Empathy is such an important virtue for a candidate to demonstrate due to the *primacy* of emotion. As stated earlier in this book, the emotional gut is "the first brain." Because of our earliest days fighting for survival, humans are wired to feel before they act.

However, that doesn't mean other activity isn't going on simultaneously in the brain when our emotions are aroused. Let's examine empathy's fascinating effect on our minds.

THE BRAIN SCIENCE OF EMPATHY

Years ago, in a science lab in Italy, neuroscientists observed the brains of monkeys who were gesturing. One monkey swung his arm up to grab a fistful of leaves, and his brain lit up in a specific region. Another monkey sat nearby, watching the first. Although the second monkey was still, his brain lit up in the identical area as the first monkey that was moving. Just watching, just studying, coded the second monkey's brain like the first, confirming the saying "Monkey see, monkey do." This study pioneered the work on mirror neurons.[158]

What are mirror neurons? They are imitative brain cells that play a role in action and intention, understanding, motivation, speech, and emotional feeling. Whenever your brain tells your body to act—whether that's laugh, smile, jump, or run—your brain activates motor neurons, just like the motor in a car gets the wheels to turn. However, you don't have to be moving for motor neurons to be firing off.

If you're sitting completely still, your brain will still activate motor neurons when you watch someone doing an action, like kicking a soccer ball. These cells reflect activity, almost like a reflection in a mirror—hence the name, mirror neurons.

Think of a pair of best friends who have adopted the same phrases, the same inflections, and the same gestures. Those friends unconsciously imitate each other because of the mirror neurons in their brains. The slow drawl of Americans from the Deep South, or the exuberant hand gestures of Italians, or the stoicism among Eastern Europeans—mirror neurons are responsible for these cultural idiosyncrasies. As people observe each other, our brains code behaviors, and it's these mirror neurons which are responsible for helping us feel empathy.

---

158 Fabbri-Destro, Maddalena, and Giacorno Rizzolatti. "Mirror Neurons and Mirror Systems in Monkeys and Humans." *Physiology.* June 1, 2008.

Empathy describes your ability to feel what another person is feeling. Someone who's lost their spouse can empathize with a recent widow, because they've both experienced similar tragedies. When you're connecting empathically with someone else—when the two of you are essentially in synch and experiencing the same feeling—your brains are activating mirror neurons. This means, according to UCLA neuroscientist Dr. Marco Iacoboni, that we are *instinctively* empathic.[159]

People incapable of empathy, classified as narcissists, can often be diagnosed as having a psychological personality disorder. In our culture, it is considered *abnormal* for one not to relate to the feelings of others. By becoming aware of our own empathic predispositions, we're better able to reflect emotions—both ours and others'—and increase our capacity to empathize.

That doesn't mean there aren't plenty of people in the world who are bad at showing empathy to others but aren't classified as pathological. Like other instinctive habits, this is a skill that people can let atrophy, or work at and improve.

STRATEGIES TO DEMONSTRATE EMPATHY

Throughout his campaigns and presidency, George H. W. Bush fell victim to gaffes which belied his genuine empathic nature and made him look insensitive. In discussing Bush's legacy, one writer wrote:

A one-termer whom the American people soundly rejected in

---

159 Daily, Mary. "Neuroscientist Marco Iacoboni on How Mirror Neurons Teach Us to Be Human." *UCLA Newsroom.* October 19, 2016.

1992, Bush was saddled with an image as a hapless, awkward, and out-of-touch patrician. "How wrong that impression was." While he disdained political theater and was uniquely unsuited to self-promotion, during critical times, Bush was "not just good at his job—he was great at it."[160]

Perhaps you, like President George H. W. Bush, "disdain political theater." Perhaps the very act of "crafting" an emotional appeal seems disingenuous.

But here's the rub: when emotional optics fail—as I experienced on the Romney campaign—candidates can be mistaken as unfeeling, uncaring, or incapable. By committing unforced errors, they mask their true selves. When emotional optics succeed, a candidate's authentic passion and character are made powerfully clear.

Optics matter! Most candidates genuinely want to make the world a better place. They take the role of being a "public servant" seriously. Paying close attention to your emotional optics will enable you to be seen as the candidate you *are:* caring, concerned, capable, and ready to lead. Consider some of the following strategies for demonstrating empathy on the campaign trail.

EMPATHY BY PROXY

Ideally, candidates communicate that they personally understand voters. If, for some reason, a candidate can't connect to a voter's experience on a personal level, they can reference someone they know who did have that experience.

---

160 "Bush 41: An Underrated President?" *The Week*, December 14, 2018.

Mitt Romney was born on third base. It was unnatural for him to relate to the experience of being raised in a family that didn't know when the next paycheck was coming. Because he couldn't identify personally, Romney's attempts to relate to the "common man" was largely cerebral. He was detached rather than attached. He was rational instead of emotional. He was sympathetic instead of empathic. In response to his opponents' attacks that as the CEO of Bain and Company his business reorganization practices caused many to lose their jobs and health benefits, he did acknowledge generally that there were many Americans unemployed. But he failed to spend enough time giving specific examples of people he *knew* personally that were out of work. As a result, his appeals to these suffering Americans fell flat.

Because I observed that Romney wasn't connecting empathically with voters, I recommended to the campaign handlers that at each stop on the stump an individual or couple be chosen that reflected the current local and national issues voters were worried about. I even volunteered to travel at my own expense to interview those selected. I suggested that we put those chosen up on stage with Mitt. He could name them and tell their story to the audience. By embracing these citizens and their anxieties up close and personal, audience members could vicariously identify and say to themselves "that story sounds like my story. That person or couple is just like me." The takeaway by association: "Romney cares about someone like me." Of course, my recommendation to the Romney campaign, like several others I made to help humanize Mitt to the public, consistently fell on deaf ears. I was told repeatedly, "You raise the money and leave the driving to us."

"Empathy by proxy" was exactly the approach Bill Clinton used when he engaged with the woman at the Town Hall debate in 1992. Clinton asked the woman questions about how she'd been affected by the downtrodden economy and then showed empathy in his response. He was only responding to one person in that moment, but those observing felt Clinton was speaking to every American who had ever felt the pinch of a bad economy on their wallets.

Vicarious empathy still accomplishes the same positive connecting effect as personal empathy: It shows voters that someone like you cares for someone like them.

USE HUMOR

Humor is amazing. It disarms, reduces tension, and gets people on your side.[161] If you can make someone laugh, you're also creating great chemical changes in the body: Laughter eases mental tension, stimulates organs, blood circulation, and relaxes muscles.[162] Laughter releases endorphins that make people feel physically good and instantly makes the humorous person seem likable.

Crack a joke! A French study published in *Psychological Reports* found that when women overhear men telling funny jokes (hopefully not vulgar), they view them as being more intelligent and attractive than men who just speak about everyday topics. According to Dr. Bogdan Wojiszke, "Men can use humor as an easy and honest—hard to fake—cue of intelligence."[163]

---

161 Mindful Staff. "How Humor Builds Empathy." *Mindful.* May 26, 2017.

162 "Stress Relief from Laughter? It's No Joke." *Mayo Clinic.* April 21, 2016.

163 Fields, Lisa. "13 Easy (and Scientifically Proven!) Ways to Look Smarter." *Reader's Digest.* October 13, 2019.

The best jokes for candidates are situational or self-deprecating. Reagan famously dismissed concerns about his elderly age during the presidential debate of 1984. When pressed whether at his age (he was seventy-three) he had the stamina required to carry out his presidential duties, he quipped, "I will not make age an issue of this campaign. I am not going to exploit, for political purposes, my opponent's youth and inexperience."[164] The audience roared with laughter. Even Reagan's Democrat opponent, Fritz Mondale, broke into a broad smile and laughed. Although Reagan consistently misremembered facts during the debates, his lack of cerebral prowess did him no harm. He won the election in a landslide, capturing forty-nine states and 525 electoral votes. His magnetic charm and likeability carried the day. After his death, staff cleaning out Reagan's desk found 365 index cards with his jokes and one-liners wrapped simply with a rubber band.

As Reagan's example proves, humor can help to dismiss potential criticisms of your candidacy. When John F. Kennedy first ran for office, many people wondered if he was simply a pawn for his wealthy father Joe Sr.'s ambitions. Kennedy joked about that early in his campaign, pretending to read a telegram from his father: "Dear Jack: Don't buy a single vote more than necessary. I'll be damned if I'm going to pay for a landslide. Love, Dad."[165]

Kennedy's joke disarmed his critics. Because JFK showed a willingness to laugh at himself, the press and his opponents had less leverage to use his father's money and influence against him. Instead, voters' potential concerns were exchanged for an

164 Wead, Doug. "Reagan and the Age Issue." *YouTube*. April 1, 2009.

165 Simon, Scott. "JFK Had The Wit To Lampoon Himself." *NPR*. November 23, 2013.

affectionate appreciation of Kennedy's wit and willingness to laugh at himself.

Avoid humor at others' expense. Mean-spirited jokes may still get people to laugh but can ultimately decrease your likeability factor, making you seem contemptuous, unkind, disdainful, or pompous. We've seen plenty of bullying humor in recent politics, but nasty humor mainly hardens partisan lines. It doesn't gather new voters into your fold who may be on the fence.

Remember the goal of the warmth virtues: to show voters that they can *trust* someone like you. Mean-spirited joking can communicate the opposite message, implying you're someone to be feared, not trusted.

Empathy puts people at ease—and good-natured humor can do much to create that sense of security and trust. Relatable humor shows voters that you *get* them and makes them feel inspired, optimistic, and understood. Laughter also *arouses emotions* in listeners—gets the oxytocin flowing—something we've established is critical for maintaining their attention. Crucially, shared laughter between voters and candidates creates the emotional connection that leads to bonding and votes.

When campaigning, make sure you have several funny anecdotes up your sleeve. Get help from a professional comedian if you struggle to do this on your own. Tell a story or joke that suits your audience—make sure it's clean, politically correct, down-to-earth, and funny.

Lightening the mood can do wonders for making you more likable and restoring an audience's attention. People love to laugh! And if your jokes are the source for voters' laughter, chances are they'll love you, too.

KNOW YOUR AUDIENCE

If your goal is to connect with your audience at a gut level, you need to know what matters to them. In the 2016 election, candidate Trump had a keen sense of what would arouse voters' emotions. He tapped into the disconnect, disenchantment, alienation, anger, and resentment which had been stewing for years across much of "middle America"—emotions that many other "elite" candidates—from both parties—had ignored. Because he understood his audience, Trump was able to ignite their passion at his rallies.

As with candidate Trump, voter enthusiasm for you is the goal. Compared to the presidential elections in 2008 and 2012, rural voters, excited that someone heard them, were propelled in droves to show up to the polls and vote for Donald Trump in 2016. Why did they like him so much? They believed he was authentic and spoke their emotional language. One article analyzing Trump's victory recognized how Trump tailored his message to the unique feelings of many small-town voters:

> 'There's this sense that people in those communities are not getting their fair share compared to people in the cities,' as Katherine Cramer, a political science professor at the University of Wisconsin, told NPR in August.

> 'They feel like their communities are dying, and they perceive that

all that stuff—the young people, the money, the livelihood—is going somewhere, and it's going to the cities,' she said.

During the campaign, Trump supporters time and again said things that seem to validate this theory: saying that they feel ignored, that the economy is leaving them behind.[166]

According to the NPR article, this "rural resentment" was what drove voters to Trump. He spoke to what they were experiencing, and that enabled him to hit them hard at a gut level.

According to Rich Danker:

> Mr. Trump may be the most copy-proof politician in modern history. Mr. Trump has shown that, in an era of polarized politics, being a brand is a better strategy than being a commodity. Most politicians are indistinguishable, interchangeable, easily copied. Their policy proposals are similar to their peers and tenuously connected to voters. They are told by consultants to "stay on message" and are respected by the media for doing so. That's why Americans are sick of their politicians—and why Mr. Trump has succeeded.[167]

Candidates must learn about the voters they're wooing. What do they care about? What issues matter most to them? What are they feeling?

Your job as the candidate is to uncover voters' feelings. Sometimes those feelings lie on the surface, like when they're blasted

---

166 Kurtzleben, Danielle. "Rural Voters Played A Big Part in Helping Trump Defeat Clinton." *NPR*. November 14, 2016.

167 Rich Danker. "A Generic Politician Can't Beat Trump." *Wall Street Journal*. December 30, 2019.

across a protest sign. Other times, however, they're buried, and you must dig deeper to reveal those emotions. The woman who posed the question in the 1992 Town Hall debate didn't initially indicate her emotions, but Bill Clinton shoveled deeper to unearth them through his follow-up questions.

Voters ask questions for a reason—usually a personal one. Emotions prompt voter questions, such as "What's your opinion on LGBTQ rights?" Perhaps this questioner has a gay son who struggled against discrimination all through high school. If you respond to any question by leading with a discussion of the facts, you'll seem insensitive and callous and will alienate yourself from voters.

Instead, gather more information from the voter asking their question. You might say, "I can tell this issue is important to you. Can you help me understand why?" A question like this will show you care and help you detect the emotion behind what a voter is asking.

Always address the voter's emotional state first. Begin with empathy. Express condolences and acknowledge pain, if needed. Speak to where the voter showed bravery or strength. Mention your personal experience and highlight your shared values.

Hopefully, at that point, the voter feels understood—and so do the other constituents standing nearby. Have people see you as someone who cares about their cares, who shares similar values, who understands their pain. At that point, and not before, will they be ready to hear your specific thoughts on the issue.

And, after listening to the needs of the voter, you will be better equipped to speak their language. With the new information you've gathered, you won't stumble out of the gate with platitudes or gaffes. You'll be on steady ground and ready to speak with thoughtfulness, tact, and clarity. Even though voters may disagree with your policy stance, they will see you as real and relatable—and that alone may ultimately secure their votes.

Role-Play Voter Interactions

Candidates can practice listening to voters' emotions through role plays. Members of the campaign team should take turns playing different voters with various concerns. You, the candidate, should practice restating the emotions expressed by the pretend voter to confirm exactly what the voter is feeling, then give a response that leads with the appropriate emotion.

Gather Data

Campaign workers can help their candidate by doing pre-assessments prior to the candidate's appearance. Staff should gather questions from the audience which will help make clear what both the local and national voter concerns are. Identify demographics and key issues through surveys or focus groups.

If the campaign has done a good job, candidates will have a series of talking points about local issues before the bus even arrives. Then, you should speak to those issues in a way that communicates, "Hey—I care about this. I care about you." And, if you are not great at empathy, remember to recruit local people with real issues and bring them up on stage with you.

Most importantly, campaign staffers should be ready with feedback for a candidate from what they glean about voter issues, especially the emotional impact these issues have on the voters they interview. Send along campaign staffers to these focus groups who have high emotional intelligence or "EQs"—people who are known for being sensitive and empathic. Enlist their help to identify the anxieties and concerns of voters in each area and then help reframe the candidate's approach to the issues accordingly. In the words of the late House Speaker Tip O'Neill, "All politics is local."

For instance, if the opioid epidemic is a priority for voters in a town or city, staffers should collect some of the personal stories of addiction and loss these voters may have experienced and then pass them along to the candidate. If you're given a question about the opioid epidemic later, you can lead with one of those stories, or another story of your own. Putting in time and effort to craft an emotional connection is the insurance that will pay dividends to help you connect with voters rather than offend or alienate them.

If you know your voters, you can tailor your message in a way that will hit them at a visceral level. You'll demonstrate you understand people like them—and that is exactly what voters are looking for. Remember, voters vote with their gut, not their brain.

REFRAME QUESTIONS USING EMOTIONAL STORIES

In the hyper-partisan animus that defines today's politics, it has never been more difficult to change another voter's point of view. Many voters will write you off the instant they know your party affiliation. If you're hoping to attract swing voters, how do you get them to listen to your message?

The process of understanding another person's take on an issue is called "perspective getting." You learn what the opposing viewpoint is and try to "get it." What's the rationale for their argument? Once you understand how and what your opponent thinks, you can engage their thinking by incorporating their views into *your* point of view to establish common ground.

Imagine the three monkeys which represent "See no evil, hear no evil, speak no evil." Symbolically, that's how skeptical listeners begin an interaction with you: hands clapped over their eyes, and over their ears, and over their mouths—determined to not give you the time of day. Somehow, you must get them to look at you and listen.

In a *New York Times* article by Rob Willer and Matthew Feinberg, the authors noted that several experiments have found that people are more likely persuaded to consider an opposing viewpoint if the candidate's message was reframed to leverage voters' own existing beliefs.[168] In other words, if you want to win somebody over to your position, don't *challenge* their beliefs. Instead, *connect* your position to their beliefs. Frame your position in line with the values of the person you want to convince.

When it comes to altering another's political ideology, this is not an easy task. According to Willer and Feinberg, "People struggled to set aside their reasons for taking a political position and failed

---

168 Willer, Rob and Matthew Feinberg. "The Key to Political Persuasion." *The New York Times*. November 13, 2015.

to consider how someone with different values might come to support that same position...You have to get into the heads of the people you'd like to persuade, think about what they care about and make arguments that embrace their principles."

Let's say you're a socially liberal candidate who is fiscally conservative, and you want to attract culturally conservative donors. One problem: your support for LGBTQ rights makes many conservative donors ready to write you off. If you approach these donors trying to prove that their socially conservative agenda is wrong—you won't get anywhere.

Instead, reframe the issue by finding common ground. What do you share with these voters? What values do you both possess? Where do those values overlap? Start your message by identifying that common ground.

For example, let's imagine you are soliciting someone's vote and they say, "Listen, we think you're a smart candidate and you've got a lot going for you. But we're just not comfortable backing someone who votes for measures that contradict our personal values."

Identify the common ground first. Perhaps you reply, "I bet our values are more similar than different. I know that you value patriotism. I do too. I know that you value high standards for integrity and morality. Me too! You want an America where families gather around the dinner table and talk. That's what I want."

When you identify commonalities between you and others who have different ideas, you increase the chance voters will be more receptive to your views—that they originally rejected. Those who disagreed with you initially may now see the legitimacy of your position. This reduces the gap between your viewpoint and theirs.

In the *Personality and Social Psychology Bulletin,* Willer and Feinberg described it this way:

> Political arguments reframed to appeal to the moral values of those holding the opposing political position are typically more effective. We find support for these claims across six studies involving diverse political issues, including same-sex marriage, universal health care, military spending, and adopting English as the nation's official language. Mediation and moderation analyses further indicated that reframed moral appeals were persuasive because they increased the apparent agreement between the political position and the targeted individuals' moral values...Recognizing morality's influence on political attitudes, our research presents a means for political persuasion that, rather than challenging one's moral values, incorporates them into the argument. As a result, individuals see value in an opposing stance, reducing the attitudinal gap between the two sides. This technique not only substantiates the power of morality to shape political thought but also presents a potential means for political coalition formation.[169]

They conclude, "The tight relationship between moral convictions and political views—so often a source of division and rigidity—can also be a basis for opinion change, political influence, and coalition formation."

---

169 Feinberg, Matthew and Rob Willer. "From Gulf to Bridge: When Do Moral Arguments Facilitate Political Influence?" *Personality and Social Psychology Bulletin.* 2015.

Remember the "See no evil, hear no evil" posture which these skeptical voters started with? Identifying common ground makes critical listeners lower their hands just enough to peek at you, listen, and allow you a moment's more to speak.

Once you've established common ground, shift gears into a story. Storytelling causes changes in the brain that help people feel connected to you and more willing to align with your vision. Make the story personal, relatable, and emotional.

You might continue to respond: "One of the reasons I love my neighbors is that they share these same values as I do. Every day, I look outside and see their flag raised. They always remember to lower it to half-mast if the White House orders it, probably because Bob was in the military. He takes the nation's flag very seriously. Bob's partner, Joe, also shows amazing leadership and spends quality time teaching their kids about morality. I remember when he walked his adopted son over to my door and guided the kid through an apology about damaging my fence. At dinnertime, I often can see them as a family through the window, sitting around their table, sharing their day. Bob and Joe are a married couple, and they're my friends. I care about them. That's why I've voted on measures that will help them have a better life and experience more of the rights that you and I enjoy."

You may not have changed a skeptic's mind—but by reframing your message you help listeners reframe their perception of you. Voters might have entered your meeting observing a blinking neon light flashing over your head: social liberal. Hopefully, by the end of the conversation, they'll see you in a new way: "This is a thoughtful individual who shares my values. Sure, we disagree on some important points, but she's caring and flexible and has a good head on her shoulders." At this point, your audience will be more inclined to take their hands off their ears and listen to what you want to express, and back you with their votes and their checks!

By utilizing the technique of "perspective getting" you become a smarter, more open, and wiser candidate. When conversing with people who have opposing viewpoints, your best approach is to learn why they believe what they do. Your attitude should not be "I'm going to prove you wrong!" but "I want to understand your perspective better." This shift in your thinking may sound counterintuitive, but it demonstrates more empathy, because you will be legitimately trying to "get" voters' concerns.

When politicians tell stories that incorporate the needs of the listener, they hit a home run. They can walk off the field having emotionally bonded with the crowd. When listeners feel understood, appreciated, and inspired, they become more than just supporters—they become scouts. They're motivated to recruit other people to your team because they'll be so enthusiastic about your candidacy.

AIM AT THE HEART

Campaign post-mortems and polls consistently show that voters choose a candidate who understands someone like them. Primarily, voters want to be understood and cared about.

As you meet and greet voters along the campaign trail, aim your words directly at their hearts, not their heads. Use the strategies

I've outlined in this chapter to establish yourself as empathic. Use stories and humor. Connect yourself to real people with real struggles. Listen well. Find common ground, even with those who disagree with you. Engage voters in conversation and show them that you are there to help.

Not only will you be a better candidate—you'll become a better human being!

CHAPTER SEVEN

FROM ARROGANT TO HUMBLE

"It is impossible for a man to learn what he thinks he already knows."
—EPICTETUS

When Ted Kennedy died in 2010, a special election was called in Massachusetts to fill his vacant US Senate seat. Martha Coakley, the state's Attorney General at the time, handily won the Democratic primary.

And then, suddenly, she stopped campaigning.

Coakley made only nineteen campaign appearances leading up to the election, compared to her Republican challenger, Scott Brown (now Ambassador to New Zealand and Samoa), who made sixty-six campaign stops. She also committed several gaffes that were equivalent to blasphemy in the eyes of her constituents—especially the rabid Massachusetts sports fans.

Coakley referred to the legendary Boston Red Sox pitcher Curt

Schilling, who won three World Series titles, as "a Yankees fan." Schilling was arguably more famous than Coakley in Massachusetts, and it's safe to say he was more beloved. In 2004, he led the Red Sox against the Yankees to their first World Series victory since 1918, thus breaking the "curse of the Bambino" that had stood for 85 years. Having myself grown up in Boston, I can attest that the Red Sox are as sacred as the Pope. The loyal sports citizens of Massachusetts did not forgive Coakley's slight.

Still, most people assumed Coakley had the win clinched. She was, after all, a Democrat. It seemed inconceivable that anybody but a Democrat would fill Ted Kennedy's seat, and Coakley didn't bother working for votes that she assumed were already automatically hers. When a reporter questioned Coakley about her halfhearted campaign style, she responded, "As opposed to standing outside Fenway Park? In the cold? Shaking hands?"[170]

Coakley's remark referred to her Republican opponent Scott Brown, who had done exactly that. As opposed to Coakley's unenthusiastic campaigning, Brown traveled the entire state in his worn pickup truck, meeting voters and having personal conversations. He wore jeans and a work shirt, presenting himself as a "Massachusetts Everyman." Brown's campaign was largely financed by mom-and-pop donations, because the Republican National Committee sent no financial support. To them, it was a waste of time and money to try to get a Republican elected a US Senator in the true-blue state of Massachusetts.

Brown's campaign ads could be considered ahead of their time and foreshadowed the political ads of live streaming today. One

170 Curtis, Bryan. "Mass Arrogance." *The Daily Beast.* January 20, 2010.

was composed almost entirely of candid clips, showing Brown walking around South Boston in a thick coat, knocking on doors, shaking hands, and greeting people cheerfully.[171] Throughout the ad, you can hear his characteristic "Southie" accent as people respond to him with pats on the back and verbal encouragement. To the people of Massachusetts, Brown—as opposed to Martha Coakley—was real, relatable, fun—and humble.

When asked by a debate moderator if he really wanted to fill Ted Kennedy's seat, Brown responded, "Well, with all due respect, it's not the Kennedys' seat, and it's not the Democrats' seat, it's the people's seat."[172]

When Election Day arrived, the people of Massachusetts responded to Brown's message—and voted him into "their" seat.

Brown's win in the Senate special election was viewed as a staggering upset. The Democrats *always* won in Massachusetts. The last time a Republican had been elected to the US Senate in Massachusetts was Ed Brooke thirty-eight years earlier in 1972. How could an upstart Republican candidate win Ted Kennedy's seat? Brown's late-surge come-from-behind victory not only shocked the state, it shook the nation. He broke the Senate's sixty-seat filibuster-proof Democratic majority and put Obama's Affordable Care Act in jeopardy.

As the election post-mortems rolled in, a consensus was reached: arrogance lost the election for Coakley. The Democrats had been overconfident to assume the seat was theirs, and Coakley's atti-

---

171 PoliticalCampaignAds. ""Momentum - Scott Brown for Senate - 2009/2010." *YouTube*. January 27, 2010.

172 Good, Chris. "'It's the People's Seat.'" *The Atlantic*. January 12, 2010.

tude had struck voters as smug. She seemed removed, disdainful, and self-interested. She'd begun the campaign thirty points ahead in November and assumed there was no way she could lose. One opinion writer quipped, "Her parents must have forgotten to read her 'The Tortoise and the Hare.'"[173]

Scott Brown's humble, go-getter attitude made the people of Massachusetts feel cared for. He drove long distances, met with people in low-income neighborhoods, and even stood outside the historic old Boston Garden in frigid weather, just to shake hands with Boston Bruins fans.

Martha Coakley, on the other hand, telegraphed directly to voters the impression that she had better things to do with her time than hang out with them. The 2.1 million independent voters in Massachusetts punished her by overwhelmingly voting for Brown, along with many Democrat defectors.[174] At the end of the day, her liberal Democratic ideology wasn't appealing enough—even in Massachusetts—to overcome her unlikable presumptuousness. Instead of joining with her Boston constituents' spirit and root for the demise of the "curse of the Bambino," she cursed herself instead.

Scott Brown worked tirelessly to make an emotional connection with voters. In his acceptance speech, he kept his focus on the people, saying, "Every day I hold this office I will give all that is in

---

173 Flynn, Daniel J. "Unsafe in Any State." *City Journal.* January 20, 2010.

174 "Scott Brown's Massachusetts Win Fueled by Independent Voters." *The Christian Science Monitor.* January 20, 2010.

me to serve you well and make you proud."[175] Ironically, Brown's power was won through demonstrating humility.

DANTE'S DEADLIEST SIN: PRIDE

Pride is known as the sin that made the angel Lucifer fall from heaven into hell—and is considered in Christian tradition as the worst of the seven deadly sins. Although Dante listed "pride" as seventh on his list of deadly sins, he made clear that he felt it was the most diabolical.

In his *The Divine Comedy*, Dante's punishment for pride was to make the sinner carry a stone slab on his neck so that his head was forced downward. The sinner was prevented from standing upright or being able to puff out his chest.

The ancient Greeks like Homer, Plato, Aeschylus, and Herodotus called pride "hubris," which they considered a sufficient vice to destroy any political order.

Aristotle had a different definition of pride. To him, pride was a virtue not a vice. He believed that a proud person was someone able to acknowledge and appreciate their own greatness.

Who's right?

Is all pride terrible? When Lee Greenwood sings, "I'm proud to be an American"—is that so malevolent? When a parent boasts about their child—is that so bad?

---

175 News, CBS. "Scott Brown's Victory Speech." *YouTube*. January 19, 2010.

Cross-cultural studies have shown that pride is a universal signal of status.[176] Every culture—even those isolated from nearly all forms of contact with the outside world, and people born blind—contains expressions of pride which look identical. In proud moments, like after winning a competition, people expand their chests, pull their shoulders back, and smile broadly. The expression of pride is universal and innate. It's hardwired.

It's also appealing. One study of corporate hiring showed that in job interviews, regardless of the strength of a resume, those who displayed pride more often were hired above people who showed signs of shame.[177]

Pride is valuable, provided it's the *good* kind. There are two types of pride: authentic pride and hubristic pride. One is positive. The other—well, just ask Dante what he thinks about the other kind.

THE GOOD KIND: AUTHENTIC PRIDE

Authentic pride describes the sense of accomplishment you feel after putting in the time and effort to achieve something beneficial. When you successfully fix the car, complete a program, or watch someone you love triumph, that's authentic pride. It's pride that fosters compassion and a focus on caring about others.

Good pride is *other-directed,* the opposite of being self-centered. Authentic pride leads a person to generosity and empathy. That good sense of accomplishment you feel with authentic pride comes from your personal efforts to help other people. It's all

---

176 Tracy, Jessica. *Take Pride.* New York: Houghton Mifflin Harcourt, 2016.

177 Ibid.

about making the world a better place and making yourself a better person.

THE BAD KIND: HUBRISTIC PRIDE (I.E., ARROGANCE)

Bad pride is narcissistic. Dante describes it as a love of self which is so extreme that it's perverted into hatred for your fellow man and contempt for others.[178] People who display hubristic pride believe they're fundamentally better than everyone.

Remember Martha Coakley, who thought it beneath her to shake hands outside Fenway Park? Whether she genuinely felt superior to "the common constituent," she was guilty of communicating hubristic pride. More commonly, we think of this pride as arrogance. It's the emotional response to any success one feels occurred simply because of who they are. The only motivation to work hard is to impress other people.

Whereas authentic pride fosters a focus on others, hubristic arrogance leads to selfishness. When you think of yourself as being above other people, you shove your needs ahead of theirs. You're being egocentric. In other words, it's all about me, myself, and I.

People with hubristic pride *do* think about others but focus mainly on other people's impression of *them*. They want desperately to be liked. President Trump felt slighted that the British ambassador, Kim Darroch, called the Trump administration "dysfunctional and inept." Trump, of course, never lets a slight go unanswered. Dan Henninger, deputy editorial director of the *Wall Street Jour-*

---

178 "Seven Deadly Sins." Canto 28, Compare Side by Side Translations of Dante's Inferno by Longfellow, Cary, and Norton.

nal, considers Trump "the best mixed-martial-arts fighter in political history."[179] Trump went on a Twitter tirade and called the ambassador a "stupid guy" and a "pompous fool." The *Wall Street Journal* commented, "Mr. Trump's over-blown response reminds the world how sensitive to criticism the president is."[180]

Voters want to feel that you like them, understand them, and care about them. If you come across as arrogant, selfish, or demeaning, you're telegraphing to voters that you think you're better than they are.

When voters sense that you don't care about them, their gut instinct immediately signals that you are foe, not friend. How will that turn out at the ballot box? I'm sure that Martha Coakley, Mitt Romney, and Hillary Clinton could fill you in.

The Trump Exception

Let's take a moment to consider Trump's 2016 presidential victory and the sin of hubristic pride. President Trump has been described as narcissistic—even clinically so.[181] The Diagnostic and Statistical Manual of Mental Disorders (DSM-5) criteria for narcissism seems to be a dead-ringer for the forty-fifth president: he expects superior treatment, exaggerates his life, shows a need for constant attention and admiration, has difficulty empathizing, demeans and bullies others, is thin-skinned, and has a pompous demeanor.

---

179 Henninger, Daniel. "Joe Biden Isn't Going to Make It." *The Wall Street Journal.* October 16, 2019.

180 "A Not-So-Special Relationship." *The Wall Street Journal.* July 11, 2019.

181 Barber, Nigel. "Does Trump Suffer from Narcissistic Personality Disorder?" *Psychology Today.* August 10, 2016.

In *Take Pride,* Jessica Tracy writes:

> To be clear, narcissists are not losers—in fact, in certain domains
> like politics, narcissists tend to be quite successful. Bill Clinton, who
> never missed an opportunity to extol his successes in office, was
> determined from personality ratings made by 121 presidential biog-
> raphers and other experts to be only the seventh-most-narcissistic
> president in American history (Lyndon B Johnson was first).[182]

If arrogance is one of the candidate's "seven deadly sins," how
did Donald J. Trump manage to be victorious?

First: We return to the power of Trump's master narrative. He
made an emotional connection with voters and told a story that
was ultimately more compelling than Hillary Clinton's.

Second: It's worth remembering that Hillary Clinton lost the
electoral vote—but won the popular vote. Although Trump made
himself likeable enough in a few key Midwest swing states to win
the Electoral College, he was still viewed by thousands of those
voters as personally unlikable. Many voted for him over Hillary
because he was the "least unlikeable." They backed his policies
of "Making America Great Again" but held their nose when it
came to his demeanor.

Trump won the presidency despite his excessive pride. When he
boasts on Twitter or picks a fight over something related to his
vanity, the response from his base of voters has mostly been irritation. They'd rather their president focus on running the country

---

182 Ibid, Tracy.

and bringing back high-paying American manufacturing jobs than wasting time defending slights to his ego.

Today, many Democrats are unhinged and driven into a rage frenzy by what is termed "Trump Derangement Syndrome." Initially used as a description of Republicans whom some felt had lost their minds backing Trump, it is now applied to any demonstration by President Trump of insult, demonizing, or self-centeredness, which proves to Democrats undeniably that he is a phony, racist, homophobe, misogynist, and pathological liar. Their goal is to drive him from office.[183]

According to Jessica Tracy, "Over time, narcissists become hostile, insulting, and aggressive...Despite their initial popularity, the most narcissistic presidents are also the ones most likely to face impeachment."[184]

THE SIN OF ARROGANCE

Donald Trump, Hillary Clinton, and Martha Coakley are not the only politicians who commit the sin of arrogance. It's one of the most common sins committed in politics.

Politicians like control. Most love having power. Powerful people are not always team players. They want to run the show, and they expect blind loyalty from others to follow their directives. But for candidates, this hubristic pride can easily ruin an otherwise successful campaign—or stint in office.

---

183 Cillizza, Chris. "What is 'Trump Derangement Syndrome'—and Do You Have It?" *CNN Politics.* July 20, 2018.

184 Ibid, Tracy.

The great Greek and Roman tragedies portrayed hubris as the heroes' undoing. Overconfidence is what led to the downfall of the greats.

Success often prevents candidates and politicians from recognizing their flaws. They fail to do what's necessary to overcome these deficiencies and emotionally connect with voters. Remember: politicians represent the will of the people. That means, ideally, you're *listening* to the will of the people. If you act arrogantly, like you already know everything you need to know, voters will sense you're not interested in listening to them.

The Greek philosopher Epictetus said, "It is impossible for a man to learn what he thinks he already knows." Good leaders remember that they have weaknesses. They listen. They continue learning. Whereas arrogance prevents growth in leaders, humility leads to greater strength.

Arrogance keeps a focus on achievements. Humility concerns itself with character. Candidates who focus only on *what* they want to accomplish can easily forget *who* they want to be. Consider: What qualities will define you in private? What qualities do you want others to praise you for at your eulogy?

Think about your character, not just the prize of victory. Remember: You always have something new to learn.

There are several missteps that will advertise an impression of personal arrogance. Unforced errors, ironically, stem from feelings of insecurity. Insecure candidates, because they lack inner confidence, pump themselves up outwardly by bragging.

Arrogance rears its ugly head when a candidate acts rude or remote. Rudeness is obvious. Perhaps Donald Trump's most insensitive moment came in late 2015 on the campaign trail when he appeared to mock a *New York Times* reporter by mimicking his disability. Although Trump claimed that was not his intention, the emotional optics were poor. According to one poll, voters believed that incident was Trump's worst offense.[185] Showing arrogance through disrespect makes you look cruel, rude, and uncivil.

Martha Coakley kept her distance while campaigning, demonstrating little eagerness to mingle and get to know voters or experience life alongside them. By being remote, voters decided that she didn't like them, and they didn't like her.

You can't connect with voters emotionally if you install a personal firewall. If voters see you as untouchable, they won't feel relaxed. They'll consider you "foe" rather than "friend." Oxytocin won't get released, and they won't bond to you emotionally.

CONCEITED & CONDESCENDING

When Al Gore debated George W. Bush, he had just completed almost eight years as vice president under Bill Clinton. He had every reason to feel confident—but that confidence quickly turned to arrogance.

During one debate, in an apparent attempt to throw Bush off

---

185 Carmon, Irin. "Donald Trump's Worst Offense? Mocking Disabled Reporter, Poll Finds." *NBCNews.com.* August 11, 2016.

guard, Gore walked right up to him while he was speaking. Voters didn't just scoff at Gore's blatant attempt to physically intimidate Bush; they were put off by his continuous disrespectful eye rolls and sighs at Bush's remarks. These observations left the public feeling that Gore treated Bush as if he were an idiot. Gore's pompous behavior made voters think of him as a bully—not as a world leader.

Going into debate with someone you think you can clearly beat—be on guard. Your superior competence can easily be communicated as superior arrogance. Don't condescend. Always focus attention on the well-being of voters and treat your opponent with respect and seriousness. If you're condescending, voters will feel like you've put them down as well.

"POLITICAL ADD"

Many candidates and politicians are guilty of what I call "Political ADD" (PADD) or Political Attention Deficit Disorder. Rather than take time with individual voters to make eye contact, share a few comments, and build a genuine rapport, candidates suffering from "Political ADD" are easily distracted and self-centered. They rarely stop to focus on the person in front of them. Instead, they constantly scan the crowd, always looking for the next person to talk to. Often, those with PADD look to trade up to someone they think can help them better.

Although the goal for "Political ADD" politicians is to connect with as many voters as possible, paradoxically, they don't end up connecting with anyone. They're too distracted.

Imagine yourself in the voter's shoes. If you've been waiting for hours to meet a candidate, and that candidate is finally shaking your hand, how would you feel if their eyes continually shifted away or they never even looked into your eyes? That would be a disappointment. You'd feel overlooked and dismissed as unimportant.

If that candidate shook your hand warmly, made solid eye contact, grinned, and asked you how your morning had been—you would feel seen and cared for. You might feel enthusiastic enough to donate to the campaign, volunteer, or plant a campaign sign in your yard.

As a political candidate, take your constituents' grievances and anxieties seriously. Don't dismiss their questions—listen to them. Acknowledge the importance of what they ask. Work to show each voter that you see them, hear them, and care about them.

NONVERBAL BEHAVIOR

As with many of the other sins and virtues I address, body language can pack a negative wallop when it comes to communicating arrogance. Al Gore's conceit in the debate with George W. Bush was chiefly communicated through his nonverbal emotional optics.

Psychologist Dr. John R. Schafer, author of *The Like Switch*, provides a list of body language cues that act as "Foe Signals."[186]

---

186 Schafer, John R., and Marvin Karlins. *The Like Switch: An Ex-FBI Agent's Guide to Influencing, Attracting, and Winning People Over.* New York: Simon & Schuster, 2015.

These cues generally communicate to people that you don't like them, or don't like what they have to say.

Foe Signals, Indicating a Lack of Rapport

- Furrowed eyebrows
- Eye rolls
- Cold stares
- Prolonged eye closure and/or gaze aversion
- Asynchronous posture (the opposite of mirroring the other person)
- Leaning away from another person
- Aggressive stance and/or "attack" posture
- Closed body posture
- Creation or use of barriers/obstacles
- Eye squints
- Fake yawns
- Negative head shakes
- Scrunched nose
- Self-preening

This list is long, but not exhaustive. Any number of subtle cues can indicate arrogance to voters. For instance, folding your arms across your chest means you're not that open. Turning your feet away from someone when standing and talking with them is a sign you're not connected. Not smiling is another negative cue.

The method of Deliberate Practice can help you modify arrogant body language. Use role-play exercises and videos of yourself to help identify potentially harmful nonverbal cues.

THE VIRTUE OF HUMILITY

Humility gets a bad rap among the rich and powerful. To be humble, some think, is to be a doormat: you fail to assert yourself. It can seem antithetical to leadership.[187]

C. S. Lewis provides one of the better definitions: "true humility is not thinking less of yourself but thinking of yourself less."[188]

When Scott Brown made voters the focus of his candidacy, calling Ted Kennedy's seat "the people's seat," that was a demonstration of humility. Constituents in Massachusetts didn't get the impression that he was concerned about his own power or reputation—they felt he was genuinely interested in *them*. That's humility.

J. Bryan Bennett with Miramed agrees with C. S. Lewis' definition, noting, "Humility is...the self-awareness that you are no better than the person next to you or across from you. Sometimes known as modesty, humble people make everyone feel special."[189]

Bennett goes on to describe characteristics of humble leaders:

> Leaders exhibit humility by making themselves available to the people they work with. Their time is valuable, but it is not so valuable that they can't take the time to listen or discuss something that is important with others. It is very easy for people to identify leaders with authentic humility. They are the ones who return phone

---

187 Freifeld, Lorri. "Leading with Humility." *Training Magazine*. October 22, 2013.

188 Lewis, C.S. *Mere Christianity*. San Francisco, CA: Harper Collins, 2001.

189 Bennett, J. Bryan, MBA, CPA, LSSGB. "The Innate Qualities of Professional Leadership." *MiraMed*. September 18, 2017.

calls, respond to e-mails and engage with others, not as a leader-to-subordinate, but as a person-to-person...[Humility] 'is not the absence of self-worth, but the validation of self-worth.'[190]

Humility is an important virtue to show as a candidate and critical for effective leadership. Bennett identifies it as the top predictor of successful leaders. Humble leaders promote good morale among their staff, prioritize continued learning, and effectively deal with their own weaknesses. President George W. Bush, when asked in a television interview what he thought was the number one trait a president should have, said "humility."

David Axelrod says, "Humility is the order of the day," commenting on Hillary's second bid to be president:

> In 2007, her campaign was the juggernaut of inevitability and it was a top-down experience. Voters don't like to be told that their decision is predetermined. They want to be asked for their vote and more than that they want to have a genuine connection with the candidate...After she lost the Iowa caucuses in 2008, she threw caution off and her vulnerabilities were more obvious and her identification with people's struggles was more obvious and I think she was a more effective candidate.[191]

Author Jim Collins found in his research that "leaders with 'gargantuan personal egos' were more likely to contribute to the demise or mediocrity of companies in the long run."[192]

---

190 Ibid.

191 Noble, Jason. "Axelrod Calls Clinton On Track with Authenticity." *Des Moines Register.* April 14, 2015.

192 Freifeld, Lorri. "Leading with Humility." *Training Magazine.* October 22, 2013.

Politicians often avoid showing humility because they think acting that way makes them look weak. However, many of the signature traits of true humility are incredibly likable: self-deprecating humor, embracing vulnerability, and elevating the needs of other people. Who doesn't like that?

Genuine expressions of humility will strengthen your warmth as a candidate and make you a more effective leader. Provided—that is—you don't practice the bad form of humility.

BAD FORM OF HUMILITY

There are two rules for making sure the virtue of humility doesn't backfire on you:

1. Don't hide your strengths.
2. Don't make people question your competency.

Mitt Romney was guilty of breaking the first rule. He failed to publicize many of the good charitable deeds he'd accomplished personally and professionally over the years. I truly believe that the public was denied the chance to learn the full measure of his strengths because, due to his excessive modesty, he hid them. (Bad modesty.)

Bernie Sanders was careful to follow the second rule. During the 2016 campaign, Sanders didn't work hard to earn voters' affections—he was already equipped with the warmth virtues. His challenge was convincing voters that as a socialist he could realistically be president. With some exceptions, Sanders generally avoided using self-deprecating humor so as not to cast any doubts on his strength and competency.[193]

What are specific ways you can effectively demonstrate humility? Start by thinking of yourself less and thinking of others more.

Others-Focused

You're more likely to possess both authentic pride and genuine humility when you focus on the well-being of others. Ask yourself: do you know how those you interact with every day are doing? What do they care about? What are they worried about? How have you served them lately?

If you're able to easily answer those questions—congratulations! You're already strong in the virtue of humility.

Humble people make a conscious effort to see the value in every person, regardless of their position in life. Get to know the names of your campaign volunteers and interns. Take the time to converse with people who aren't fluent in English. Create strategies to intentionally check your own ego at the door.

Gracious & Grateful

There's usually a moment at the start of political debates when candidates shake each other's hands and thank the moderator. That's a nice moment. Graciousness and gratitude play well.

---

193 Nussbaum, Jeff. "Voters like Pols Who Can Laugh at Themselves. Why Can't These Candidates Pull It Off?" *The Washington Post.* March 4, 2016.

Thank people for their efforts. Be appreciative to reporters and media representatives who track your campaign. Know them by name. Affirm voters for their questions. Compliment your campaign workers on their hard work.

Graciousness and gratitude are key components of demonstrating respect for those around you. When you fail to show appreciation, you easily commit the sin of arrogance.

Be humble and accept your limitations. Most accomplishments of your campaign are a result of many people's efforts. Share the credit and affirm your team.

George H. W. Bush was known for his graciousness. His mother had raised him to "never be a braggadocio," and that was reflected in his character during his presidency. When the Berlin Wall came down—an event that he played a large part in accomplishing—he didn't take the credit. In his 1992 State of the Union address, he said, "By the grace of God, America won the Cold War."[194]

During Bush's funeral in 2018, his humility was a theme that came up repeatedly. One speaker, former Wyoming Senator Alan Simpson, said "He was a man of such great humility. Those who travel the high road of humility in Washington D.C. are not bothered by heavy traffic."[195]

A big ego is common among politicians, but eventually it might

---

194 "State of the Union; Transcript of President Bush's Address on the State of the Union." *The New York Times.* January 29, 1992.

195 Cummings, William. "Humor Was Always at the Center of Sen. Alan Simpson's Life, and He Brought It to Bush's Eulogy." KTVB. *USA Today.* December 5, 2018.

undermine your leadership and your appeal with voters. Instead, travel the high road. Be gracious. Be grateful.

Use Inclusive Language & Discuss Your Strengths within a Story

Despite G. H. W. Bush's strengths, he couldn't convince voters that he deserved a second term. Why? Partly, he lost to the charisma of his opponent, Bill Clinton. And Bush was too modest by not highlighting his accomplishments with voters.

Now, here's a catch-22: travel the high road of humility, but still make sure you talk yourself up. How do you manage that?

Use stories as a vehicle to share your strengths and accomplishments without coming across as arrogant.

G. H. W. Bush should have shared stories about key moments with world leaders that led to his remarkable foreign policy accomplishments. He could have expressed what life experiences prompted him to create the Americans with Disabilities Act and could have shared snippets of conversation he'd had with the nation's governors, whom Bush led to collectively establish a minimum academic standard for the nation's schools. Most critically, he could have shared the story of his decision-making process to compromise with Congress on raising taxes, rather than pinning the announcement on a one-page statement in the White House press room—a move that many saw as cowardly.[196]

Stories can help mask arrogance. Donald Trump boasted at the

196 Duffy, Michael. "President George H.W. Bush Did More Than He Got Credit For." *Time*. December 1, 2018.

FROM ARROGANT TO HUMBLE · 227

Republican National Convention, "Nobody knows the system better than me, which is why I alone can fix it."[197] The statement seemed self-centered and unprecedented in its claim to power—but it was a detail that fit within Trump's narrative. He was the Avenger, ready to "drain the swamp" of Washington, to root out the corruption and self-dealing of the big-monied interests and restore the traditions and values that America was founded on. As a result—he got away with a godlike boast.

EMOTIONAL OPTICS OF HUMILITY

Scott Brown's drive across the state of Massachusetts in his worn pick-up truck established an impression of humility. Other politicians roll up their sleeves, kiss babies, attend pig roasts, fish and steak frys, or crack self-deprecating jokes. Let's consider some of the factors that will help you demonstrate the emotional optics of humility.

Tell Your Story

Just telling stories related to your accomplishments is not enough. Voters want to hear *your* story.

Relate to voters your personal history, especially if you came from humble beginnings. Then focus on stories that illustrate what you've learned in life about kindness and helping others.

Stories centered on how you're raising your children can highlight your values and increase your relatability. Most people can identify with the challenges that come with parenting.

---

197 "Full Text: Donald Trump 2016 RNC Draft Speech Transcript." *Politico.* July 21, 2016.

Remember to incorporate emotional language in your narrative to target the voter's gut. Stories offer an opportunity to connect with voters on a human level. Be real, embrace vulnerability, and share the stories that define your candidacy.

Give Thanks for Your Blessings

To demonstrate gratitude is to verbalize thanks for your blessings. If you're fortunate enough to run for office, chances are you have a lot to be thankful for. Voice that gratitude.

You might say to voters, "I've been blessed. I've had hard times, and out of those hard times have come life lessons." Then share a story about a hardship you've endured and then acknowledge what lesson you learned. Bring listeners on your journey from the tough times in your life to the good times.

When you recognize the gifts that came from challenges, you show yourself as optimistic, relatable, and humble. You demonstrate an awareness of pain and suffering but also hope and blessing.

You'll also be in a better position to discuss your strengths because you have begun by painting yourself as an underdog. Barack Obama made his life story a focal point of his campaigns. When asked during a *60 Minutes* interview if he was an elitist, Obama responded with a description of his humble background:

> Look at how I came up. Raised by a single mom. Family had very little money growing up. We were on food stamps at some point. Went to school on scholarships. Michelle, coming from the south

side of Chicago to a working-class shift worker who never...went to college, and a stay-at-home mom. That's our background.[198]

Obama's stories of financial struggle made it easier for voters to see him as a humble leader rather than an arrogant elitist. He expressed gratitude for the people and experiences that helped him find his way to the White House.

Be Kind

On August 18, 1988, George H. W. Bush accepted his party's presidential nomination. He called for a "kinder, gentler nation." Unfortunately, thirty years have passed, and with today's political vitriol and incivility, we are no closer to Bush's vision for America.

According to Dr. Arthur C. Brooks, former director of the American Enterprise Institute, "There is no inconsistency between kindness and effective, winning leadership."[199] A Republican member of Congress told him that "he feels anguished because to stay in office, he often has to be a person he doesn't admire. He has to say harsh and unkind things, he said, even though he wants to be friendly and tolerant." Brooks says that kindness "requires self-control and maturity, like anything else that is worthwhile. It means seeing ourselves in others and actively practicing gratitude. But with commitment and repetition, we can become kinder people, leaders admired by others, and a greater force for good in a troubled world."

---

198 CBS. "Obama, McCain On Elitism." *YouTube*. October 15, 2008.

199 Brooks, Arthur C. "Kindness Isn't Just Nice—It's More Effective. Just ask Obama and DeGeneres." *The Washington Post*. November 4, 2019.

Be Underestimated

Candidates who perform best in debates are likely those no one expects to do well. They are the underestimated—those with low name recognition or considered outliers. When these underestimated candidates distinguish themselves on the campaign trail, voters are surprised and impressed by their performance.

Take a lesson from those moments. If you are kinder, more articulate, and more gracious than people expect, you'll be a surprise. You'll solidify a good first impression as you surpass their expectations.

I love being underestimated, and I've found it to be a great way to build connections with others. People like you when you underplay your accomplishments. That expression of humility seems down-to-earth.

Being underestimated is much better than being overestimated— especially if you pretend to be someone or something that you're not. When Trump boasted about having the biggest inauguration crowds in history, he was mocked and his claims were disproven.[200] When the male candidate lied about his college degree, he was caught and humiliated. Hyping yourself, especially when the facts don't back you up, rarely pays off.

Also, don't excessively boast. President Trump recently said in a TV interview, "I've kept more promises than I've made." In two other tweets to his 65 million followers, Trump touted his "great and unrivaled wisdom" and wrote in the other tweet, "Actually, throughout my life, my two greatest assets have been mental sta-

---

200 Qiu, Linda. "From the Archives: Sean Spicer on Inauguration Day Crowds." *Politifact.* January 21, 2017.

bility and being, like, really smart. I went from VERY successful businessman, to top TV Star. I think that would qualify as not smart, but genius...and a very stable genius at that!" President Trump's supporters may be immune to the hyperbole as "Trump being Trump," but many others, even in his own party, will be turned off.

Many politicians have fought to win arguments for the sake of winning but made themselves look terrible in the process. Remember, humility is a warmth virtue. It's what makes you *likable*. When you are blatantly trying to impress others, or fight to prove you're right, you make yourself *less* likable. People see right through this.

Instead, be consistent with your kindness and gestures of respect.

Laugh at Yourself

When former New Jersey governor Chris Christie appeared on David Letterman's late-night talk show, the famously rotund politician was ready to make a joke at his own expense. Early into the interview, he pulled a donut out of his pocket and said, "I didn't know the interview was going to take this long."[201] *The Washington Post* reported that viewers who watched Christie's donut stunt were more likely to vote for him.[202] Through his self-deprecating putdown, he'd made himself more likable.

We discussed the value of humor for connecting with voters in

---

201 Chanel, ABŞ Voice. "New Jersey Gov. Chris Christie on The Late Show with David Letterman." *YouTube.* November 30, 2014.

202 Ibid, Nussbaum.

the previous chapter on empathy. There's no question that self-deprecating humor can be a valuable tool in communicating humility. Laughing at yourself makes you seem human, relatable, and likable and can help you address potential voter concerns. Recall the example when JFK joked about his father's unwillingness to "pay for a landslide." By jesting about it, he diffused concerns that he was merely a pawn of his father's ambition.

President Trump, using self-deprecating humor, flashed a glimmer of humility when he spoke recently about visiting the hospital room of Steve Scalise the day the congressman was shot. "There was his wife crying hysterically at his bedside. I said to Steve, 'my wife would never do that.'"

Whereas arrogant people try to make others feel beneath them, self-deprecating humor helps minimize status distinctions.[203] Making a joke at their own expense levels the playing field, reminding voters that the candidate is aware of their own vulnerability. Aggressive humor, on the other hand, exaggerates status distinctions. Insult humor (i.e., jokes made at *other* people's expense) can be effective in the short run—by elevating you above your opponents—but will eventually come back to haunt you. Voters usually don't see these jokes as being funny but as mean-spirited.

Jeffrey Nussbaum for *The Washington Post* notes, "Insult humor is the easiest to do and the surest way to get on the news. But it doesn't help build the candidate's larger persona."[204] This kind of

---

203 Hoption, Colette, Julian Barling, and Nick Turner. "It's Not You, It's Me: Transformational Leadership and Self-deprecating Humor." *Leadership & Organization Development Journal.* 34, no. 1 (2013): 4–19.

204 Ibid, Nussbaum.

humor will make you seem arrogant in the long run and decrease your likability.

In the same article he points to self-deprecating humor as a surefire way to boost likability: "as Dannagal Young, a professor of political communication at the University of Delaware (who performs in an improv comedy troupe), puts it, 'If your goal is to appear human, authentic and relatable, it makes sense to deploy self-deprecation as a tactic.'"

My friend Senator Rick Scott ran against Charlie Crist for governor of Florida in 2014. The two are very different in appearance. Scott is tall, pale-skinned, and bald. Crist is shorter and perpetually tanned with a full head of long flowing gray hair. I suggested the following to Scott: if the debate moderator were to ask, "Governor Scott, is there anything you can say that's positive about your opponent?" Scott's answer could be, "Great hair." That line and that visual, I assured him, would be on the cover of every newspaper the next day.

Are you struggling to connect with voters? Do voters think you seem distant, cerebral, or wooden? Make them laugh. Do you get accusations of appearing arrogant or elitist? Crack an appropriate joke at your own expense and diffuse the criticism. Hire a professional comedian if you need help with your timing or coming up with good one-liners.

Humble people are likable because they don't take themselves too seriously. What *do* they take seriously? The well-being of their voters. Now *that's* likable.

CHAPTER EIGHT

FROM RIGID TO AGILE

"Those who cannot change their mind cannot change anything."

—GEORGE BERNARD SHAW

At the Colony Resort in Longboat Key, Florida (not far from my home), debate prep for the 2000 Presidential election was underway. The man standing in for George W. Bush began to detect signs of animosity stemming from the performance of democratic nominee Al Gore. Paul Begala, Bush's stand-in, describes his experience with the Vice President:

> Right away I picked up a problem about Gore during debate prep: a raw, unbridled contempt he had for Bush. It wasn't the usual 'my worthy adversary and I have different ideas.' He would sometimes sigh when I was talking, or frown, or roll his eyes. And his tone and language too—it all communicated that Gore thought Bush was an idiot. 'You don't deserve to be on stage with me' was Gore's basic attitude.[205]

---

205 Healy, Patrick. "Debacle: What Al Gore's First Debate Against George W. Bush Can Teach Hillary Clinton." *The New York Times*. September 25.

Gore's debate team coached him on his nonverbal emotional optics. He was instructed not to grimace in response to anything Bush said. He was explicitly ordered to not invade Bush's personal space. Despite those warnings, Gore continued to use intimidation tactics during the practice sessions.

Gore couldn't help himself. His contempt for Bush was palpable.

Gore's behavior during the actual debate with Bush has already been described in earlier chapters as abysmal. He acted aggressively, he grimaced—in fact, one member of his debate prep team acknowledged, "[Gore's reactions were] somewhat inexplicable—as if the things that Gore had been told not to do became his to-do list."[206]

Gore's rigidity was easy to see externally: his posture was rigid and his voice often monotone—not to mention, he became verbally fixated on his Social Security term, "lockbox." He repeated the word "lockbox" seven times—a gaffe which was ruthlessly mocked on *SNL*'s rendition of the debate. The skit portrayed Gore as inflexible, unyielding, and wooden.

But Gore's real problem was his *internal* rigidity. He was so set in his opinions—especially his negative opinion of Bush—that he couldn't adjust his emotional optics—even at the recommendations of his team.

Begala said, "For all of Gore's good answers, his feelings for Bush was his fatal flaw. You can't afford to look across the stage with that kind of contempt at someone who millions of people have

---

206 Ibid.

nominated as their standard-bearer, and not have it bleed over to the audience and have them see you negatively."[207]

When a candidate, or politician, is rigid in their thinking, this can easily translate to outward rigidity. Gore's *external* reactions stemmed from his *inner* contempt. His *outer* stiffness revealed his *inner* inflexibility. Even his repetition of "lockbox" was likely an indication of inward rigidity—he was unable to shift gears and adopt new words or phrases.

Many politicians commit the sin of rigidity. Sometimes their rigidity is outward: They look awkward, remain too serious, or become overly repetitive.

Often though, the rigidity is internal. Some candidates lack the agility to navigate multiple views of an issue and get stuck captaining the only points they're ready to discuss. Maybe they're unsure, and they feel more comfortable following the instructions of their handlers. Sometimes they're stubbornly dogmatic in their thinking and can't find ways to move off a position. Or maybe—like Gore—they feel a negative emotion so strongly that it stymies their ability to communicate.

Effective candidates and politicians tack. They have the flexibility to adapt to changing circumstances. That doesn't mean you flip-flop or change your mind. You're adjusting your sails so that you can keep your boat moving in the direction *you* want.

You need that same agility in your physicality, personal inter-

---

207 Ibid.

actions, and policy thinking if you're going to accomplish your agenda—and win your election.

THE PSYCHOLOGY OF RIGIDITY

Deadlocked. Hyper-partisan. Tribal. Polarized. Stuck.

The words above describe uncompromising politicians. These political stances are not productive. Yet more and more, this is where our elected leaders have taken us. Why so rigid?

According to one researcher, the rigidity traces back to issues of self-esteem. Jonathan Keller of James Madison University writes, "When a situation arises that arouses a leader's core sources of self-validation—the criteria by which one judges one's worth as a political leader—the leader becomes willing to endure enormous political opposition and policy setbacks in order to remain faithful to the policy that has become identified with their self-worth."[208]

If a politician has staked their campaign on a single promise—think George H. W. Bush's line, "Read my lips, no new taxes!"—then they risk their identity as a politician if they back down. There's good precedent for heeding this risk. After all, George H. W. Bush failed to win re-election after breaking his promise.

Keller explains that some politicians are driven by internal validation which emerges from their personal ideology or mission. Ronald Reagan was like that. His personal journals reveal a sense

---

208 Keller, Jonathan W. "Explaining Rigidity and Pragmatism in Political Leaders: A General Theory and a Plausibility Test from the Reagan Presidency." *Political Psychology* 30, no. 3 (May 8, 2009): 465–98.

of mission, and he was not easily persuaded to change policies that reflected his core principles.

Other politicians, like Donald J. Trump, are externally validated. They live for the approval of their voters and party leaders and will do anything to avoid disappointing their base.

In either case, politicians want assurance that they're doing the job. Compromise feels like unconditional surrender. One journalist, Tom Jacobs, explains, "For many, bending would mean betraying their sense of who they are and why they're in office."[209]

Let's return to the example we discussed in chapter 3 when we covered the dangers of campaign hyperbole. Donald Trump promised during his 2016 run for the White House that he would build a "big, beautiful" border wall between the US and Mexico, and that Mexico would pay for it. His strident voter base loved the idea of Trump's wall. He was elected with the expectation that he would get the wall built.

That was part of his appeal as a candidate. When elected president, he reinforced his pledge: the wall. "*I'll* get it built," he reassured his audience during his 2019 State of the Union address.[210] Trump sought validation externally. He was determined to keep his promise to his core voters.

However, Trump couldn't get that wall approved in Congress. He resorted to declaring a national emergency to get his wall funding. As his approval ratings dropped, he dug in his heels. For Trump,

209 Jacobs, Tom. "The Psychology of Political Stubbornness." *Pacific Standard*. July 28, 2011.

210 "State of the Union 2019: Read the Full Transcript." *CNN*. February 6, 2019.

because of his strong policy stance against illegal immigration, there was no option but to build the wall. His campaign promise had led to total rigidity. He couldn't tack.

For some politicians, the rigidity is worth the risk—even if it results in a loss. Arizona senator and prisoner of war hero John McCain's views on certain issues, like opposing the CIA's enhanced interrogation techniques for terrorist detainees at Guantanamo, bucked his own party's position. Prior to securing the 2008 Republican presidential nomination, McCain was asked if he would compromise on certain issues to appeal to more Republicans.

McCain responded, "I don't want it that badly...I will continue to do what is right. I will continue to pursue torture, climate change. If that means I can't get the Republican nomination, fine. I've had a happy life. The worst thing I can do is sell my soul to the devil."[211]

Good candidates and leaders show conviction. Voters should expect politicians to make good on the goals and promises they made when they ran. Most Americans admired McCain for his convictions, which often were in opposition to the GOP. McCain was nicknamed a "maverick," because he had backbone. One journalist wrote, "McCain was a conservative Republican, but his work in the Senate was marked by a zest for bipartisanship which often put him at odds with his own party. McCain reached across the aisle on several occasions to push for action on issues like campaign finance reform, climate change and immigration."[212]

---

211 Ignatius, David. "Opinion: John McCain Refused to Sell His Soul." *North Jersey.* August 27, 2018.

212 N'dea Yancy Bragg, "Six Memorable Moments When John McCain Earned a Reputation as a 'Maverick,'" *USA Today,* August 26, 2018.

But a backbone is made up of solid bones, connected by flexible tissue. A healthy backbone bends. Candidates and politicians need a *balance* of ideological conviction and flexibility. As one writer notes, "The politician should be flexible enough to accommodate new thoughts, ideas, and suggestions as the emerging situations demand. After all, there is a famous saying that politics is the art of compromise."[213]

If your sense of self-worth is primarily determined by the opinions of your supporters—you set yourself up for rigidity, just like President Trump.

If your sense of self-worth is reinforced by the failures of others, you set yourself up for rigidity like Al Gore.

If your sense of self-worth is a function of dogmatic adherence to an ideology—you set yourself up for rigidity, like many of the Tea Party candidates or the "Squad," the name given by *New York Times* columnist Maureen Dowd to four current congresswomen.[214] Alexandra Ocasio-Cortez (AOC), one of the four, describes her group this way: "it's a shorthand," showing that "you might be someone who sees the world the way that I do."

If you believe, however, that getting legislation passed—even if it isn't everything you wanted—is a sign of doing a good job, you set yourself up to be agile. If you're willing to entertain opposing ideas and alternate positions, you exchange arrogant rigidity for humble agility. If you have a sense of self-worth that is independent of what people say about you on Twitter—you

---

213   Khan, Nasir. "Politics: The Art of Compromise." *Daily Times*. August 2, 2018.

214   Anna North, "How 4 Congresswomen Came to be Called 'the Squad,'" *Vox*, July 17, 2019.

have more agility than the insecure politician who's desperate for the approval of others.

As one writer points out:

> [Compromise] does not mean that you have to surrender your personal convictions and always level the decision-making process to the lowest common denominator. This does not mean everyone is unhappy because they only get half a solution. But it does mean that effective leaders have to keep an open mind and be able to identify the greater good and the lesser of two bad solutions, and then make a timely choice, in good faith, to the best of their ability.[215]

Physical rigidity is easy to see in a candidate's outward bodily signals, like stiff posture or a clenched jaw. Rigid thinking more often lies deeper below the surface because it connects to a politician's underlying beliefs about who they are and what gives them worth.

Rigid candidates and politicians can quickly come across as unlikable. They appear defensive, hostile, dogmatic, fixed, and closed. They often take themselves too seriously and lack a sense of ease or humor. In fact, their stiffness can make them the *butt* of jokes: rigid politicians make great material for late-night comedy punch lines.

Chevy Chase famously impersonated President Gerald R. Ford on *SNL* as a stiff, bumbling, accident-prone, inept goof. Several

---

215 Ibid, Khan.

SNL skits in the 2016 election portrayed Hillary Clinton wearing pantsuits to bed and to the beach.[216]

INSECURITY

Ironically, it's often strong candidates who give into their insecurity and commit self-sabotage. Going into the presidential debate, Gore's experience should have equipped him with a strong sense of self-assurance. Likewise, Marco Rubio's natural gifts of public speaking and thinking on his feet should have provided him self-confidence. But anxiety reared its ugly head and drove these two accomplished politicians to gaffe.

Stop the downward spiral that fear can trigger before it starts. Throughout the book, we've discussed strategies to help you build confidence and assurance. Amy Cuddy's power poses, Tasha Eurich's *Insight* tools, and Deliberate Practice are all helpful methods to deal with fear and insecurity.

UNYIELDING

Intransigent politicians refuse to think outside their own close-minded opinions and mindset. They enter conversations with a confirmation bias and quickly veto opposing arguments.

It's like a teenage game of chicken with cars: two opposing forces barrel towards a collision, daring the other to swerve first. Although an unyielding stance is usually meant to force sub-

---

216 Outi J. Hakola, "Political Impersonations on *Saturday Night Live* during the 2016 U. S. Presidential Election," *European Journal of American Studies,* 2016.

mission from the opposing side, it can tragically result in your own crash.

When Trump was fighting for wall funding, Congress originally gave him the option of $25 billion to completely fund the wall, provided that 1.8 million Dreamers—the name given to children who came to the US illegally but were protected under the Deferred Action for Childhood Arrivals (DACA) policy—be given a ten- to fourteen-year timeline for a pathway to citizenship. But President Trump thought this time period was too generous and wouldn't yield to any concession that allowed Dreamers to sponsor their parents for citizenship. He turned the deal down.[217]

The $25 billion funding for a border wall was offered well in advance of the 2018 midterm elections, which ushered in a wave of new Democrats who took control of the House. Trump was then in a much weaker bargaining position. Democrats knew it. When Trump proposed a new deal, this time asking for $5.7 billion for the wall, Democrats, knowing they were now in the driver's seat, flatly rejected his plan. The government shut down for a record thirty-five days while Trump and the Speaker of the House, Nancy Pelosi, played chicken, each daring the other to swerve first.

Bluffing only works until someone is forced to give. Be forewarned: it might be you. In the end, Trump relented. With his approval ratings in freefall, President Trump agreed to reopen the government with no wall funding approved.

Effective politicians move their agenda forward by being resilient.

217 Newell, Jim. "Why Didn't Trump Just Take the Border Wall Deal?" *Slate Magazine.* March 28, 2018.

They can flex as needed. Consider: are you able to incorporate new information and make a shift? Can you be cognitively flexible enough to pursue your bigger goals and compromise on the smaller details? You will need this agility to be productive in politics.

EMOTIONAL OPTICS OF RIGIDITY

Gore repeated himself. Marco Rubio repeated himself. Trump repeated himself. Why would repetition come up so often as a sign of rigidity?

There are several reasons. First, when candidates memorize policy points or rebuttals, it's a sign that they want to guarantee an appearance of knowledge or find it difficult to be spontaneous and think outside the box. When candidates regurgitate the same points over and over, they are viewed as rigid, inauthentic, and robotic. That's not great.

Through good preparation and solid talking points, you can show that you recognize the ramifications of your ideas. With genuine understanding of policy complexities, you'll come across as better informed, more confident and authentic—and less wooden.

Repetition can occur when you've been unexpectedly challenged, as Rubio was by Chris Christie. Direct attacks on you personally or your policy ideas can instantly create a feeling of insecurity and make you feel threatened and cornered. As anxiety floods your brain, mental fog rolls in quickly, preventing you from thinking clearly.

How do you clear the fog away? Practice. Comedians constantly deal with hecklers in their audience, and you'll need to learn the same tactics they employ to neutralize taunts and insults. Remember: you are the boss of your campaign. Don't be limited to only a few approved responses. Tight boundaries will only increase your nervousness.

To think better on your feet, use the methods of Deliberate Practice. Watch films of candidates who respond well to criticism or unexpected questions. Study how they respond, and practice by asking some of your campaign team to heckle you.

Candidates also perseverate when they don't have much to say. If you have limited understanding about an issue, you can easily get stuck saying the only lines you've prepared—and saying them over and over.

To avoid being stuck verbally like a broken record, you need to learn both the pros and cons of a given issue. Candidates get trapped when they don't have a comprehensive knowledge of the policy facts or evidence to support various perspectives of the argument. If you're well-informed, though, the opposition is going to have a much harder time making you look foolish or ill-informed.

Rigidity often results from being unprepared. Think of athletes getting ready for a game. If they don't stretch and warm up, they set themselves up for injury.

Likewise, you need to be on your game: mentally and physically prepared. Do your homework. Strengthen your cognitive flexibility. Get your political coach to help you identify your weaknesses and bad emotional optics.

When you enter the arena, you'll have the agility you need to score your points—and avoid injury to your campaign.

THE ART OF AGILITY

There was a period in history when a political leader's agility spared us from disaster. The time was the Cuban Missile Crisis, and the leader was John F. Kennedy.

Kennedy's presidency hadn't begun well. Early on, he was humiliated by the outcome of the Bay of Pigs invasion. The CIA. had recommended that Kennedy invade Cuba with a small group of ex-pat Cubans. The goal was to overthrow Fidel Castro in a coup and seize control of the Communist government. Instead, Castro was tipped-off to the coup in advance and easily squashed the invasion. One hundred and fourteen soldiers were slaughtered on the beach, and 1,100 more taken prisoner.[218]

Kennedy was shamed and unnerved by the failed mission. He regretted the invasion, which he'd doubted from the beginning. There wasn't much time for mourning though—the Soviet Union had begun to surreptitiously muscle its way into Cuba. Testing the mettle of America's new, young, inexperienced president, Nikita Khrushchev, the Russian premier, began erecting secret missile sites in Cuba.

Somehow, without starting a nuclear war, Kennedy had to stand

---

218 "Bay of Pigs Invasion." *History.com.* October 27, 2009.

up to Khrushchev and respond to his aggression with force and strength.

Kennedy's responses to the Soviet Union's threat show masterful decision-making. Each day brought new tensions, and there often seemed like no way out but war. Kennedy's generals urged him to bomb Cuba—but how much, and where, and how? JFK felt that America's values had to be considered. He realized that if the US initiated a first strike by a surprise bombing of the island, the United States would appear equally as guilty to the world as the Japanese were when they infamously bombed Pearl Harbor.

Kennedy had the option to ignore Khrushchev's encroachment into Cuba entirely. But he wouldn't capitulate. JFK considered Khrushchev's boldness of encroaching fifty miles off US soil as an indication that the Soviets wouldn't stop there and intended to take over West Berlin. He wouldn't let that happen on his watch.[219]

Kennedy opted instead for "a quarantine," better remembered today as the blockade. He prevented any Soviet ships from bringing in new nuclear missiles. JFK also revealed publicly to the American people the presence of Soviet missiles in Cuba. His intent was to buy himself time and gather a coalition of support from other nations. Kennedy faced Khrushchev down. In the end, the Soviets backed off and withdrew their missile installations after reaching a compromise in a silent nonpublic deal where the United States withdrew its missiles from Turkey.

---

219 May, Ernest R., PhD. "History - World Wars: John F Kennedy and the Cuban Missile Crisis." *BBC*. November 18, 2013.

The details of that crisis are numerous and complex, but one factor emerges clearly: Kennedy had to pivot time and again over thirteen days in October 1962. With each new move from the Soviets, he evaluated our nation's safety, values, and interests abroad. JFK remained firm in his convictions but was flexible in what he considered the best path forward. He listened to his advisers but also trusted his gut. In the end, he put on a show of personal strength for Khrushchev. He allowed the premier to save face, forced the Soviets to reverse direction, and managed to avoid starting a nuclear war.

Kennedy's actions are a great example of agility. It's all about bending, adapting, and getting creative, while sticking to your guns and following what you believe is right. It's a series of pivots—not ones which move you from side to side or opinion to opinion but enable you to move forward in the direction you want to go.

Political agility is not easy. One journalist summed up the two extreme positions that are more common in politics, writing, "Politicians: They're slick and soulless, shifting positions shame-lessly to stay ahead of public opinion. Unless they're ridiculously rigid and inflexible, sticking to their principles even when doing so courts disaster."[220]

Rigidity versus flexibility—walking that tightrope can feel as har-rowing as responding forcefully to Khrushchev's missiles in Cuba. Being too rigid is bad—nothing gets done when there's no room for compromise. But being too flexible is also not good. When you overaccommodate, you run the risk of slipping off the wire

220 Jacobs, Tom. "The Psychology of Political Stubbornness." *Pacific Standard.* July 28, 2011.

and being called a hypocrite and a flip-flopper. How do you strike the right balance?

That's what the rest of this chapter will discuss.

BECOMING A TIGHTROPE WALKER

Kennedy was a smart politician—but his gifts for analysis were not all inherent. He worked hard, and he worked smart. He surrounded himself with a gifted team of diverse thinkers and sought advice.

Political agility is a virtue that can be developed and honed. To achieve it, you will need to focus on developing some of the following skills.

FLEXIBILITY

Florida governor Rick Scott had a perfect A+ rating from the NRA for his history of voting for Second Amendment gun rights. However, the horrific and tragic mass shooting at Marjory Douglas Stoneman High-School in Parkland, Florida, that took seventeen lives of students and staff prompted Scott to reevaluate his longtime opposition to gun control.[221]

On March 9, 2018, Scott signed into law red-flag provisions that allow judges to issue risk-protection orders. Authorities are now able to temporarily confiscate guns from those deemed by a court to be a threat. Also included and bundled with the Marjory Stoneman Douglas High School Public Safety Act are provisions

221 Yan, Holly. "Florida Gov. Rick Scott Signs Gun Bill." *CNN*. March 10, 2018.

that raise the age to purchase a gun from eighteen to twenty-one and a ban on bump stocks.

Rick Scott told NBC's Meet the Press, "We sat down with law enforcement, the mental health counselors and educators and said 'what would really work?' And so we passed historic legislation within three weeks."[222] These increased measures for gun control were the first enacted in Florida in over twenty years.

In changing his longtime stance, Scott risked angering the powerful NRA and many of his fellow Republicans who didn't support the bill. He also risked angering Democrats who believed the gun control provisions didn't go far enough. His move was not politically safe. It was, however, what Scott believed was right.

The protests and passionate speeches from Parkland students had led Scott to consider new views. As the father of two daughters and several grandchildren, he empathized with the victims and parents and told the press that he wondered how he would feel had it been his child who had been shot or killed. Scott didn't abandon his Second Amendment allegiance—in fact, his US Senate campaign later in the same year emphasized his continued support for gun rights. But he flexed. For good reasons, Scott adjusted his stance to introduce "common sense" measures for increased public safety.

Scott's school safety control legislation reflects the kind of cognitive flexibility that candidates need to display. He didn't ignore the protesting students and parents—he listened to them,

<hr />

222 Scott, Rick. "GOP Sen. Scott Says Laws to Combat Mass Shootings Should Focus on Mental Illness." *NBC News.* September 1, 2019.

identified with their pain, and responded in a pragmatic and thoughtful way.

Cognitive flexibility allows you to shift gears and think about something in multiple ways. Rather than stay fixated on a specific viewpoint, you open yourself to consider a range of possible courses of action. Then, after considering different viewpoints, you return to what you think is the best approach and why. That's what Rick Scott did.

Even John F. Kennedy said, "Change is the law of life. Those who look only to the past or present are certain to miss the future." You've got to be ready to respond to any crises or cultural changes with cognitive flexibility.

What is the best way to adapt to change? Start by breaking complex issues or tasks into bite-sized chunks. Then, consider a variety of strategies to meet the different types of challenges that each small chunk represents.

This will require innovative thinking. When President Kennedy confronted the Cuban Missile Crisis, the most obvious solution—bombing the island—was just one option. After gathering the facts and consulting with various trusted advisors, his choice to quarantine the island was a more creative alternative and helped avoid war.

If you're not naturally innovative, surround yourself with creative thinkers. Some of your policy stances are going to alienate voters, and you need to become comfortable with that reality. As Abraham Lincoln famously said, quoting the poet John Lydgate,

"You can please some of the people all of the time, you can please all of the people some of the time, but you can't please all of the people all of the time." You will need to push beyond your conventional mindset to make the most effective decisions, both in your campaign and in office.

THINK ON YOUR FEET

In March of 1981, Ronald Reagan was shot outside the Washington, DC, Hilton in an assassination attempt by John Hinckley, Jr. His attacker was immediately subdued, and to the relief of the nation, Reagan, even though wounded seriously, recovered quickly.

Several years later, Reagan was giving a speech in West Berlin when suddenly a balloon popped. The bang sounded just like gunfire, but Reagan didn't miss a beat. Interrupting his own speech, he quipped, "Missed me."[223]

Comedians—and comedic politicians—are gifted at thinking on their feet. Yet behind Reagan's quick sense of humor was his famous discipline. He knew his principles, he knew his vision, he was well-informed about what was happening in the world—and he could easily crack a joke. The weight of his understanding enabled the lightness of his agility.

Politicians open to learning will have the edge here. The more prepared you are on the campaign trail—the more self-aware, the more acquainted with the issues, the more you grasp the pros

---

223 Arterton. "Reagan Was Giving a Speech in West Berlin When a Balloon Popped Very Loudly." *YouTube.* November 3, 2018.

and cons of your policies, the more you've learned about your audience—the more agile you will be.

Be open, be receptive, and pursue genuine understanding, not just memorized factoids. Practice improvising with your team—an acting or political coach can help. And take a note from Reagan: always maintain your sense of humor!

QUICK LEARNING

George W. Bush had been branded as an intellectual lightweight by the Democrats and media during the 2000 presidential election. He did the smart thing: he fought that branding. Leading up to his debates with Gore, Bush rigorously prepared so he would show the American people that he was self-assured and knowledgeable.

George W. studied and learned during those debate prep weeks. During the actual debate his agility was on clear display and he was able to adapt to the various questions that were pitched to him. He also managed to remain unfazed by Gore's verbal and nonverbal reactions to his comments.

During the debate, Gore's sighs and eye rolls were meant to communicate to America that George W. was not credible, but his efforts backfired. Gore looked like a spoiled child, not like a Commander in Chief. By comparison, Bush's professionalism and decorum showed the voters that he was more ready to be President of the United States than the existing Vice President.

Work hard and smart. Find out *what* you don't know, and then absorb that info quickly. Make sure to focus effort towards improving your weaknesses. Just like an athlete working to correct bad technique or rehabilitate an injury—deliberate practice is where you'll best increase your agility.

OTHER STRATEGIES TO DEVELOP AGILITY

I want to make you aware of several tools you can use to help increase agility. I've already discussed Tasha Eurich's book *Insight*, which is excellent. Here are some other great resources:

First: take **Shane Snow's Intellectual Humility** quiz.[224] A quick Google search will bring the quiz up for you. This assessment helps highlight where you make unknown assumptions and where you are genuinely open to new knowledge. For people who are unaware of their biases, this is an invaluable tool. You'll need a friend to complete the assessment.

Check out Sean Munson's online tool called **The Balancer**.[225] This program gives you real-time feedback about your online news reading habit. If "The Balancer" determines that you're only reading liberal media sources, you will be prompted to consult more conservative sources to balance out your news media intake. Just like athletes studying videos of an opposing team, reading opinions from both sides of the spectrum helps build your agility in discussing issues.

Finally, try to learn Karl Popper's method called **Falsification**.[226]

224 "Take The Intellectual Humility Assessment." *Shane Snow*.

225 "Balancer." *Balancer* :: How Balanced Is Your News? :: BALANCE Study.

226 "Falsifiability." *Explorable* - Think Outside The Box - Research, Experiments, Psychology, Self-Help.

The process of falsification requires you to interrogate your opinions so ruthlessly that you end up proving them false. Recruit your staffers to help you. If you're campaigning on a platform for single-payer healthcare, your team should lay out enough evidence to prove that single-payer healthcare would never work.

Why would you want to practice these techniques? Because as you examine every angle and potential pitfall of your platform, your argumentation skill is forced to become more fine-tuned. You need to gather *counter*evidence and develop ways to respond to strong criticisms. Most of the points your team brings up will be thrown back at you by your opposition. By enlisting the process of falsification, you will be better prepared to counter whatever curveballs are thrown your way.

Candidates and politicians get trapped and commit the sin of rigidity when they don't have all the facts, and their opponent makes them look stupid. The process of falsification will force you to get smarter about your issues, make better decisions, become aware of your cognitive biases, and help you clarify what you already know along with the evidence you've gathered to back it up.

UNDERSTAND BOTH SIDES

When armed with this knowledge, your debate skills will improve. You can, in fact, learn to think differently about issues. As you solidify your political and moral principles, you will discover your biases. Where do you assume your opponent has it all wrong? If you're convinced your opponent is truly an idiot, that bias and contempt will become visible, just like it was for Al Gore. That's not good for you!

If you learn the arguments for both sides of an issue, you will have more respect for the voters who disagree with your policy. Remember, reframe policy points to get people on your side. Tom Jacobs, author of "The Psychology of Political Stubbornness" speaks to this:

> Those trying to strike a bargain need to a) understand what motivates individual members, and b) reframe issues so that less-extreme positions are no longer a threat to their sense of self-worth... The key to getting a member to switch their vote is reframing the issue in such a way that it aligns with the impulse that provides them with their sense of self-worth.[227]

If you shy away from learning what motivates voters, what issues are connected to their self-worth, and how their opinions feel connected to their survival—you'll be unable to reframe their concerns in a way that resonates with them. But if you do understand what voters need and feel strongly about, you will respond empathically and thoughtfully, while still being true to yourself.

DETERMINE YOUR DEFICIT: STRENGTH OR WARMTH?

George W. Bush arrived at the presidential debate already strong in the warmth virtues. He was folksy, affable, candid, and appeared authentic. Therefore, during debate prep, he worked on his strength virtues. He rigorously prepared to talk policy.

Gore came to the debate with robust strength virtues. He was confident, decisive, and he had clear plans for where he wanted to take the country. But he neglected to work on his warmth vir-

---

227 Ibid, Jacobs.

tues and came across as unlikable. His lack of warmth squelched any appearance of national policy strength, which was the main attribute he had going for him.

The 2000 presidential election results were famously contested: George W. Bush lost the popular vote to Gore but ultimately was declared winner by the Supreme Court based on approximately 500 votes in Florida. But Gore's campaign team said later they felt Gore would have won a decisive victory if it were not for his unlikable performance in the debates.[228]

When voters don't like you or feel you understand them, they won't trust you. If they can't trust you, they won't feel safe committing to you. If they won't commit to you, they won't vote for you.

As you implement the methods of Deliberate Practice, get your campaign team to help assess whether you need to work on strength virtues or warmth virtues—or both. Watch videos of yourself. Unfortunately, we all have a biological disadvantage for determining how we look to other people. You can't physically see yourself—except on film or in a mirror! However, your "loving critics" can give you honest feedback, and videos will help as well.

Once you've analyzed what virtues most need to improve—get to it, using the strategies laid out in each of these chapters.

GATHER AN AGILE TEAM

John F. Kennedy's decision to invade Cuba at the Bay of Pigs was

228 Ibid, Healy.

strongly recommended—by just a few people. They were mostly hawks, bent on military intervention as the best solution. New to the presidency, Kennedy didn't think he was permitted to consult with anyone who wasn't officially sanctioned to discuss the plan—so the advice he received was limited and lopsided.

Following the Bay of Pigs fiasco, Kennedy was determined to surround himself with a wider group of expert opinions, and he put together a team known as "ExComm." The BBC describes who specifically was on Kennedy's new team:

> Included in the ExComm were the regular participants in National Security Council meetings, plus Kennedy's brother, the attorney general Robert Kennedy, and the President's chief speechwriter, the White House counsel Theodore Sorensen. Both of these men could help Kennedy to think about the domestic political aspects of the crisis. The President also invited several other key advisors to join the group: C. Douglas Dillon, who had held high posts under Eisenhower and who gave Kennedy a link to the Republican leadership; Dean Acheson and Robert Lovett, who had served under President Harry Truman and could help Kennedy see the current crisis in longer historical perspective; and a former ambassador to the Soviet Union, Llewellyn (Tommy) Thompson, probably the person in the President's circle who was best acquainted with Khrushchev.[229]

Kennedy gathered around him people that knew him well and how he thought. He engaged both domestic and foreign policy experts. He included historical thinkers, Republican thinkers, and scholars who were familiar with Russian strategy. He gathered a

---

229 May, Ernest R., PhD. "History - World Wars: John F Kennedy and the Cuban Missile Crisis." *BBC*. November 18, 2013.

team that would help him be far more agile in decision-making than when he first pondered the Bay of Pigs invasion.

Some campaign strategists are like the hawkish generals that initially counseled Kennedy to invade Cuba: they're a one-trick pony. They know one strategy well, and they'll push for that every time. They're not flexible—and that's a recipe for bad decision-making.

Flexibility is difficult to learn if the people around you aren't flexible. Gather an agile team! Take a lesson from JFK and surround yourself with people from various walks of life to help you grasp all the different elements of your campaign.

You will, of course, need qualified campaign strategists. That's a given. But whom else do you need to circle yourself with? Hire an acting coach to help you better display your emotional optics. Find a comedian—a professional, or just a funny friend—to help write one-liners and appropriate jokes. Enlist Republican and Democratic political experts to help you hone your policies and comprehensively understand both sides of the issues. Get a political coach to help you with your Deliberate Practice. Lastly, get a loving critic who will be honest with you about your campaign sins and the ways to turn those into virtues.

FIND YOUR VOICE

Easy enough for Kennedy to seem agile—he was smart, naturally funny, and a gifted public speaker. But how do you avoid being anxious when speaking to a crowd?

George W. Bush was not a great public orator. He was famously mocked for his Leo-Gorcey-like malapropisms such as mispronouncing "nuclear" and making up words like "misunderestimated." But he rolled with it, often poking fun at himself. Once, after making a language mistake, he noticed his mother's expression and quipped, "She gave me a look that only a mother could give a child."[230]

Bush's speaking foibles were mocked by his opponents as evidence that he was dim-witted. But for the most part, people saw his speaking gaffes as proof of his authenticity. He seemed human, and that was appealing.

Know the content of your policies and that of your opposition— and then *relax*. Deliver the information in your normal way, and if you make a mistake, acknowledge it with lightheartedness. People will see you as human.

You already have a uniquely personal speaking style—although you may not realize it. During your Deliberate Practice work, observe the aspects of your speaking style that are unique to you. Identify the weaknesses, and work on those.

Aside from any coaching, most aspects of your speaking style should be embraced. Your speech will be a way people distinguish you from your competitors. By embracing your style of communicating, you can relax into greater agility because you won't feel constrained or on-guard by what you should or shouldn't say.

To practice honing your public speaking, pick out a few people whose verbal style you feel is compelling and attractive. It might

230 CBS. "8 Years Of 'Bushisms'." *YouTube.* January 8, 2009.

be a newscaster, politician, or an author you've heard talk. Look for any clues as to what makes you pay attention to what they are saying. How do they hold their body and what hand gestures do they use? What is their cadence? What common words do they use and emphasize? Then pick a topic, and practice speaking about it by trying to incorporate some of what you have observed from these speakers. Remember, you're not aiming to orate like Ronald Reagan or Dr. Martin Luther King. Discuss something you're passionate about. Practice speaking when you're looking in the mirror, or practice discussing the issue with a friend or spouse. Get feedback on your mannerisms and body language. Ask what works well and what doesn't. Pay attention to your unique vocabulary and speaking idiosyncrasies.

If you're still struggling, seek out training. **Toastmasters** is a great organization which gives coaching in public speaking. Or hire a personal verbal coach to help you develop your voice. Former British prime minister Margaret Thatcher hired a voice coach because she felt that the tone of her speaking voice was too deep to be taken seriously.

President Trump is by no means an accomplished and fluid public speaker. But his style is successful and works for him. It's visceral, off-the-cuff, unfiltered, and taps right into voters' guts. Sarah Palin was also not a polished speaker, but people found her folksiness endearing.

Find your own voice. It's you, after all, who's running for office. When elected, you will draft the proposals and legislation and issue public statements. You must take control, just as Kennedy did in the Cuban Missile Crisis.

You're the boss, the person ultimately in charge of what you want to say and accomplish. Embrace who you are, own your candidacy, learn to be agile, and speak your thoughts and ideas as only you can.

THOUSANDS OF TALLIES

There's a story about a time a journalist interviewed the famous New York Yankee baseball player Joe DiMaggio. DiMaggio, nicknamed "Joltin' Joe," was known for his unbelievable talent as a hitter. He still holds the Major League Baseball record of fifty-six consecutive games with a hit, the longest streak in baseball history. The journalist asked Joe how it felt to be so "naturally" gifted at hitting.

DiMaggio led the reporter down to his basement. In the dim room, he began practicing a series of hits. He would call out a pitch—"fastball, low and away"—and then swing. He'd call out another one, adjust accordingly, and then swing again. After repeating the routine for a long series of pitches, DiMaggio put the bat down and wrote a tally mark on the wall, signaling the completion of a practice session.

Then, DiMaggio turned on the lights. The wall was covered with thousands of tally marks. Legend has it that DiMaggio then turned to the journalist and said, "Don't ever tell me that I'm a natural hitter again."[231]

Agility. Flexibility. Responsiveness. These are traits that are practiced, built, and developed over time.

---

231 Clear, James. "The Myth and Magic of Deliberate Practice." *James Clear.* September 1, 2018.

To practice effectively, you need to first learn what your areas of rigidity are. Where are you externally inflexible? What are your nervous tics, your visible signs of negative emotion? Remember that the outer signs of rigidity usually connect to *inward* rigidity.

Hopefully, you now understand that the virtues I've shown you build on each other. Having more humility will make it easier to confront your inner biases and learn opposing views. Owning your authentic self will better enable campaigning with confidence and flexibility. Developing a clear sense of your values will help remain consistent and be deliberate.

Don't let a lack of understanding of the Candidate's 7 Deadly Sins drag down your campaign or your efficacy as a leader.

You have great abilities, ideas, and strengths to offer. Do the hard work to transform your vices into virtues—and help lead us all towards a better tomorrow.

CHAPTER NINE

THE ART OF THE TELL

"Seek out that particular mental attribute which makes you feel most deeply and vitally alive, along with which comes the inner voice which says, 'This is the real me,' and when you have found that attitude, follow it."

—WILLIAM JAMES

As the black and white cartoon begins, a grinning Uncle Sam figure swaggers onto the screen, sporting a button that reads loudly, "I Like Ike!" Cheerful music accompanies his walk, and other smiling cartoon characters bound into the screen—painters, farmers, chefs, firefighters, mothers pushing strollers. They all carry signs emblazoned "IKE." Singers chant in the background: "You like Ike! I like Ike! Everybody likes Ike!"[232]

General Dwight D. Eisenhower, America's thirty-fourth president, was a war hero. As Supreme Allied Commander during WWII, he led the army of troops who liberated Europe. There

---

232 "1952 Eisenhower Political Ad - I Like Ike - Presidential Campaign Ad." *YouTube.* February 14, 2012.

was little doubt Ike was strong and competent as a military commander. But his TV ad says nothing about Eisenhower's war time experience, intelligence, or leadership skills. Instead, the singing cartoon characters, designed by the animator Roy Disney, focus purely on "Everybody likes Ike!"

This was 1952 and advertising experts were taking charge of political campaigns. Likeability would headline their efforts. Rosser Reeves, an ad executive, wanted to champion Eisenhower's likeability. According to Claire Bond Potter, professor of history at the New School, Reeves worried about what he called Eisenhower's "inept" speaking style, so he put him in "controlled settings where his optimism, self-confidence, humor and nonpartisanship could be emphasized over his political inexperience."[233]

Before neuroscience findings, prior to the era of political televised debates, before the Gallup polls—Dwight D. Eisenhower understood the critical power of establishing an emotional connection with voters. His attachment to the American public was so strong that he had an overall approval rating of 66 percent for all eight years of his presidency!

Eisenhower got more than his money's worth from his marketing team. Another Eisenhower political ad discusses the general's leadership experience but fails to list his war victories. The spot doesn't recite his opponent's flaws or Eisenhower's good qualities. Instead, the ad tells a story.

A good story is the best vehicle for bonding and victory. The newer TV ad opens by showing Eisenhower as an everyday citi-

233 Ibid, Potter.

zen, beginning with his humble roots in Abilene, Kansas. Then, Ike is portrayed as a war hero. Images of the Arc de Triomphe in Paris appear, along with descriptions of Eisenhower's critical leadership to help America defeat the Nazis and win WWII.

The ad then creates a threat and stokes the audience's fear. A commentator asks, "The big question: 'General, if war comes, is this country really ready?'" Eisenhower is shown answering the commentator decisively: "It is not. The administration has spent many billions of dollars, yet today, we haven't enough tanks for the fighting in Korea. It is time for a change." Eisenhower establishes the villain responsible for the perceived threat, blaming the current administration—and offers himself as the solution.

The ad resumes, showing clips of Eisenhower with foreign leaders, and describes Ike as the hero that America needs. It ends with an image of Eisenhower lifting his arms above his head at the Republican National Convention: victory.[234]

Eisenhower campaigned on a narrative. He had plenty of work experience to discuss, and no shortage of ideological principles, but that's not what he marched with. Instead, he crafted a story which began with his humble roots, moved to his wartime leadership, and ended with him being recast from general to president: Commander in Chief. He was able to produce the first truly powerful presidential commercial in TV history.

One ad focused on likability, and one told a story. When you're trying to craft communication that creates an emotional connection with voters—it doesn't get better than that.

234 "1952 Dwight Eisenhower for President Campaign Ad." *YouTube*. September 8, 2009.

STORYTELLING: THE POLITICIAN'S BEST WEAPON

Stories make up close to 65 percent of our conversations.[235] For over 40,000 years, we've been communicating through stories. Jesus instructed his followers with parables, and Aesop with fables. The ancient Greeks and Romans built their religion around stories, as did the Norse and the Egyptians. Stories have shown up in every culture, in every land, almost since the dawn of humanity.

According to Dale Raphael Goldberg:

> We use storytelling as a way of gaining allies, conveying ideas, and seeking empathy. You might share a story with your colleague about an interesting trip you took or tell your spouse about a rough day at work. You might tell a story to your children as a way of teaching them.[236]

When we look at information by reading written text, two areas of the brain are activated, Broca's area and Wernicke's area. These cerebral centers process language and translate it into meaning. However, when we hear a story, additional areas of the brain get aroused, which helps process the language and translate it. Stories get the whole brain humming.[237] In a study on neural coupling, both a listener and a storyteller were measured by fMRI. When the storyteller's brain displayed activity in one specific area, the listener showed the exact same activity in the identical part of their brain. Dale Goldberg says, "In other words, simply by

---

235 Hsu, Jeremy. "The Secrets of Storytelling: Why We Love a Good Yarn." *Scientific American Mind*. August 2008.

236 Goldberg, Dale Raphael. "The Science of Storytelling." *Polymath Innovations*. January 9, 2017.

237 Ibid, Hsu.

telling a story, the storyteller could plant thoughts and emotions in the brain of the listener."[238]

We are hardwired to communicate through narrative. Goldberg writes, "Broken down into the simplest form, a story is a connection of cause and effect, and that is exactly how we think. We create narratives in our minds to help us justify and understand our decisions." The reason we need the narrative can be traced back to our earliest efforts at survival. To exist, humans innately look for patterns and causalities.[239] We instinctively try to discover why a certain event happened: What caused it? How can I do it again? Or what can I do to avoid it next time?

The brain's ability to recognize and remember patterns is what allows us to tell the difference between a tiger and a tree. Once the pattern is identified, the brain acts on autopilot as we discussed in chapter 1, determining if we're dealing with friend or foe. Is this situation dangerous, or is it safe? For example, an entire generation of beachgoers that watched the movie "Jaws" was sensitized to feel anxious when they went swimming in the ocean.

Stories capitalize on these patterns and provide an avenue to stroll on because they place the pattern down the center of a narrative, as its theme. Famed political strategist Mark McKinnon, who advised President George W. Bush and John McCain, says forming a story is a critical step candidates must take to help voters organize the various data they're presented with: "Every election,

---

238 Ibid, Goldberg.

239 Stephens, Greg J., Lauren J. Silbert, and Uri Hasson. "Speaker-Listener Neural Coupling Underlies Successful Communication." *Neuroscience, Psychological and Cognitive Sciences.* July 26, 2010. 107(32): 14425-30.

we're bombarded by billions of bits of information, and we want it organized so it has meaning...Voters think in very simple ways. They want things communicated in an organized, compelling, but simple fashion. There has to be a narrative arc."[240]

This narrative arc answers the question many voters start with: "I see threats to my survival—why are they there, how I can avoid them, and who will help me?" A story clarifies that pattern and helps voters find solutions to manage these survival questions.

Stories also provide context—which connects to our experience—and emotion, which lays the story down in our primitive limbic system to make it deeply memorable. The more emotion in the story—either positive or negative—the more we pay attention. The more we pay attention, the better we'll remember the message and the more meaning it has for us. In fact, "messages delivered as stories can be up to 22 times more memorable than just the facts."[241]

Stories evoke how we feel, and they give us moral options for how to act. The emotional journey of the story encourages us to alter our behavior for the better. Narratives link events and information and fuse together both an emotional and a behavioral response.

Stories are engaging, memorable, and they have the power to

240 Klein, Sarah, Tom Mason, and Mark McKinnon. "How to Win an Election | Op-Docs." *YouTube.* February 18, 2016.

241 Zandan, Noah. "The Science of Stories: How Stories Impact Our Brains." *Communication Analytics Platform - Quantified Communications.*

move people to action. These are powerful motivators for any political candidate looking to connect to an audience of voters!

Neuromarketing, or the field of persuasion science, is nearly twenty years old. Dr. Christophe Morin, an expert in the field of advertising on the brain of adolescents and young adults says, "To be persuasive, target your messaging to your customer's primal brain." Morin adds that "because of the dominance of the primal brain, we like to say that persuasion is a bottom-up effect. So to optimize your chances of getting results, you need to first and foremost make your messages friendly to the primal brain."[242]

Morin believes a story must contain "persuasion biases." Initially, a story must be **personal** because the primal brain "has no patience or empathy for anything that does not immediately concern its well-being. This primitive brain scans for threats before it attends to pleasure."

Second, the story must be **memorable** by placing the most important content at the beginning and then repeating it at the end. And, a story must be **emotional** because the primal brain is triggered by emotions, and emotions trip off neurochemicals that process and remember information. Dr. Morin concludes, "In fact, you simply can't remember events unless you have a strong "emotional cocktail...No emotion, no decisions."

Tell your audience a story—make it beautiful, or sad, inspiring, or scary. Make it *emotional*. Get your listeners' brains to synchronize with yours and move them to action.

242 Morin, Christophe. "Neuromarketing." Interview with Roger Dooley. October 7, 2019.

At a campaign stop in Columbus, Ohio—a state with a long coal-mining history—Hillary Clinton made a comment that she later described as the most regrettable moment in her campaign.[243] To an audience packed with people connected to coal-mining, she said, "We're going to put a lot of coal miners and coal companies out of business."

Ironically, Hillary was trying to inspire her audience. The message she wanted to communicate was that she had a plan to create hundreds of new jobs in Ohio by promoting and developing the clean energy industry. But the sound bite no one could forget was her promise to put coal miners out of work. Her gaffe would have hurt her anywhere—but it especially hurt in Ohio, a state she ended up losing to Donald Trump. And remember, no Republican has ever won the White House without winning Ohio!

To tailor your story to each unique audience, it's best to have an arsenal of personal tales ready to relate. These stories should not be just random bits of history from your life—they should be intentionally chosen, and thematically driven.

Make a list of your values and brainstorm stories from your life that testify to those different values. Ahead of campaign stops, as you gather data about that community, think of stories that will establish common ground with those voters.

Study your life! You can draw upon any number of personal experiences and bring them to the table as points of connection.

---

243 Relman, Eliza. "Hillary Clinton: Here's the Misstep from the Campaign I Regret the Most." *Business Insider.* September 6, 2017.

Don't be afraid to be vulnerable with your audience. Real stories about you demonstrate your humanity and relatability. That, in turn, makes voters feel safe, emotionally connected to you, and most importantly, makes them *like* you and feel understood. That translates to votes.

Your goal as a candidate is to align *your story* with the *voters' emotional needs*. If you do that, you'll create a positive feedback loop between yourself and voters. As you share stories, they'll see you as authentic and real and increasingly feel closer to you. Consequently, there's a domino effect whereby you'll feel affirmed and demonstrate more confidence and authenticity. The result: they'll feel that you understand them, and you'll feel they understand you. That's the goal!

CREATING YOUR MASTER NARRATIVE

Every candidate is a human being with a personal history and story to tell. To connect emotionally with voters, you need to tell *your* story. When crafting a compelling personal narrative, you need to know who you are, what you stand for, and what you have to offer.

When Bill Clinton campaigned in 1992, he was initially perceived as a two-bit hick governor from a small southern state. Rather than allow those criticisms to stick, Clinton—a consummate retail politician—spun his personal experience into the web of his appeal, advertising himself as "The Man from Hope." By owning his association with Hope, Arkansas—a small town and Clinton's boyhood home—he applied the connotations of "Hope" to present himself as the candidate that could restore faith, hope, and optimism to a Jimmy-Carter-jaded America.

Clinton went on to discuss his "small state" experience as proof of his attachment to the American people: he was from a small town, where he knew almost everyone's name. He built his master narrative upon a foundation of relating to common people and making them believe that he was just like them. The story stuck, people were hooked, and Clinton's populist homespun narrative helped carry him to victory.

Studies have shown that our brains are more attuned to marketing messages presented as narratives than just "lists of facts." This is a valuable finding for campaign ad consultants who see the sharing of a candidate's story as their primary goal.

Media is drawn to good stories. Personal narratives are a vehicle to get your side heard, even if you don't have an oversized budget. According to Brendan Steinhauser and Josh Eboch, paid media, "if done strategically, can help an underdog candidate with a great story to tell beat big-money rivals."[244]

Dan McCready, a Democrat and small business owner, ran in 2018 for Congress in North Carolina's Ninth District. McCready, a thirty-five-year-old father of four, is a good example of a candidate who never held elected office and almost flipped a deep red district that hadn't elected a Democrat since 1963. McCready ran on his personal story:

> I built trust with voters by talking about what motivated me to serve. I felt a calling to serve because I thought politicians needed to bring our country together, not tear it apart. I explained to voters that I

---

244 Steinhauser, Brendan, and Josh Eboch. "A Playbook for the Midterm's Insurgent Candidates." *VoterTrove. com*. August 6, 2018.

had a similar calling after Sept. 11, 2001, which led me to join the Marine Corps. I wasn't afraid to show how my faith led me to run, and then helped me press on through challenging times. I likewise emphasized my business experience. When I built a solar energy company, I collaborated with Republicans and Democrats to put people to work.[245]

McCready lost in a general special election after the North Carolina State Board of Elections called for a new election in the district following a months-long inquiry into alleged absentee ballot fraud. McCready felt this way about the election outcome: "In the end, voters told me they trusted me because they got the real me. It's a great lesson. We all have our own stories to tell. Lead with the heart, and the rest will follow."

Although conventional wisdom assumes that the candidate with the most money and name recognition wins, Steinhauser believes that if you identify and target your audience with a candidate's compelling story and run a multichannel communications offensive, you will develop an audience that will show up at the polls on primary day. In 2017, Republican Dan Crenshaw of Texas was another novice Congressional candidate with a personal story to sell.

At a time when more veterans are winning political office—like Martha McSally and Tulsi Gabbard—Crenshaw had a unique story to relate. He was wounded by an IED while serving in combat as a Navy Seal. He lost his right eye in battle and now proudly wears his familiar eye patch. He holds a master's degree

---

245 McCready, Dan. "I Almost Flipped a Deep Red District. Here's What I Learned." *The New York Times,* October 14, 2019.

in public health from Harvard. His background and his desire to win made the thirty-three-year-old Crenshaw's story compelling.

Between online branding, knocking on thousands of doors, and volunteers placing tens of thousands of phone calls, the Crenshaw campaign was able to refine their digital advertising to drive voters to early voting and on primary day. Steinhauser and Eboch comment:

> More than 20,000 voters turned out to cast their runoff ballot for the Navy SEAL who had given his right eye for his country and still wasn't done serving. On May 22nd, Dan Crenshaw, who had been essentially unknown in his own district, earned nearly 70 percent of the vote—the largest margin of victory for any congressional candidate that night in Texas…The candidate with the most money and the highest name ID doesn't always win. A good candidate with a great story can overcome even the biggest obstacles in campaigns.

Your narrative is your curb appeal. Think of Eisenhower's storytelling ad: in one minute, he presented a narrative of who he was, what mattered to him, and what problems he intended to solve. He offered himself to voters as an everyday American who rose from humble roots to greatness as a war hero.

Use your master narrative to communicate why you are the right person to be elected and why the right person *right now*. Blend your story with what's happening currently in society. What are the major social and cultural trends and issues? What do people feel needs to be addressed and changed? And why are you qualified, in particular, to lead? The story you share with voters must provide a viable answer to those questions.

Your master narrative should be an appetizing mixture of the following ingredients:

- Your life story and experiences
- Your principles, ideals, and vision
- Your focus on what voters need

When you mix those elements together and bake it into a story, the effect is appetizing.

When I meet with candidates to form their narratives, I work to get a comprehensive portrait of their personality. In my interview, I tease out the most compelling aspects of their life history and values. Through lots of questions, quizzes, and responses, I gather information about many of these key points:

- What matters to you?
- Who are the important people in your life, both past and present?
- Where do you come from? What was it like growing up?
- What have been your successes and failures?
- What have been the happiest moments of your life, and what down periods have you experienced?
- What has your work meant to you? What do your personal relationships mean to you?
- What social and cultural issues are you really concerned about?
- What do you have a passion for?
- What are your wishes, fears, values, strengths, weaknesses?

I gather lots of other information, too. If I was working with you,

I'd want to know what stories you could tell me about how you relate to your peers, learn from mentors, and problem-solve with colleagues. I want to understand how you will handle stress, conflict, and difficult issues that are presented to you.

A typical person's life is a chronology of facts, experiences, and emotion. But once you've assembled a full and complete picture of your history and values, you can begin crafting the master narrative. Identify the needs your voters want met (such as clean air and water, healthcare, and housing) and adopt those as your themes. As I tell candidates: we are all cloned. There are only so many human themes. And there are only some many variations on those themes. Ultimately, your goal is to come up with a narrative that is authentic to you, fits the times and location, and is inspiring to voters. Hit those points, and you will connect at the voter's gut level.

CAMPAIGNING ON A STORY: MCKINNON'S MODEL

George W. Bush managed to keep his hands on the reins of his own branding, largely thanks to the help of his chief media advisor, Mark McKinnon. McKinnon's strategy for helping Bush ride into the White House revolved around storytelling.

In an op-ed documentary titled *How to Win an Election*, McKinnon states, "The stakes of telling a good story in politics are winning or losing. Good stories win. Campaigns without a story lose."[246]

McKinnon, co-host with John Heilemann of the award-nominated

---

246 Klein, Sarah, Tom Mason, and Mark McKinnon. "How to Win an Election | Op-Docs." *YouTube*. February 18, 2016.

documentary political cable show *The Circus* and chief media advisor to both Bush and John McCain, established steps to create a narrative arc that would offer voters a compelling story, something he calls a "filter." McKinnon's steps serve to explain to voters the pattern behind the seemingly disconnected data they're dealing with.[247]

1. **Identify a threat and/or an opportunity.** By either stoking fear (through identifying a threat) or hope (through identifying an opportunity), the story aims at the gut and seizes on voters' emotions immediately. This emotionally arousing start makes listeners alert, engaged, and invested in finding the answer.

2. **Establish victims of the threat or denied opportunity.** Establishing victims does two things: first, it shows any voter who feels like a victim that they are seen, cared about, and heard. Second, it promotes a clear need for a new leader.

3. **Suggest villains that impose the threat or threaten opportunity.** Creating a villain elevates the candidate as the one who knows how to beat them.

4. **Propose solutions.** Offering solutions proves to voters that the candidate can turn around a bad situation, give them hope, and lead them into an improved future.

5. **Reveal the hero.** The hero, of course, is the candidate. By this point in the story, the stakes have been raised, emotions have been aroused, voters are invested and ready to place their bet on a convincing hero.

Let's take a closer look at how a candidate can incorporate McKinnon's formula into one brief campaign ad. Twenty-eight-year

247 Ibid, Klein

old Alexandria Ocasio-Cortez (AOC), 2018 winner of New York's Fourteenth Congressional District, applied McKinnon's formula masterfully to create a viral campaign ad which helped her topple ten-term incumbent congressman Joe Crowley. She became the youngest woman ever elected to Congress. Political commentators across the country were dumbfounded by her success. She had far less funding, fewer political ties than Crowley, and she was a political newcomer. However, one look at her campaign ad helps explain her victory.

AOC begins, "Women like me aren't supposed to run for office. I wasn't born to a wealthy or powerful family: mother from Puerto Rico; dad from the South Bronx. I was born in a place where your zip code determines your destiny." Ocasio-Cortez is pictured tying back her hair and applying mascara in a modest bathroom. From the start of her ad, she presents herself as someone voters can relate to.

Ocasio-Cortez goes on to list her emotional connections with voters in her district and describes the frustrations many of them feel. She identifies **the threat**, and implies that **the villain** is Joe Crowley: "But after twenty years of the same representation, we have to ask, who has New York been changing for? Every day gets harder for working families like mine to get by. The rent gets higher, healthcare covers less, and our income stays the same. It's clear that these changes haven't been for us..." Her words show that **the victims** of Crowley's supposed villainy are the people of her district—including her.

Ocasio-Cortez then identifies herself as **the hero**: "We deserve a champion. It's time to fight for a New York that working families can afford. That's why I'm running for Congress." She lists her political goals and **proposed solutions**. Finally, she ends with hope and inspiration: "We can do it now. It doesn't take one hundred years to do this. It takes political courage. A New York for the many is possible. It's time for one of us."[248]

Regardless whether you share AOC's far-left progressive political beliefs, this ad received millions of views.[249] *Adweek* raved about it, saying:

> Fleeting hallmarks of empathy and authenticity are everywhere in this work. For all the talk of storytelling, the little more than two minutes in the film is a master class in compacting passion, honesty and, yes, empathy and authenticity into a compelling package. Ocasio-Cortez isn't merely telling her story; she's telling everyone's story in the district.[250]

AOC had less money. She had less experience. She had no backing from the Democratic Party. She lacked a powerful ground game. She wrote the ad herself and utilized the help of volunteers to get it produced.

But what did she do so successfully? She nailed the emotional connection. Using her story, she was able to highlight her values and passion in a way that convinced voters she was the real deal hero that they needed. AOC now has over 4 million Twitter followers, and with her New Green Deal, and as a member of

248 Ocasio-Cortez, Alexandria. "The Courage to Change | Alexandria Ocasio-Cortez." *YouTube*. May 30, 2018.

249 Sherman, Erik. "The DIY Viral Ad That Will Change Politics Forever." *Inc*. June 29, 2018.

250 Zanger, Doug. "Alexandria Ocasio-Cortez Went DIY on Her Campaign Ad, and It's a Runaway Hit." *Adweek*. June 27, 2018.

four Congresswomen known as "The Squad," she has become a disruptive, controversial politician in Congress. Some in the media feel she has become such a powerful competitor to House Speaker Nancy Pelosi that they even call AOC "Madam Speaker." But there's no question she used wisely McKinnon's storytelling formula as a powerful campaign tool to win her election.

Think of storytelling as the small, smooth stone that David used to defeat Goliath. You don't have to be overpowering to win, if you get the aim right.

As McKinnon explains, the narrative should serve to frame your story for the current times. When McKinnon was working with George W. Bush in 2000, Bush had to overcome his formidable opponent, Al Gore. Gore, two-term vice-president, had high name recognition. He hoped to ride into the White House on Bill Clinton's coattail, so the story Bush's campaign told voters was targeted against Clinton. Because of President Clinton's affair with his White House intern Monica Lewinsky, the story threat proposed was that Americans faced diminished morality and values. The victims were the American people, and President Clinton was the villain responsible for the moral degradation of the country. Bush offered his own values and ideals as the solution and presented himself as a hero.

In 2004, there was a different cultural context, so the narrative arc changed along with it. The terrorist attacks of 9/11 had traumatized the American mindset, and that's where McKinnon started. The new threat was terrorism, and the victims were Americans. The villain was Osama bin Laden. Bush's re-election campaign touted the military efforts he'd made to combat terrorism and emphasized the need for continuity and steady leadership. Once again, Bush presented himself as the hero who could be counted on to guide the country through an era of increasing terrorist threat. Despite low approval ratings and repeated opposition attacks against his personal morals, President Bush managed to convince the American people that he deserved a second term.

Candidates need to provide voters with a full portrait of who they are. You must convince voters that you have the passion, values, and the experience to save them from a perceived threat and bring them a hopeful opportunity. If you fail to do that, you fail.

TIPS FOR POWERFUL STORYTELLING

McKinnon's storytelling formula gets to a larger truth: some forms of communication light up the brain, and others leave it dim. Emotional or interesting communication creates persuasive brain synchronization. Bad communication bores us and we quickly tune out.

Stories are a powerful way to get the brain of your listeners blazing with activity. Stories can wake up tuned-out listeners, secure their attention, and help you establish yourself as relatable and likable—provided, that is, your story is told *well*. I'm sure that you've listened to someone relate a painfully long-winded or boring anecdote. A poorly told story makes listeners want to run for the hills. Fortunately, there's plenty of research that spells out exactly what makes for rich, engaging communication.

There's a reason the Pro-Choice movement doesn't call itself "Anti-Life." There's a reason the Pro-Lifers don't call themselves "Anti-Choice," and "Global Warming" is now termed "Climate Change." Or, that the "Estate Tax" is not called the "Death Tax." Words pack a punch, and in the political realm, you want to make the most of words with positive connotations.

Dr. Frank Luntz is the guru of political focus groups who pioneered the "Instant Response" focus group method. In his book *Words that Work*, Luntz says that effective words are interactive, direct, and clear.[251] There are seven words he has found especially persuasive in politics:

1. *Consequence*: conveys having a stake in something
2. *Impact:* implies a measurable difference that can be felt or heard
3. *Diplomacy*: delivers peace of mind to somebody
4. *Dialogue*: delivers peace of mind, through interactive communication with voters
5. *Reliability*: shows your trustworthiness
6. *Mission*: explains what you do, why you do it, and why you care
7. *Commitment*: connects passion and devotion to a cause

Your goal is to use words that are loaded with charge that makes voters' minds connect to positive ideas. Pronouns are important, too. Studies on brain measurements using fMRI show that words with a focus on others like, "your," "you," "theirs," and "ours" activate the brain much more than when candidates use words

---

251 Luntz, Frank I. *Words That Work: It's Not What You Say, It's What People Hear.* New York: Hachette Books, 2015.

like "I" or "me."[252] Voters appreciate when candidates speak *to* them rather than *at* them.

Luntz's book title, *Words That Work,* refers to his description of ten rules that promote good communication. By following these rules, candidates connect with their listeners on a gut level and ensure that what they *say* is consistent with what the audience *hears.* I've unpacked for you many of those rules in the sections that follow.

USE EVERYDAY WORDS

Luntz's first two rules are similar: One, use small words. Two, use short sentences.[253] When candidates use highly complex language, or theoretical concepts without examples, they'll "sin" politically. They're boring, they're confusing, and they're targeting the "blue coasts" of the brain, rather than the gut, which means they're failing to make an emotional connection.

Instead, candidates should give simple explanations. They should speak in the present tense and make their ideas actionable—not theoretical.

When John McCain campaigned for president in 2008, he discovered the impact of shifting his language during a stop in south-central Pennsylvania. Politico describes McCain's speech, and the effect on his audience:

---

252 Diaz, Michele T. and Gregory McCarthy. "A Comparison of Brain Activity Evoked by Single Content and Function Words: An fMRI Investigation of Implicit Word Processing." *Brain Research.* July 28, 2010. 1282: 38–49.

253 Ibid, Luntz.

The Republican nominee had opened by promising a country-over-party approach to politics, recalling his compromises with Democrats like Ted Kennedy: 'We'll have our disagreements, but we've got to be respectful.' The Republican crowd sat in silence. McCain then denounced Vladimir Putin's incursion into independent Georgia, warning that 'history is often made in remote, obscure places.' No one seemed interested in that remote and obscure place.

McCain couldn't connect with the crowd, until he unleashed a garbled riff about how Congress shouldn't be on recess when gasoline prices were soaring. 'My friends,' he said, 'the message we want to send to Washington, D.C. is: "Come back off your vacation, go back to Washington, fix our energy problems, and drill and drill now, drill offshore and drill now!"'...The York Expo Center suddenly erupted with raucous cheers.[254]

McCain's initial words were cerebral and boring: "disagreements," "respectful," "remote," and "obscure." Although these aren't complex vocabulary words, they lack the simplicity that makes phrases visceral and memorable. When he simplified his words and intensified them—"Drill, and drill now!"—the crowd's brain's lit up and they roared in approval.

Half the adults in the US can't read a book written at an eighth-grade level. Therefore, it's important for candidates to explain their ideas as they would to a class of sixth graders.[255] Words speak volumes about where you're from, and how relatable you might be. As voters listen to you, they are evaluating you: "Is this

---

254 Grunwald, Michael, Jesus Rodriguez, and Jack Shafer. "How Everything Became the Culture War." *POLITICO*. November/December 2018.

255 Strauss, Valerie. "Hiding in Plain Sight: The Adult Literacy Crisis." *The Washington Post*. November 1, 2016.

candidate speaking my language? Does this person understand someone like me?" If you use language voters don't understand, the assumption is that you wouldn't understand them, either.

Voters don't want to hear technical terms or pretentious vocabulary—like "irrational exuberance," "lockbox," or "gerrymander." Most memorable political phrases have been composed of simple words, with straightforward grammatical structure. Consider the following:

- "Speak softly and carry a big stick."—Theodore Roosevelt, 1900
- "The only thing we have to fear is fear itself."—Franklin Delano Roosevelt, 1932
- "Ask not what your country can do for you—ask what you can do for your country."—John F. Kennedy, 1961
- "I have a dream..."—Martin Luther King Jr., 1963
- "Mr. Gorbachev, tear down this wall!"—Ronald Reagan, 1987
- "Read my lips: no new taxes!"—George H. W. Bush, 1988
- "When they go low, we go high."—Michelle Obama, 2016

Compare those simple, straightforward phrases with the forgettable slogans of Al Gore, a candidate who gravitated towards more theoretical, complex speech: "Prosperity and Progress" and "Prosperity for America's Families." Hillary Clinton's multisyllable words in her slogan, "Stronger Together," were far less memorable than the phrase some voters coined for her: "I'm With Her." On the other hand, Trump's visceral gifting was apparent in his coining of such stuck-in-your-head phrases as "Make America Great Again," "Build that Wall," "Lock Her Up!", and "Drain the Swamp!"

Candidates should practice using everyday language through role play exercises with their campaign teams and practice using McKinnon's storytelling formula. Remember that audiences need to recognize something in your story is there for *them*. The goal is to be memorable, which requires clear language, brevity, and everyday words. Save the technical language for the policy meetings!

INCORPORATE DRAMA

The stagecraft optics Donald Trump created during his appearance at the Republican National Convention in 2016 earned comparisons to Batman emerging from the Batcave.

While Queen's "We Are the Champions" blasted through speakers in the giant auditorium, Trump emerged in silhouette, with brilliant lights backing him, diffused in a hazy fog. As he walked forward, a podium rose up from the floor as if by magic. Finally, the lights shone on Trump's face. To an audience which included many fierce "Never Trumpers" within his own party, Trump smiled and spoke: "We're going to win! We're going to win so big."

Nominee Trump's gift for theatrics gave all RNC viewers the drama they might have expected from a reality TV star. He epitomized Luntz's fifth rule: "Novelty is important. Offer something new."[256]

You don't need Queen playing at one hundred decibels or fancy lighting to create this effect. Often, the impact is just as powerful when told through a good story.

---

256 Ibid, Luntz.

Modern-day audiences are media-saturated and have shorter attention spans than before our attachment to devices took hold in 2000.[257] Candidates, therefore, would be wise to incorporate drama into their messaging. A powerful story can get the job done, and additional special effects don't hurt.

USE SENSORY LANGUAGE

There's a difference between saying, "The singer had a pleasing voice," versus "The singer had a velvet voice." The latter example sticks in our heads and helps us to understand the beauty, smoothness, and warmth of a singer's voice far more than the first example. Changing just a word increases understanding and resonates more powerfully in the brain.

When you read sensory words like "velvet," "perfume," or "coffee," your brain lights up like the Fourth of July fireworks. Words that activate our senses wake up the parts of our brains that normally lie dormant when we're only processing language. Sensory language activates additional neural tracks which process feeling, seeing, smelling, and hearing. Then oxytocin gets released to establish a bond.

It's why Luntz's sixth rule is "Sound and texture matter. You have to construct your language and make it pleasurable to hear and repeat."[258]

According to Emory University psychologist Dr. Drew Westen, the more neural tracks a speaker's message activates in the

257 McSpadden, Kevin. "Science: You Now Have a Shorter Attention Span Than a Goldfish." *Time*. May 14, 2015.

258 Ibid, Luntz.

brain with words, images, and tone, the better the message is reinforced.[259] Sensory language—and all the brain-fireworks that go along with it—establishes loads of neural connections to make the message appealing, and the more likely it will make an emotional connection.

President John F. Kennedy was masterful at using sensory images. Consider his use of imagery in his 1961 inaugural address: "together let us explore the stars, conquer the deserts, eradicate disease, tap the ocean depths and encourage the arts and commerce."[260] Kennedy makes use of stunning images and chooses words with musical vowels and soft consonants, which sound beautiful: "stars," "deserts," "depths," "encourage," and "commerce," which all work to create a pleasing sound texture.

Effective candidates use words, emotions, stories, images, analogies, metaphors, sounds, and music to be emotionally resonant and create an emotional bond with listeners.

USE INTERESTING RHETORIC AND FIGURATIVE LANGUAGE

In his 2005 Inaugural Address, George W. Bush said, "By our efforts, we have lit a fire as well. A fire in the minds of men. It warms those who feel its power. It burns those who fight its progress. And one day this untamed fire of freedom will reach the darkest corners of our world."[261]

---

259 Ibid, Westen.

260 "Transcript of President John F. Kennedys Inaugural Address (1961)." Our Documents - Interstate Commerce Act (1887).

261 "President Bush's Second Inaugural Address." *NPR*. January 20, 2005.

Bush's stirring metaphor epitomizes Luntz's eighth rule: "create visuals: paint the picture."[262]

Linguists estimate that we use metaphors like the "fire in the minds" image about every twenty-five words.[263] We think with metaphors. If you've ever thought to yourself, "I feel down," instead of "I feel sad," you've swapped out a figurative term for a literal term. In other words, you're thinking metaphorically.

Metaphors are embedded in our everyday language. Because we're used to them, they go unnoticed. However, metaphors are powerful tools of persuasion, especially for politicians. Emerging psychological and neuroscience research shows that a single metaphor can have profound consequences in how we think about issues. If candidates and politicians are armed with the ability to use these powerful tools, they can shape opinions.

In a series of five experiments, Paul Thibodeau and Lera Boroditsky from Stanford University have shown how powerful and influential metaphors can be. In one study, participants were presented with brief passages about a crime in a hypothetical city. Half of the passages described the crime as a virus, infecting the city. The other half described the crime as a beast, preying on the city. In all other ways, the passages were identical.[264]

Those key metaphors changed the participants' beliefs about how the crime should be legally addressed. When asked to come up

262 Ibid, Luntz.

263 Rathje, Steve. "Metaphors Can Change Our Opinions in Ways We Don't Even Realize." *Quartz*. March 31, 2018.

264 Yong, Ed. "Is Crime a Virus or a Beast?" *National Geographic*. February 23, 2011.

with consequences for the crime, those who read the passage with the beast metaphor thought the crime should be dealt with by using more punitive solutions, including more jail time. Those who read the passage with the virus metaphor thought the crime should be addressed using more palliative measures, like social reform.

Metaphors are useful, because they allow us to substitute a complex and remote concept with a term that feels simpler and more familiar. For instance, when Obama wanted to discuss the importance of equality in our nation in his 2009 inaugural speech, he described it as a "precious gift."[265] The implication was that equality should be valued, cherished, treasured, and protected.

Metaphors are powerful because they activate areas of the brain where emotion resides. These brain regions would stay dark if we were just fed facts. For instance, if you read a sentence, "He had a rough day," instead of "He had a bad day," the part of your brain associated with texture lights up. Metaphors turn a boring speech into something which is visceral, persuasive, and emotionally evocative.

Don't neglect other tried-and-true elements of good rhetoric, either! Make sure your speeches *sound* compelling and emotionally arousing. President Trump's rallies run on metaphoric emotional fuel.

Candidates should watch videos of powerful speakers like Dr. Martin Luther King Jr., John F. Kennedy, or Ronald Reagan. Notice their tone and cadence. Notice their use of repetition and

265 Obama, Barack. "Obama Inaguration Speech." *Huffington Post*. December 6, 2017.

the way they inspire their audience through brain synchronization. Strong oratory is a skill that can be honed, practiced, and used for powerful effect.

NESTLE THE FACTS INTO A STORY

Facts, data, and statistics are important. Political policies are shaped around research and facts. But facts are boring. How, then, do you discuss data that informs voters but also makes them feel and care?

Candidates who are naturally cerebral, like Paul Ryan, Mitt Romney, Jeb Bush, or Hillary Clinton, don't have to discard data points altogether when giving speeches—they should rev up listeners' brains by embedding the facts within a story.

Like pet owners hide a dog's medication inside a mouthful of peanut-butter, facts can be swallowed and digested—as long as there's an appealing vehicle of delivery. The information must be bonded to emotion through a story. Facts are important, but without a story, facts become forgettable. *Within* a story, facts become memorable and actionable, so Luntz names as his tenth rule "provide context and explain relevance."[266]

This is not *The Art of the Deal*.[267] This is "The Art of the Tell."[268] You can grab listeners' attention by packaging your data within

---

266 Ibid, Luntz.

267 Trump, Donald, and Tony Schwartz. *Trump: The Art of the Deal*. New York: Ballantine Books, 2017.

268 Guber, Peter. *Tell to Win: Connect, Persuade, and Triumph with the Hidden Power of Story*. New York: Crown Publishers, 2013.

a story, thereby making your content knowledgeable and interesting.

HAVE A POINT

Most everyone has attended a wedding where the toasts went on painfully long. As mesmerizing as a good story can be, long-winded anecdotes can be annoying to listen to and alienate your audience rather than make them like you. Your stories should ultimately be a vehicle for a message—so have a point.

If a story goes on and on, and a politician doesn't seem to know when to stop talking, the message becomes boring, alienating, and may ultimately seem arrogant, awkward, and out-of-touch.

Storytelling is an incredible tool for effective communication. If you harness this skill well, you will be off to the races, and the audience will be wanting to saddle up too. Voters will be engaged and tuned in. They will like you and view you as humble and authentic.

And, if you get the narrative right—they'll recognize you as the hero they need.

THE FUTURE OF STORYTELLING

During the presidential race of 2016, a four-person team of neu-roscientists was working on a stealth project in Manhattan, New York. Their objective: develop a way to measure how different stimuli in the brain affect our emotions. Called Spark Brainwave, this new tool was intended to be the holy grail of political marketing. By watching and measuring a person's physiological response to a stimulus—such as a campaign ad—the neuroscientists hoped they could develop a model to predict the person's behavior—such as which candidate they would vote for.

Independently, a political campaign company hired Spark Brainwave to study GOP presidential candidate Trump's ads. Trump deployed ads in both Pennsylvania and Florida—states that would be crucial to his win—showing that illegal immigrants would hurt workers by taking their jobs. He positioned himself within this narrative as the only hero who could stop this.

The Spark Brainwave team decided to focus solely on independent voters in both states. The team equipped their voters with a headset to measure electrical signals from the brain through an electroencephalogram (EEG). Researchers also measured electrical signals in the voters' sweat, called the galvanic skin response (GSR), which reflects a person's emotional state. Then, the Spark Brainwave team showed Trump's speeches and campaign ads to a sample of voters. They followed up with a personal interview.

Spencer Garrol, head of Spark Brainwave, was shocked by the results. The team discovered that many independents were really "hidden Trump voters."[269] These supporters fell into two different camps, "those who were afraid to admit to pollsters that they supported Trump because they didn't want to be judged," and "people who honestly believed they didn't know who they'd vote for, but were actually very likely to vote for Trump, based on their physiologic response to his ads and speeches."

269 Lazauskas, Joe. "The Neuroscience Technology That Could Change the 2020 Election." *Medium.* February 10, 2019.

As the voter responses from the ads came in, Garrol said, "We started to realize that a lot of these people—who were answering the poll undecided—were not undecided." In a *Medium* article on the research, Joe Lazauskas reported, "In other words, Spark's neurotechnology revealed something about voters that they didn't even know about themselves."

The chief neuroscientist, Dr. Ryan McGary, became so confident in the team's findings that he bet everyone he could that Trump would win.

HILLARY'S WARNING SIGNS

When Spark Brainwave's team then turned to study Hillary's speeches and ads, they found very different results. Clinton's ads scored poorly. The culprit, researchers concluded, was that she failed to tell a good story.[270]

Hillary's presidential announcement video opens with Clinton telling the story of her mother Dorothy, who was abandoned as a young girl and at age fourteen began working as a housemaid. Lazauskas says, "Listening to it, I was on the edge of my seat. How was her mom saved? This was a side of Clinton I didn't know. But the story stops there, summed up with a generic platitude, followed by a plug reminding us that Clinton is a Methodist. By the thirty-nine-second mark, the ad has abandoned any kind of story in favor of reciting her resume."

When Spark Brainwave researchers showed the ad to independent voters, their engagement "fell off a cliff after the twenty-second

---

270 Ibid.

mark. By the twenty-five-second mark, Clinton's ad was generating one of the lowest engagement scores possible." It failed to grab voters' attention. Lazauskas remarks, "Who knows how starting with a good story would have changed the narrative around Hillary's candidacy—an election that she lost by just 70,000 key votes."

The Spark Brainwave research accurately predicted Trump's win in Florida and Pennsylvania. It also pointed to his winning key states in the Midwest, enough for him to pull an inside straight and win the Electoral College.

Garrol says, "It's not rationally saying: I'm going to vote for this crazy reality TV show guy yelling on TV. But emotionally, he's making me feel something. And, so when I get to the ballot box, my emotional brain is going to (respond to that)."[271]

Garrol's research has rich implications for those running for political office. Focus groups, polls, and surveys don't tell the whole story. A better way to predict whom a person will vote for is to measure their physiological and neurological responses to a candidate's ads and speeches.

The field of biometrics is increasingly used today to read voters' true feelings that they are often reticent to admit. With newer technologies, it's possible to monitor microexpressions on constituents' faces, read positive and negative signals in their tweets, and even tweak search engine algorithms as voters look for news and political information online.

---

271 Ibid.

Using brain scans and facial recognition to uncover voters' true feelings might be seen as dystopian overreach and a George Orwell 1984 rerun. But consider that candidates and campaigns already use databases of consumer preferences—what they read, what music they like—and apply computer algorithms to target their appeals to the voter's gut. With neuropolitics, campaign messages can now be microtargeted to specific voter emotions.

All this data serves to prove when it comes to winning an election, emotion rules the day.

New disruptive technologies claim they can bias a voter's emotions—positively or negatively—to modify their perception for one candidate over another. Unfortunately, this is increasingly true. But, for me, in political campaigning, you can't replace the human interaction—handshake, door-to-door visits, rallies, yard signs, town halls, or bar-b-ques. Nothing creates that positive emotional connection better than individual direct contact and a relatable, personal story.

CONCLUSION

"Elections are won or lost in the marketplace of emotions."

—DR. DREW WESTEN, *THE POLITICAL BRAIN*

On January 17, 2014, a documentary premiered at the Sundance Film Festival titled *Mitt*.[272] The movie poster featured a close-up portrait of Mitt Romney, showing the upper half of his face. Most noticeable in the poster is Mitt's hair: It's sticking up in the back.

It's not smooth or combed. Not like an eight-by-ten-inch glossy. His hair, quite obviously, is out of place.

The documentary features candid footage of Mitt as he navigated his 2008 and 2012 presidential campaigns. The footage of Romney shows a man unlike the stiff, formal, and wooden presidential candidate most voters were programmed to remember.

One clip shows Mitt ironing his shirt cuffs while still wearing the shirt. Another clip shows him wrestling his grandchildren in

---

272 Netflix. "MITT | Official Trailer [HD] | Netflix." *YouTube.* December 18, 2013.

the snow and then all of them riding down the hill in sleds held together with duct tape. Another shot shows him giving his wife, Ann, a light tap on her bum.

What's most revealing are Mitt's observations from the campaign trail. He grimly sums up the description many voters assigned to him: "the flipping Mormon." At one point he admits to his campaign team, "I may be a flawed candidate." On the night of his election loss to Obama, Romney sits quietly in a hotel room in Boston while his family and aides try to comprehend his loss. Finally, Romney says, "By the way, does anyone have the number for the president?" He laughs. It's an easy, authentic laugh. "Hadn't thought about that!"

The reality movie reveals Mitt as the genuine candidate voters never got to know during the 2012 presidential campaign. Although Romney's aides kept the candid footage closely under wraps during the campaign season, Romney finally allowed the documentary to be released two years later. Why?

Perhaps Mitt felt he could afford to be shown as less formal and uptight now that the political stakes weren't so high. Or maybe he realized that the revelation of his humanity in the documentary was more what voters had wanted to see all along. They needed to know Romney was real.

My guess is that Mitt wanted to shed his outward buttoned-up self. However, sometimes he overshot his reveal. Rather than looking authentic, Mitt comes off looking surprisingly odd because his behavior was so far removed from his customary political presentation.

For example, in 2015, Mitt volunteered for a charity event and stepped into a boxing ring with famous heavyweight boxer Evander Holyfield, the only boxer in history to hold undisputed championships in two separate weight categories. Mitt was shirtless, in shiny red boxing shorts. The announcer introduced sixty-eight-year-old Mitt: "...Weighing in at a ready 179 pounds, he'll make his boxing debut here tonight in Salt Lake City, Utah! His political record: one win, and one very big loss."[273] Videos of the match show Mitt cracking up at the joke. Then, he starts moving around the ring, tossing punches at Holyfield.

One day before taking the oath of office as the incoming freshman US Senator from Utah in 2018, Romney continued to step out of his former "play it safe role." He risked his political goodwill by publishing a scathing op-ed on President Trump in *The Washington Post*. He wrote:

> I will act as I would with any president, in or out of my party: I will support policies that I believe are in the best interest of the country and my state, and oppose those that are not...I do not intend to comment on every tweet or fault. But I will speak out against significant statements or actions that are divisive, racist, sexist, anti-immigrant, dishonest or destructive to democratic institutions.[274]

Despite taking heavy incoming flak from fellow Republicans, Romney decided to enter the fray as a moral critic. He came out with both guns blazing and has reloaded his weapon several times since.

---

273 CNN. "Mitt Romney vs. Evander Holyfield." *YouTube*. May 16, 2015.

274 Romney, Mitt. "Mitt Romney: The President Shapes the Public Character of the Nation. Trump's Character Falls Short." *The Washington Post*. January 1, 2019.

Another example of Romney's "reveal" included unmasking an alter ego operating a secret Twitter account under the handle "Pierre Delecto." When asked to confirm that this was his account, he said, "C'est Moi." Tweeting from this alias, Mitt has been caustic in his criticism of President Trump's personality and what he feels are impetuous presidential executive decisions.

Public reactions have ranged from support to derision and anger at his lack of candor. One questions why now, after working hard to turn his political sins into virtues, would freshman Sen. Romney want to hide his identity while protesting the president's personal behavior and decisions that he feels are dangerous and immoral?

Hopefully, this clandestine tweeting effort is not a fallback to his previous sin of being emotionally tone-deaf to his constituents. Rather than rock the boat with a current fellow-party president under impeachment attack, some pundits feel that Romney's newfound chutzpah would have better served him in his 2012 run for the White House.

The public probably didn't know whether to laugh along with Mitt—or be confused by this newly revealed side of his personality. We want our candidates to show their many sides. But when the sides are so incompatible and startling, the voters may wonder: Is this behavior genuine? Why didn't we see this side come out during his campaign in 2012? How do we reconcile these extremes of his personality? Should we applaud or be turned off?

Romney's behavior, regardless whether you approve of it, is different now. Obviously, he feels he must speak out and that his moral outrage is necessary. And he seems to be demonstrably excited about issues and having fun expressing them.

Where Romney was once tentative, he now seems more sure-footed. He's more deliberate in shaping his own branding, seems less canned, and is far less inhibited. His demonstrations of vulnerability in the documentary *Mitt*, and evidence of his humor, show a more empathic quality. He's more confident. As he told USA Today, "My career, my family, my faith: Those define who I am. And so I'm free emotionally...to do entirely what I believe is absolutely right...My future is behind me."[275]

For candidates whose futures are beginning, the ups and downs of Romney's political journey provide important lessons: authenticity and emotional connection are critical to gaining voters' trust—and winning elections.

To paraphrase Kenny Power's eulogy for JFK, "Mitt: We hardly knew ye."

EMOTIONS ARE YOUR CURRENCY

When voters step into the voting booth, their hands are guided by their emotions. They'll vote with their gut, not their brain. Voting is an emotional decision. Think of emotion as the currency that buys votes. When you run an emotionally compelling campaign, your stock rises, your interest increases, your dividends pay more. Not to mention, people are more likely to give you

---

275 King, Ledyard and Christal Hayes. "Mitt Romney: A Solitary GOP Voice Battling Trump for the Soul of the Republican Party." *USA Today*. October 28, 2019.

actual currency in campaign contributions. Voters will bank on you and stick with you.

People may claim that emotion-based decision-making is irresponsible. But it's not. Fundamentally, this is how we function. Neuroscience shows that human connections are made through the arousal of emotion. Our brains are hardwired to listen to our guts. And what drives our gut instincts, our fight-or-flight reactions? It's emotion.

I'm not advocating principles and recommendations that manipulate voters. Using lessons from neuroscience, history, and psychology, my goal is to help you reveal your true self in a way that's memorable, trustworthy, likable, and emotionally compelling.

Emphasizing emotions as a campaign strategy can be anxiety-provoking. Tangible goals, like fundraising, knocking on doors, and developing a ground game, feel much easier to target. Those strategies are important—but equally important is your emotional connection with voters.

Hillary Clinton had a massive fundraising machine and a prolific campaign organization. Al Gore had the full backing of the Democratic Party and was a sitting vice president. George H. W. Bush had an impressive first presidential term and plenty of funding. Mitt Romney had movie-star good looks and piles of cash. But they all struggled to make an emotional connection with voters. And three out of four failed in their quest to grab the political brass ring: the American Presidency.

TAKE ACTION

You've read the book—now it's time for you to act.

Start with an audit to assess which of the 7 deadly political sins you are committing. Enlist people you trust to give you feedback on where you can best improve as a candidate. Studies show that people defensively over-exaggerate what they know about themselves. Take a few personality inventories or insight quizzes to diagnose your deficits.

Ultimately, voters want to be persuaded to like you, value what you have to offer and feel connected. We have an inherent desire to attach and acquire. From a consumer's perspective, a candidate running for office is offering themselves as a product with some of the assurances you'd get when buying other goods. We don't always buy a product because it is the least expensive or more attractively packaged. We feel compelled to obtain items because they instinctively appeal to our need for survival. Whether we're choosing a new car or a new city commissioner, we first must be drawn to that brand and devote a level of trust to what it represents or promises us. If we buy into the promise, we'll likely purchase the product.

As a political candidate you must give a voter something to believe. You can't rely only on talking points or plans to forge the emotional connection between you and the voter. To sell yourself, empathy and understanding are key ingredients. That's what voters will trust.

Once you've defined and identified your political sins, you can begin the process of turning them into virtues. Remember Joe

DiMaggio, who in 1941 hit successfully in fifty-six consecutive games. He put thousands of tally marks on his wall. It takes a lot of practice swings to get as many hits as Joe—but, if you put in the time and hard work, you'll be successful too.

WISH FOR THE WIN

I'm a psychologist, couple's therapist, and political coach. Let me give a piece of advice that touches all these areas.

When you enter a relationship, you don't expect to radically change, but you do expect to grow. Similarly, you don't get involved to change your partner, but you do expect you'll learn together.

As a candidate, your goal is not a complete self-overhaul but to learn communication skills that improve the way you show care to other people.

Politics is a marriage between policy and personality. As Frank Luntz says, "What matters most in politics is personality. It's not issues; it's not image. It's who you are and what you represent."[276]

Speak to voters and make them feel cared for. Relate to each audience so they know you understand their viewpoint and individual needs. Your goal: Be a truer, more authentic, kinder, and more capable human being first and candidate second.

My best advice: follow what *The Like Switch* author Dr. Jack Scha-

---

276 Ibid, Luntz.

fer calls The Golden Rule of Friendship—"If you want people to like you, make them feel good about themselves."

Above all, if you try to tell a voter how to feel, you will lose them. But if you show them how to feel, they're yours.

Make the connection—and win the election.

ACKNOWLEDGMENTS

In completing this book, I have several people I wish to acknowledge. First, I'd like to thank the smartest and nicest person I know: my wife, LeslieBeth (LB). She always provides unconditional love and support. When I was stuck on an idea or couldn't articulate a concept, she was there to figure it out. LB helped me outline the nomenclature of some specific sins and virtues and edited parts of my writing.

I want to thank student interns Christopher Campbell at Ringling College and Thomas Ghebrezgi and Sydney Anderson of New College who spent their time and energy summarizing research studies and articles.

And thanks to Scribe Media for Tom Lane, who assisted with my outline, and Greta Meyers, the scribe who listened for many hours while I dictated the book contents and research to her. And, finally, to my publisher Emily Gindlesparger, whose editorial skills guided me through my revisions.

And I want to thank Mitt and Ann Romney, two decent, sincere, honest, and moral people whom I've had the pleasure to know and work with. Thanks to the former Romney financial campaign staff, Mason Alexander and Kevin Hofmann, who tirelessly worked behind the scenes to coordinate events to make my fundraising job easier and more fun to do. To the Romney team communications director Eric Ferhnstrom and Mitt's wingman, Bob White, thank you for listening to my ideas and believing I had more to offer the campaign than just bundling donations.

Finally, my gratitude to Mark McKinnon, talented political strategist and media consultant to President George W. Bush and Senator John McCain and co-host of the award-nominated political cable show *The Circus*. Mark graciously offered to write the foreword. I am honored by his support and kind words. Mark's pioneering model of storytelling was invaluable to writing this book.

I do not in any way regret the two and a half years of nonstop fundraising and attending debates and retreats to help Mitt Romney be elected president. The time spent traveling was frustrating yet invigorating and a significant life experience that exposed me to the scores of hard-working, involved American patriots and dedicated politicians who want only the best for everyone in our country. The working Joes and the billionaires I hung out with taught me great life lessons.

Today, politics has become a blood sport that is too tribal and partisan. Hopefully, good candidates for public office—at all levels of government—will step up to serve because they are not disillusioned with the process of campaigning and the uncooperative and uncivil behavior of legislators. I encourage those who want to make an impact to get involved and go for it.

Unfortunately, time and hard work invested doesn't guarantee victory. Winning sometimes comes long after the fact. In writing this book, eight years past a painful loss, I hope to help future candidates—Democrat, Republican, or Independent—learn from my experience and succeed where we fell short. That's my triumph.

ABOUT THE AUTHOR

During a prominent career as a clinical and academic psychologist, **DR. WISH** also became a fundraiser, campaign coach, and strategist to political candidates. He served on Mitt Romney's 2012 National Presidential Finance Committee and has advised Republican and Democratic candidates in state, congressional, senatorial, and gubernatorial campaigns.

Listed in *Who's Who in American Men and Women of Science*, and *Who's Who in America*, he has been quoted by over 200 newspapers and magazines, including the *New York Times, USA Today, Time, Newsweek, L.A. Times, Cosmo*, and the *Wall Street Journal*.

Dr. Wish wrote "The Family Experience" syndicated UPI column for the *Boston Globe*, hosted *Psychologically Speaking*, on CBS radio, and was a guest consulting psychologist on *The Good Day Show* at WCVB-TV Boston. Wish has appeared on *Nightline, Good Morning America*, and *The Today Show*. He won the prestigious National Media Award from the American Psychological Foundation and was awarded the Public Communications Award by the Massachusetts Psychological Association. He lives in Sarasota, Florida. Contact: drpwish@political-coach.com.

Made in the USA
Monee, IL
15 July 2021

73693452R00184